UNDERSTANDING STATE WELFARE

UNDERSTANDING STATE WELFARE:

Social Justice or Social Exclusion?

Brian Lund

SAGE Publications
London • Thousand Oaks • New Delhi

SAGE Publications Ltd
6 Bonhill Street
London EC2A 4PU

SAGE Publications Inc
2455 Teller Road
Thousand Oaks, California 91320

SAGE Publications India Pvt Ltd
32, M-Block Market
Greater Kailash - I
New Delhi 110 048

British Library Cataloguing in Publication data

A catalogue record for this book is available
from the British Library

ISBN 0 7619 6768 0
ISBN 0 7619 6769 9 (pbk)

Library of Congress Control Number: 2001132923

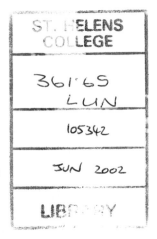
Typeset by SIVA Math Setters, Chennai, India
Printed in Great Britain by Biddles Ltd., Guildford, Surrey.

Contents

Acknowledgements

Thanks are due to my colleagues at the Manchester Metropolitan University who read various chapters in the manuscript, especially to John McHugh who read all the chapters and made many valuable suggestions. The usual disclaimers apply. Thanks also to Sukey, Ted, Sue, Gordon, Chris, Rod, Elaine, Gerry, Barbara, Dan, Rachel, George, Milligan and Meg, whose company and conversations, in and outside the Bell, were welcome distractions.

1

State Welfare: Distributive Principles

WHAT IS STATE WELFARE?

'Welfare' has numerous meanings but it has been co-opted to refer to specific elements of public policy. In the United States, the term is construed narrowly as relating to the means-tested, residual, 'assistance' dimensions of state provision whereas, in the United Kingdom and most other European countries, it has acquired a broader meaning. Here, the policy areas most frequently encompassed under 'welfare' – sometimes called 'social welfare' – are income security, health, 'social' housing, education and the personal social services. The rationale for this delineation is opaque but seems to be based on the notion that these five services share a common orientation towards meeting individual needs (Taylor-Gooby and Dale, 1981: 3, Goodin, 1988: 11).

The term 'welfare state' came into use in the 1940s and embodied a British tradition in political philosophy born in the late nineteenth century. This tradition regarded the state as the embodiment of the 'common good' with the corollary that its specific welfare programmes must be in the interests of every citizen. Over time, the tradition developed a welfare discourse – a theory *for* welfare aimed at promoting efficient, fair, state-directed 'social administration'. In contrast, theories *of* welfare developed since the 1970s, try to explain 'how the organisation of social relations ... comes to express the particular pattern that it does, what social forces and struggles underpin ... particular distributions, inclusions and exclusions' (O'Brien and Penna, 1998: 4). Theories *of* welfare usually adopt a broader definition of 'welfare' than theories *for* welfare. Included, for example, are employment programmes – aimed at promoting work and thereby reducing the requirement for income maintenance – plus the fiscal system with its capacity to redistribute income and encourage desirable behaviour. Theories *of* welfare also embrace the idea of a welfare society (Robson, 1976; Rodger, 2000). They explore the roles of the voluntary sector, the family, for-profit organisations and friends and neighbours, not as adjuncts to state welfare, but as welfare systems in themselves. When focused on the activities of the state, theories *of* welfare choose to refer to 'state welfare' because the term avoids the assumption of benevolence locked into the expression 'the welfare state' (Gough, 1979).

THE MARKET AND SOCIAL JUSTICE

The nineteenth century … was concerned with the creation of wealth: the twentieth century will be concerned with its distribution. (Archbishop Lang, 1911, cited in Hay, 1978: 74)

In the late nineteenth century, a number of political movements emerged in Britain each demanding greater collective involvement in the distribution of the 'social product'. Their demands were made from the baseline of the shares in income and wealth generated in the nineteenth century when a template of property ownership, forged in earlier times, was permeated by market principles of distribution. The promoters of social justice wanted to mend the old order by modifying the entrenched links between acquisition and distribution. At the core of their programmes was the identification of the 'social product' – the economic gains accruing from a co-operative and harmonious society – as belonging to the 'community' and hence legitimately available for *re*distribution. Progress towards social justice, they claimed, would yield greater social harmony and hence faster economic growth (Webb and Webb, 1913; Hobhouse, 1974 [1911]; George, 1979 [1879]).

The advocates of social justice held different views on the role of state welfare in promoting a fairer society. The Fabian Socialists awarded the state the major role in redistribution of wealth and income through the direct provision of welfare services aimed at delivering 'national efficiency' alongside social justice. The 'new' Liberals were more circumspect in their support for the state and tended to portray government as the remover of material obstacles to full participation in the civic life of the community. Nonetheless, both streams of thinking regarded the state as the primary mechanism for promoting social justice. In contrast, the followers of Karl Marx believed the state would 'wither away' when, in the transition from capitalism to communism, people produced goods to satisfy human needs including their need to work to master nature. Under communism, the process of production would be organised to satisfy human needs so there would be no requirement for a *re*distributive state (Heller, 1974; Young, 1990: 15). Thus, a tension developed between 'socialist' supporters of the common ownership of the means of production and the 'social democrats' – an amalgam of Fabian Socialism and 'new' Liberalism – who believed state economic management plus a redistributive welfare state were sufficient to deliver a fair society. By the late 1950s the application of Keynesian demand management techniques to deliver full employment had swung the debate on the left towards the social democratic approach. The willingness of the Conservative Party to accept state intervention to secure full employment and the basic elements of a 'welfare state' produced a period of alleged consensus on the primary institutions of British society lasting from 1945 to 1976 (Pimlott, 1989; Marlow, 1997).

John Rawls: justice as fairness

John Rawls' *A Theory of Justice* (1971) – described by the Commission on Social Justice (1993: 6) as the 'most famous' account of social justice – supplied a philosophical rationale for this consensus. Rawls, claiming his theory encapsulated universal 'intuitive' understandings of a fair society, set out to justify the 'patterned' approach to distribution that had animated social democratic programmes during the twentieth century. 'Although a society is a co-operative venture for mutual advantage,' says Rawls, 'it is typically marked by conflict as well as by an identity of interests' (Rawls, 1971: 4). Social co-operation makes possible a better life for all by enlarging the social product, but there are potential conflicts about how shares in the enhanced social product are to be distributed. Thus 'a set of principles is required for choosing among the various social arrangements which determine this division of advantages and for underwriting an agreement on the proper distributive shares' (Rawls, 1971: 4). These are the principles of social justice. They provide a way of assigning rights and duties in the basic institutions of society and define the appropriate distribution of the benefits and burdens of social co-operation.

The original position   To establish basic principles of justice Rawls asks us to imagine ourselves as our society's founders. He constructs a hypothetical 'original position' in which individuals are placed in a situation of impartiality – behind a 'veil of ignorance' – when discussing their potential participation in society.

> It is assumed, then, that the parties do not know certain kinds of particular facts … no one knows his place in society, his class position or social status; nor does he know his fortune in the distribution of natural assets and abilities, his intelligence and strength, and the like. (Rawls, 1971: 137)

In this 'original position' potential participants in society construct principles for the allocation of what Rawls calls 'primary goods' – those necessary for the pursuit of a plan of life whatever the specifics of that plan may be. Primary goods include rights and liberties, opportunities and powers, income and wealth and a sense of one's own worth (Plant, 1991: 99).

Principles of distribution   Rawls claims that the distributive principles agreed by the participants in the debate on the just society will be, in priority order.

> First Principle: each person is to have an equal right to the most extensive total system of equal basic liberties compatible with a similar system of liberty for all. Second Principle: social and economic inequalities are to be arranged so that they are both:
> (a) to the greatest benefit of the least advantaged ... and
> (b) attached to offices and positions open to all under conditions of fair equality of opportunity. (Rawls, 1971: 102)

The agreement on the primacy of liberty is defended by Rawls with the argument that all individuals desire self-respect, liberty is necessary to self-respect and hence equal liberty is necessary if human beings are to 'express their nature in free social union with others' (Rawls, 1971: 543). The second principle – the 'difference' principle – arises because, under the conditions of the 'original position', participants will adopt a *maximin* strategy. They will attempt to optimise the worst possible outcome in case they are in this position in 'real' society. Rawls starts with the assumption of an agreement on an equal distribution arguing that structuring a society to produce inequalities will be regarded as legitimate only if such inequalities work to the advantage of the worst off. An individual with natural talents will be allowed to utilise these talents and become unequal but the *maximin* principle provides insurance against the possibility an individual may not be endowed with natural abilities.

'Rational' social allocation of the kind advocated by Rawls was the predominant force in academic and political discourses on social justice in the twentieth century. Using established techniques of political theory, such as the notion of a 'social contract', Rawls produced a justification for a market-capitalist economy but one extensively modified by state intervention to supply 'property rights' in the collectively created 'social' product (Rawls, 1987). Such a system had evolved in most western industrial democracies after 1945 but, according to Rawls, had lacked a systematic rationale.

Hayek and the mirage of social justice

Soon after Rawls' justification of 'welfare capitalism' was published it was challenged by an academic and political movement labelled the 'New Right'. Friedrich Hayek was the New Right's most important guru.

At the heart of Hayek's thinking was the rejection of the application of the notion of 'social justice' to a market system. Hayek believed the market to be a 'spontaneous order', characterised by the maximisation of individual liberty, wealth enhancement and the achievement of 'greater satisfaction of human desires than any deliberate human organisation can achieve' (Hayek, 1976b: 33). Justice, Hayek argued, can be applied only to 'situations which have been created by human will' (Hayek, 1976b: 33) hence the concept is 'entirely empty and meaningless' (Hayek, 1976a: 11) when related to the particulars of a 'spontaneous' order such as the market. In a market there are no principles of *individual* conduct available to produce a pattern of distribution that can be called 'just'. Individuals engaged in market exchanges make their decisions in ignorance of their general outcomes because general outcomes depend on the behaviour of a myriad of others. So, said Hayek, although

it has of course to be admitted that the manner in which the benefits and burdens are apportioned by the market mechanism would in many instances have to be regarded as very unjust if it were the result of a deliberate allocation to particular people. This is not the case. (Hayek, 1976b: 64)

If Hayek's notion of the market as a 'catallaxy' or spontaneous order, untouched by human design, is accepted then the idea of 'social' allocations designed to alter the outcomes of market mechanisms is at best misguided and at worst dangerous. 'It must lead to the extinction of all moral responsibility' (Hayek, 1976c: 129) and is a grave threat 'to most other values of a free civilisation' being 'the Trojan Horse through which totalitarianism has entered' (Hayek, 1976a: 66–7, 136). This is so because the achievement of social justice involves imposing a predetermined pattern on the *unintended* outcomes of market processes and the passing of laws affecting *specific* forms of behaviour. According to Hayek the only laws compatible with freedom are general, abstract laws concerned with procedures such as 'the rules of the law of property, tort and contract' (Hayek, 1976b: 109). Specific laws designed to produce particular outcomes must infringe liberty.

In Hayek's discourse the philosophical justification of redistribution via state welfare disintegrates. However, as Kley (1994: 24) has indicated, Hayek runs together the idea that social justice has no meaning in a market system with the notion that social justice is an illegitimate concept to apply in *any* type of society. Hayek assumes the market order is the 'natural' order but, because we know about the general outcomes of markets and because we can construct alternative systems, there is no reason why we should accept market outcomes. Shklar makes this point succinctly in stating 'It is evident that when we can alleviate suffering, whatever its cause, it is passively unjust to stand by and do nothing' (1990: 81). We can choose between unfettered markets, regulated markets, a combination of markets with a welfare state or a communist system. Hayek's rejection of the idea of social justice creates what Hirsch has called the 'tyranny of small choices'.

> The core of the problem is that the market provides a full range of choice between alternative piecemeal, discrete, marginal adjustments but no facility for selection between alternative states ... (Hirsch, 1977: 18)

Robert Nozick and rectification

In *Anarchy, State and Utopia* (1974) Robert Nozick starts from a similar position to Hayek but comes to recognise reluctantly how historical injustices in acquisition negate the current legitimacy of market outcomes. Nozick begins with the assertion 'Individuals have rights, and there are things no person or group may do to them without violating their rights' (Nozick, 1974: ix). A minimal state, 'limited to the narrow functions of protection against force, theft, fraud, enforcement of contracts, and so on', can be justified (Nozick, 1974: 10–25). A more extensive state, involved in the redistribution of resources already acquired, violates individual rights because current justice in holdings depends on how they were acquired. Assets secured without coercion – by creation, barter or as a gift – are legitimately the property of the individual who now holds them. Reapportioning this original distribution, according to some 'patterned principle' such as 'justice', violates the rights of the first holders of the resources. Thus, according to Nozick (1974: 169), 'taxation of earnings from labour is on a par with forced labour' and the only legitimate principle of justice is 'from each as they choose, to each as they are chosen'. So far, so Hayek, but Nozick makes some important qualifications to the notion that the market produces legitimate outcomes. He recognises that market distributions:

> seem arbitrary unless some acceptable initial set of holdings is specified, or unless it is held that the operation of the system over time washes out any significant effects from the initial set of holdings. (Nozick, 1974: 160)

First, there is the problem of how individuals can acquire rights to natural resources such as land. Nozick tries hard to reconcile market outcomes with established rights to natural resources but, twist and turn as he does, he cannot find a solution to fit his entitlement theory. He concludes that one is entitled to a part of a natural resource if one leaves 'enough and as good' for others to have some use of it and if the position of others is not worsened by the act of appropriation. This opens the door to extensive state intervention in the distribution of holdings for we must ask 'enough and as good' for what? Since a primary purpose of the use of natural resources is to satisfy basic needs then 'enough and as good' for needs satisfaction must be the answer to this question thereby giving the state a legitimate role in needs satisfaction.

Nozick is also troubled by the compounding impact of resources obtained in the past through force and concludes compensation has to be made for historical injustices in acquisition.

> ... a rough rule of thumb for rectifying injustices might seem to be the follow-ing: organise society so as to maximise the position of whatever group ends up least well-off in the society ... Although to introduce socialism as a punishment for our sins would be to go too far, past injustices might be so great as to make necessary in the short run a more extensive state in order to rectify them. (Nozick, 1974: 152)

Although short on answers to the issues raised, at least Nozick identifies the problem of rectification. Hayek does not even consider the issue. He is what Nozick calls a 'current time-slice' theorist believing that, if a market is created today, then its outcomes are legitimate regardless of what people bring to the market as a consequence of their heritage.

The ideas of Rawls, Hayek and Nozick illustrate the contested terrain of mainstream philosophical thinking on social justice. During the nineteenth century ideas similar to Hayek's were dominant although elements of Nozick's approach can be discerned in the attacks made by the emerging middle class on the rights to the 'unearned income' derived from land. In the twentieth century thinking grounded in the basic structure codified by Rawls became prominent albeit against a background of radicalism generated by Karl Marx's theory of exploitation and working class pressure for social and economic change (Lavalette and Mooney, 2000).

Distributive domains

Hayek and Nozick identified principles of distribution to be applied to all goods and services. Rawls made a distinction between 'primary' and other goods but his 'primary' goods definition – 'rights and liberties, powers and opportunities, income and wealth' (1971: 62) – was so broad that few domains remained in which different principles could be applied. However, what actually emerged in Britain during the twentieth century was a 'welfare state' – a system that 'decommodified' certain goods and services and allocated them according to criteria at odds with market principles. The establishment of the 'welfare state' thereby produced a situation corresponding to Michael Walzer's notion of 'complex' equality.

Walzer has been described as a 'communitarian' because he is critical of theorists who artificially abstract human beings from their cultural experiences and present a model of human thinking as 'disembodied and disembedded' (Edgar and Sedgwick, 1999: 46). In *Spheres of Justice* (1983) he argues that egalitarianism's origins were in abolitionist politics; its aim was to eliminate the experience of personal subordination and create a society 'free from domination' (Walzer, 1983: xiii). Freedom from domination is achievable by full recognition that different spheres of life generate disparate meanings about their purposes and hence each domain requires a specific principle of distribution. Allowing each separate aspect of life to embody a particular distributive principle ensures that no single source of power (material wealth for example) can dominate society. Hence medical care, if thought of as a special 'needed good' 'cannot be left to the whim, or distributed in the interest of, some powerful group of owners and practitioners' (Walzer, 1983: 89). Likewise education, being 'a programme for social survival' expressing 'perhaps, our deepest wish: to continue, to go on, to persist in the face of time' (Walzer, 1983: 197) will also generate its own distributive principles. Thus, says Walzer, 'No social good x should be distributed to men and women who possess some other good y merely because they possess y without regard to the meaning of x' (1983: 20). Against Hayek and Nozick, Walzer makes the point; 'A radically laissez-faire economy would be like a totalitarian state, invading every other sphere, dominating every other distributive process. It would transform every social good into a commodity' (1983: 119–20). Certain exchanges are 'blocked' because they belong to separate spheres of justice.

SOCIAL EXCLUSION

The expression 'social exclusion' entered British academic discourse in the early 1990s. Although the meaning of the term is opaque, supporters of its use claim it poses the right questions and is a 'comprehensive and dynamic concept' (Anderson and Sim, 2000: 11). It is 'comprehensive' because, unlike the term 'poverty', it covers different dimensions of integration – civic, social, economic and interpersonal (Cummins, 1993: 4) and 'dynamic' in that it directs attention to *processes* rather than *outcomes*. However, the alleged 'comprehensive' and 'dynamic' nature of the idea has allowed different ideological perspectives to shelter under its wing.

Levitas has divided these perspectives into three 'discourses'. What she calls 'RED' (the redistributionist discourse) posits 'citizenship as the obverse of exclusion', addresses 'social political and cultural as well as economic citizenship' and 'implies a radical reduction of inequalities plus a redistribution of resources and power' (Levitas, 1998: 14). In contrast 'SID' (the social integrationalist discourse) 'narrows the definition of social exclusion/inclusion to participation in paid work' (Levitas, 1998: 28) and therefore, according to Levitas, excludes gender and class from the debate. 'MUD' (the moral underclass discourse) has a focus 'on the behaviour of the poor rather than the structure of the whole society' and presents a gendered discourse identifying a 'socially excluded underclass as culturally distinct from the mainstream' (Levitas, 1998: 21). Inclusion by participation in paid work (SID) has been a dominant theme in economic and social policy in the nineteenth and twentieth centuries although the focus has now switched from male to female involvement in the paid labour force. The 'MUD' discourse has also featured strongly in social policy debates. Reoccurring disquiet about 'the pauper class', 'the residuum' and 'the underclass' has resulted in state welfare simultaneously incorporating both inclusionary and exclusionary tendencies.

Distributive 'subjects' and the politics of identity

Levitas' formulation of the RED perspective on social exclusion combines elements of traditional 'left' concerns about the distributive justice of outcomes with the 'identity' politics associated with the growth of 'new' social movements in the 1970s. It directs attention to the structural causes of social exclusion.

Gender   Rawls, Nozick and Hayek belong to a tradition of writing on distributive justice, sometimes called 'liberalism' (O'Brien and Penna, 1998), whose 'subject' is 'homo economicus'. The mission of this tradition has been to establish the 'correct' relationship between 'individual economic man' and 'collective economic man'. It developed in response to the pressing demands of organised male labour and has regarded the alliances formed in households, families, groups, friendships and neighbourhoods variously as 'spontaneous', 'voluntary' and 'sentimental'. Such bonds are adjudged to be outside the 'public' sphere and inappropriate for analysis by political philosophy. (Hayek, 1988, 66–7; Goodin and Pettit, 1993, cited in Gray, 1995: 12; Pateman, 1995: 54). In the 1970s a variety of 'new' social movements emerged, each challenging this restricted notion of the 'subjects' of political philosophy. Some identified oppressive distributive systems within seemingly 'voluntary' and 'private' affiliations. Take the family for example. It is possible to represent marriage as a voluntary contract with the partners perceived as a two-person 'firm' improving their efficiency through a specialisation and voluntary division of labour. On the other hand it can be portrayed as a reflection of the power relationships generated and maintained from outside the domestic sphere 'through marriage law, divorce law, abortion law, day care law, etc' (Eisenstein, 1980: 61). Barrett and McIntosh (1982: 55), for example, claim 'marriage is a form that is sanctified by tradition, not justified by rational social debate. The tradition is one that carries with it the whole historical baggage of male power and patriarchal authority'. Hence, in discussions of social justice, many feminists assert the family must be 'disaggregated' so its impact on men and women can be assessed separately.

'Race' and ethnicity   In the 1950s and 1960s the UK government adopted a 'colour blind' approach to the production of official statistics on social difference, a reflection, in part, of a concern with the absorption of 'coloured' immigrants into the mainstream community. The initial government response to immigration was an attempt to assimilate the newcomers into the 'British' culture by dispersal and tutelage in 'identity' within the 'universal' social services with their alleged ethos of promoting equality of status. The notion that these services might require modification to suit the cultural requirements of the new arrivals received scant consideration, indeed, meeting cultural requirements was sometimes viewed as a reaction to 'demand' rather than 'need' and therefore a barrier to assimilation. However, as the newcomers became established, 'they formed communities with their own distinct lifestyles' (Parekh, 1991: 187) and developed the confidence to claim their cultures should be respected and incorporated into welfare provision. The idea that the social services should reflect cultural diversity rather than assimilate 'strangers' gathered momentum in the 1960s and was reflected in Roy Jenkins's definition of integration expounded when he was Home Secretary. 'Integration does not mean a flattening process of assimilation', he said, 'but equal opportunity accompanied by cultural diversity in an atmosphere of mutual tolerance' (1966). Cultural pluralists in the Jenkins mould tend to analyse distributive outcomes in terms of 'ethnicity' – a subjectively assigned category containing 'notions of shared origins, culture and traditions' (Nazroo, 1997: 8). In contrast the 'anti-racist critique', developed in the early 1980s, claimed the institutions of state welfare treated 'racialised' minorities on systematically less favourable terms than members of the white majority. 'Race', usually interpreted to mean a socially constructed category ascribed in terms of biological/genetic determinants, was studied through examining the 'subjective', 'institutional' and 'structural' dimensions of racism (Ginsburg, 1992).

The social movements instrumental in adding new dimensions to studies of distributive outcomes also introduced a 'recognition' factor into the analysis of social justice. 'Recognition' refers to the degree of respect awarded to differences in ethnicity, gender, sexuality, age, and physical differences. If the dominant culture fails to respect 'minorities', indeed if there is a 'dominant culture' with others seen as 'minorities' (Parekh, 2000: xxiii), then the designated 'minorities' suffer a distortion in self-identity 'as a result of repeated encounters with the stigmatizing gaze of a culturally dominant other' (Fraser, 2000: 109). Thus 'injustice in identity' includes being 'subject to an alien culture, being rendered invisible in one's cultural specificity, and being subject to deprecating stereotypes and cultural representations' (Young, 1990: 52).

STATE WELFARE

Although the quest for social justice has been a major stimulant to the development of state welfare in Britain other factors have also been important. In the nineteenth century, the endeavour to control the 'externalities' produced by urbanisation led to state regulation of building standards and eventually to the municipal supply of 'public utilities' such as sewerage and water. Another strand in the story of state welfare has been 'the continuing endeavour to provide the environment required for industrial progress by ensuring a more efficient labour force' (Donnison, 1965: 16). Marxist historians stress the development of state welfare as a 'recognition by property of the price that has to be paid for political security' (Saville, 1957: 5). The recent 'cultural turn' in social policy analysis has led to an emphasis on the role of state welfare in underpinning a 'national identity' with its associated identification of 'outsiders' to cement the unity of 'full citizens' (Lewis, 1998; Burden et al., 2000). Given these divergent inputs it is not surprising the contemporary welfare state is a complex mixture of different principles of intervention and distribution.

Primary intervention

A tenuous but useful distinction can be made between 'primary' and 'secondary' intervention by the state. Primary intervention involves direct interference in the economy and social life to promote socially desirable outcomes, whereas secondary intervention *re*distributes resources already allocated via market transactions and social and political interaction. The most important forms of 'primary' economic intervention have been demand management, job creation, regional policy, prices and incomes control, employment subsidies and minimum wage legislation.

Economic intervention   The foundation stone of the welfare state as constructed between 1942 to 1948 was the attempt to manage demand 'to secure the maintenance of a high and stable level of employment' (White Paper *Ministry of Reconstruction*, 1944: 3). Successful demand management in the period 1945 to 1974 produced high levels of employment. This shaped the distribution of income by ensuring work was available for people who wanted to work and by allowing organised labour to press for higher wages without fear of generating unemployment. The rising unemployment of the mid-1970s meant work creation returned to the political agenda in the form of the Job Creation programme, targeted at 16–18 year olds (1975), and the Community Industry and Work Experience Programme (1976). The mounting unemployment and high inflation of the mid-1970s also prompted direct state intervention in the labour market in the form of a prices and incomes policy. Although the primary objective of this policy was to control inflation it also embraced 'social justice' objectives by allowing the lowest paid to negotiate the largest pay increases (Ormerod, 1991: 57; Heath, 1998: 416).

Regional policy began in the 1930s when central government gave grants to local authorities and voluntary agencies in designated areas for water supply, sewerage, hospital building and new factories. After the Second World War the policy consisted of advance factory building, the payment of regional development grants to firms setting up in assisted areas and the use of industrial development certificates to encourage new and expanding industries to set up in areas of high unemployment. Direct payments to employers to recruit or retain workers started in the mid-1970s but were abolished in the 1980s only to return in the late 1990s, under New Labour's 'New Deal', in the form of subsidies to employers to hire the long-term unemployed.

The notion of a statutory defined 'living wage' was in wide circulation towards the end of the nineteenth century. The Trade Boards Act 1909 established statutory machinery for the establishment of minimum wages in the female dominated trades of tailoring, box-making and lace-making and in 1912 a minimum wage was set for coal miners. Later, other industries and services were brought within the scope of Trade Boards but, in the 1980s and 1990s, the Conservatives scaled down and then eliminated state involvement in the setting of minimum wages. Under New Labour the National Minimum Wage Act 1998 provided for the introduction of a single National Minimum Wage throughout the United Kingdom. One of the principal arguments put forward in support of this measure was that it would reduce the need for the state to support wages through the 'secondary' intervention of the social security system.

The Politics of 'representation'   The primary/secondary distinction can also be applied to the social domain albeit with the same caveat on the fragile nature of the distinction. In *Justice and the Politics of Difference*, Iris Young argues that 'instead of focusing on distribution, a full understanding of social justice should begin with the concepts of domination and oppression' (1990: 3). She is critical of mainstream political philosophy for its tendency 'to focus thinking about social justice on the allocation of material goods and things, resources, income, and wealth' and its neglect of the social structure that 'helps to determine distributive patterns and influences "non-possession issues" such as culture' (Young, 1990: 16, 23). For Young 'oppression' is produced by:

> Systematic institutional processes which prevent some people from learning and using satisfying and expansive skills in socially recognized settings, or which inhibit people's ability to play and communicate with others or to express their feelings and perspectives on social life in contexts where others can listen. (1990: 38)

She insists that decision-making power and procedures, divisions of labour and culture must be the central concern of political philosophy because they influence the self-respect of 'identity groups'.

Primary political intervention is necessary to promote the empowerment of hitherto dominated and oppressed groups. This requires special representation rights plus careful attention to the structures of decision making to ensure the voices of excluded groups have an impact. Young's point finds support in the recent work of Stuart Hampshire who rejects the traditional 'liberal' belief in a definitive, rational account of social justice. 'Fairness and justice in procedures', he claims, 'are the only virtues that can reasonably be considered as setting norms to be universally respected' (Hampshire, 1999: 56). Young also rejects traditional liberal objections to 'strong' versions of 'affirmative action'. Some liberals claim 'group' quotas in employment, education and housing are discriminatory against individuals but Young contends that oppression happens to groups, not individuals and, in the real world, 'merit' plays little part in distributive outcomes (Young, 1990: 192–225). Some feminists have extended Young's case for 'representation' politics by claiming to have located an 'ethic of care', more likely to be adopted by women, that gives personal circumstances more weight than the 'ethic of justice' (Ramsay, 1997: 209–21; Noddings, 1986).

Regulation   Primary social intervention can take the form of a legal requirement on people and institutions to behave in a particular way, whereas secondary intervention often involves the state in compensating for the 'diswelfares' generated in 'private' domains. Workman's compensation provides an early example of the distinction. The Employers' Liability Act of 1897 placed a legal obligation on employers to provide compensation to workers for injuries arising from accidents that took place 'out of and in the course of employment'. The legislation placed a duty on an employer to pay a man half his wages if totally incapacitated (Bolderson, 1991: 13) – a liability that, according to some contemporary observers, meant state compensation was unnecessary. Planning legislation offers a current example of the primary/secondary intervention distinction. In the 1980s the Conservatives reduced the supply of state housing mainly by awarding local authority tenants a statutory right to buy their homes. By the early 1990s, a homelessness 'crisis' had developed with 73,490 households living in temporary accommodation (Wilcox, 1997: 169). In 1991 the Department of the Environment issued circulars suggesting that the willingness of a developer to include affordable accommodation in a planned development should be regarded as a material planning consideration (Barlow et al., 1994: vii). This was an attempt to secure more 'affordable' housing to alleviate homelessness without the involvement of the state in the direct provision of homes.

Secondary intervention

During the twentieth century certain goods and services – education, health care, the personal social services and elements of housing – were 'decommodified'; that is, they were distributed through mechanisms other than the market. By the early 1970s 'need' had become the dominant principle on which these 'decommodified' goods and services were allocated. To understand this supremacy of 'need' as a distributive criterion and its relationship to social justice it is necessary to examine the organic theory of society from which the twentieth century concept of 'need' emerged.

Need   At the heart of organic theory was the notion that 'society was a living organism ... and that social efficiency and survival were determined by structural "organization" and the capacity for adaptation to external social change' (Harris, 1993: 226). According to the organic perspective, society had 'needs' that must be satisfied if it was to continue and, in the final harmony, society's requirements and the 'real' needs of the individual were as one. Seebohm Rowntree's famous study of poverty in York illustrates this unity. In *Poverty: A Study of Town Life* (1901) Rowntree declared he wanted to obtain information about 'the true measure of the poverty in the city, both in extent and depth' (1901: viii). He defined 'primary' poverty as 'total earnings insufficient to obtain the minimum necessaries for the maintenance of merely physical efficiency' (1901: 87). Because he wanted to protect his definition of poverty from any accusations of generosity (Veit-Wilson, 1995) Rowntree made no allowance for 'expenditure needful for the development of the mental, moral, and social sides of human nature' (1901: 87). His calculation was related to 'the two chief uses of food', that is, 'heat to keep the body warm' and the 'muscular and other power for the work to be done'. As Rowntree explained, people living below his poverty line:

were not necessarily chronically hungry but that the food which they eat (although on account of bulk it satisfies the cravings of hunger) does not contain the nutrients necessary for normal physical efficiency. A homely illustration will make the point clear. A horse fed upon hay does not feel hungry and may indeed grow fat, but it cannot perform hard and continuous work without a proper supply of corn (1901: 303).

Rowntree's equation of individual need with the needs of society for a productive labour force was quickly grasped by those who wanted to relate the poverty issue to the growing concern about national efficiency and the future of the British Empire. Economic competition from Germany and the United States, combined with the military incompetence exposed in the Boer War, produced the cry 'Give us efficiency or we die' (*Spectator*, 16 September 1902, cited in Searle, 1977: 1). Having read Rowntree's book, Winston Churchill wrote to a friend:

> it is quite evident from the figures which he adduces that the American labourer is a stronger, larger, healthier, better fed, and consequently more efficient animal than a large proportion of our population and this is surely a fact which our unbridled Imperialists should not lose sight of. (Churchill, 1902, cited in Bruce, 1973: 129)

Fabian socialists also absorbed the organic conception of society. Beatrice Webb's minority report of the 1909 Royal Commission on the Poor Laws 'assumed a highly organic conception of society' (Pierson, 1979: 318). She rejected the notion of unconditional insurance benefits as containing a 'fatal defect'. The recipients of benefit 'had a right to the allowance whatever their conduct' (Webb and Webb, 1909: 304) and thereby the bond between individual and community was broken.

Britain's involvement in two world wars helped to strengthen the organic notion of society (society being represented as the 'nation-state') and, after the Second World War, theorists of the 'welfare state' developed an organic, functionalist approach to justifying state welfare. In *Citizenship and Social Class* Marshall made distinctions between the civil, political and social rights of citizenship – citizenship being interpreted as 'full membership of a community' (Marshall, 1963 [1950]: 72). He defined social rights as 'the whole range from the right to a modicum of economic welfare and security to the right to share to the full in the social heritage and to live the life of a civilised being according to the standards prevailing in the society' (Marshall, 1963 [1950]: 74). Marshall believed the legislation of 1944 to 1948 embodied social rights and this legislation represented the final stage in the emergence of citizenship rights. His explanation of the development of citizenship rights was expressed in terms of the natural, 'organic' development of society towards harmony and the 'functional' requirements of any social system for bonds to unite its disparate elements (Mishra, 1981: 28). In feudal society the civil, economic and social rights of citizenship were integrated on a geographical basis but, during the industrial revolution, these rights became separated. 'When the three elements of citizenship parted company', Marshall said, 'they were soon barely on speaking terms' (1963: 76) and, during the nineteenth century, social rights became subordinate to civil and political rights. There then followed a functional process whereby the social, economic and political dimensions of citizenship rights were reintegrated in the form of the welfare state.

Richard Titmuss followed a similar line of thought. In *Social Policy: An Introduction* (1974) he set out three models of social policy and identified the 'Institutional Redistributive Model' as the template for state welfare. Titmuss claimed the 'Institutional Redistributive Model' sees 'social welfare as a major integrated institution in society, providing universalist services outside the market on the principle of need ...' (1974: 31–2). He supported his belief in this model with a variety of arguments but, at the heart of his justification, was the notion that the 'Institutional Redistributive Model' focused on:

> integrative systems; on processes, transactions and institutions which promote an individual's sense of identity, participation and community and allow him more freedom of choice for the expression of altruism and which, simultaneously, discourage a sense of individual alienation. (Titmuss, 1974: 223–4)

Conservatives also embraced elements of organic theory. After the Second World War the notion of the welfare state as an 'enormous mutual insurance covering us all against ill-health, unemployment and loss of earning power in old age' (Willetts, 1992: 142) had a strong appeal to the 'One Nation Toryism' wing of the Conservative Party. Thus by the early 1970s individual 'need' – interpreted as an objective, finite condition related to the requirements of society for functional efficiency – was established as *the* principle on which certain 'decommodified' goods and services ought to be distributed.

Desert   During the nineteenth century the market and the family emerged as the dominant mechanisms of distribution and supplied the normative baselines from which notions of 'desert' were constructed. Classical economics was opposed to any form of intervention in the labour market. Malthus summarised the conventional wisdom in saying:

There is one right which man has generally been thought to possess, which I am confident he neither does nor can possess – a right to subsistence when his labour will not fairly purchase it. (1803: 190–1)

With the exception of Malthus, the classical economists produced few reflections on the nature of the family as a social institution. They seem to have regarded the family in much the same way as their disciple, Fredrich Hayek – as a 'molecule' in society created by the natural, moral sentiments of autonomous, atomistic individuals. It was left to religion to codify these 'moral sentiments'. Under the influence of Evangelical Christianity, the family – seen as consisting of the male breadwinner, female carer and their children – acquired an almost 'sacred' status. The 1871 Census declared 'the natural family is founded by marriage, and consists, in its complete state, of husband, wife and children' (cited in Harris, 1993: 63). 'In unity of marriage', Samuel Smiles declared 'Man is the brain, but woman is the heart of humanity; he its judgement, she its feeling, he its strength, she its grace, ornament, and solace' (Smiles, 1871, cited in Searle, 1998: 134).

Notions of 'desert' were based on the ability of individuals to acquire their means of subsistence from the designated 'primary' mechanisms of resource acquisition. By the sale of their labour, single able-bodied people were presumed to be capable of earning sufficient to maintain themselves. If they failed they did so of their own volition and, after the passing of the Poor Law Amendment Act 1834, were to be incarcerated in a workhouse. On marriage, a man acquired the additional obligation to maintain his wife and children through his labour but this did not imply a corresponding right for women and children to claim maintenance directly from the male head of the household. The Acts of Settlement declared a married woman could not acquire rights of abode or assistance in a different parish from her husband (Lidbetter, 1933a: 76); any woman who left the marital home was liable to be deported to her husband's parish (Englander, 1998: 18). Unmarried mothers acquired a double stigma. They were to be incarcerated in a workhouse and, to remind them of their status as moral outcasts, 'many unions put their unmarried mothers into a distinctive yellow uniform, the colour of a ship's plague flag, the wearers being nicknamed "canary wards" ... ' (Longmate, 1974: 125).

Although the market and the family as the sanctioned mechanisms of distribution continued into the twentieth century they were gradually layered with other normative conventions such as 'worker' and 'citizen'. This allowed additional criteria, including new norms of 'desert' such as 'homes fit for heroes', to influence distribution. In the 1960s and 1970s, according to some commentators, the market and the family as *the* distributive mechanisms became subordinate to 'citizenship' rights and hence required reanimation (Murray, 1988; Etzioni, 1995; Thatcher, 1995). Today they remain important normative systems on which 'desert' is assessed (Schmidtz and Goodin, 1998) and around which concepts such as 'the underclass' and the 'socially excluded' have been constructed.

Ends and means

Some economists claim the distinction between ends and means marks the separation of the 'normative' from the 'positive'. According to Barr (1998: 4), once the question 'How much redistribution (of income, wealth, power, etc.) should there be?' has been answered, the issue of method is 'more properly the subject of technical rather than political discussion'. However, the form in which redistribution is delivered carries messages to both 'providers' and 'receivers' in the distributive process. Such messages can have implications for the acceptability of the transfer and, in turn, may influence its efficiency as a redistributive mechanism.

Income testing   Studies of income redistribution and state welfare indicate that the most efficient way to shift resources from 'rich' to 'poor' is to impose direct taxes on the 'rich' and to transfer these resources to the 'poor' via a test of income. Goodin and Le Grand, for example, found that, of the 13 services and subsidies examined, income-tested allowances were the most 'pro-poor'. They concluded that 'the best way to [produce greater equality] is to give all the resources to the poor and only to the poor' (Goodin and Le Grand, 1987: 226). However, depending on the dominant normative system operating in a particular society, the *method* of redistribution can have important consequences. Two assumptions are implicit in the endorsement of a transfer of income from 'rich' to 'poor' via a specific test of income applied to people with low incomes. It presumes the 'poor' should be grateful for their donation regardless of how the 'rich' acquired their wealth, and that the 'poor' have failed to achieve economic independence by their own efforts. These assumptions may lead to feelings of stigma and injustice within welfare recipients and result in redistributive inefficiency due to the low take-up of benefits (Townsend, 1968: 4).

Social insurance   The idea of social insurance evolved in response to the perceived necessity to encourage working people to save plus a recognition that means testing may discourage thrift (Nevile, 1838; Blackley, 1906). State 'social' insurance started in Britain in 1911 when an 'insured person' was required to pay a weekly contribution to be stored in a special fund earmarked for the payment of specified benefits. The payment of the contribution entitled the claimant to receive benefit without a test of means and therefore transferred income to the 'contingency' poor (*likely* to require income because of unemployment, sickness, etc.) from those who did not experience such contingencies. The compulsory dimension of the scheme enabled the state to pool risks not pooled in commercial or in the 'mutual-aid' schemes developed by working class communities during the nineteenth century. David Lloyd George referred to the problem, called 'adverse selection' by contemporary economists, when he introduced his National Insurance Bill to Parliament in 1911.

> Voluntary schemes of unemployment insurance ... have always failed because those men likely to be unemployed resorted to them, and, consequently, there was a preponderance of bad risks ... which must be fatal to the success of the scheme. (Lloyd George, 1911, cited in Atkinson, 1991: 7)

Until 1948, the pooling of risks in state social insurance was limited to the working class. Thus social insurance involved 'horizontal' redistribution *within* the class structure, over the lifetime of the individual according to the experience of contingencies such as unemployment, sickness and disability. The incorporation of all social classes in the post-war system of social security meant some 'vertical' redistribution of income from 'rich' to 'poor' occurred because the risk of experiencing unemployment and sickness was lower for members of the middle class. However, because the middle class live longer than the working class, the incorporation of retirement pensions as an insurance benefit may have counter-balanced this vertical redistribution.

Cash or kind?   One of the distinguishing features of state welfare in Britain is the provision of services rather than the supply of cash. This reflects the historical evolution of the current welfare system from its origins in the reformed Poor Law. Some contemporary universal social services such as the National Health Service and the 'personal social services' have evolved from the 'workhouse' system of the nineteenth century. From the perspective of the state, 'in kind' services carry the advantage that their consumption can be shaped towards the promotion of 'common good', defined in terms of the interests of the nation-state. Thus, for example, William Beveridge based his support for a comprehensive National Health Service on promoting 'national efficiency' by providing a service directed towards the prevention of disease and the rehabilitation of sick and disabled people into the labour force. 'In kind' services also offer the opportunity for the state to shape the identity of the 'subjects' of the service by incorporating its recipients into dominant notions of the 'ideal' citizen. Thus, for example, maternity and child welfare services have incorporated normative notions of 'motherhood' in their operations (Hendrick, 1994).

Looked at from the perspective of the individual the provision of 'in kind' services may be seen as 'paternalistic' and as imposing limitations on freedom of choice. The evolution of services for disabled people illustrates this point. In the nineteenth century people with a severe disability were exempt from the full rigours of the deterrent Poor Law. As the more 'deserving', so-called 'impotent' poor, they were to be the province of charity and, should they require state assistance, this would be provided by outdoor relief or in special sections of the workhouse. This different treatment of disabled people had implications for the forms of service that evolved during the twentieth century. The 'special' needs and 'worthy' status of disabled people removed them from the political struggle to establish social rights with the result that voluntary and statutory provision remained 'paternalistic' and was delivered mainly in the form of services rather than cash. This dominant paradigm of service provision remained unchallenged until the late 1970s when the Union of the Physically Impaired Against Segregation (UPIAS) rejected the conventional definition of disability 'as lacking all or part of a limb, or having a defective limb, organism or mechanism of the body'. As a replacement definition, UPIAS suggested 'the disadvantage or restriction caused by a contemporary social organisation which takes no or little account of people who have physical impairments and thus excludes them from the mainstream of social activities' (Oliver and Barnes, 1998: 17). The disabled persons' movement began to demand 'independent living' as the model for disabled persons' services and the establishment of a comprehensive disability income became a dominant element in this campaign. A reasonable income would allow a disabled person to purchase those services that he or she chose to use and thus would free disabled people from the choices made by others.

Selective services – those provided *only* for people with a low income – present similar advantages and disadvantages to selective cash benefits but in intensified form. It can be argued that the 'welfare function' of the poor is improved by the delivery of services rather than cash because the poor can consume only what is considered good for them. Moreover the transfer is 'twice blessed' because the knowledge that their resources will be used only for approved purposes enhances the willingness of the 'rich' to make provision for the 'poor' (Marquand, 1996: 23, Blair, 1999: 13). From the perspective of the recipient, however, the combination of paternalism and mistrust implicit in these arguments may induce a sense of 'spoiled identity' and/or resentment. Take, for example, the current provision of free school meals for the 'non-working' poor only. Implicit in the provision of this service is the notion that, if cash is provided, then parents will not spend the money on feeding their children. The demeaning message is difficult to escape and, in the past, has made a significant contribution to the low take-up of the service (Davies and Reddin, 1978: 82–4, 126–9).

Area selectivity   Examination of the principles of distribution applied in the United Kingdom is complicated by the system of devolved government. The UK is divided into four entities: England, Scotland, Wales and Northern Ireland, and a Scottish Parliament and a Welsh Assembly were established in 1999. Each entity has been allowed different degrees of 'de jure' and 'de facto' discretion in distributing the resources allocated from the centre – a distribution that, since the mid-1970s, has been made according to the 'Barnett formula' (Twigger, 1998). In addition the four constituents of the UK have particular systems of local government subject to specific forms of resource distribution from the 'centre'. It is further complicated by the power of the 'national executive' to bypass local distributive systems and allocate resources directly to small areas within local government boundaries. The policy of small area selectivity – often known as 'priority area policy' – has a history dating back to slum clearance areas in the nineteenth century, but was reformulated in the 1960s and 1970s. At the time it was justified with the arguments that individual deprivation was concentrated in particular areas and the existence of 'neighbourhood externalities' meant the spatial concentration of resources would provide larger aggregate welfare (Holtermann, 1978: 34). Some commentators also regarded small area selectivity as a form of 'positive discrimination', promoting social justice by bestowing *additional* welfare services to compensate for the compounding impact of concentrations of disadvantage (Central Advisory Council for Education, 1966: 50–68). Critics of area selectivity have pointed out how targeting resources on deprived areas misses the majority of deprived individuals who live outside such areas (Barnes and Lucas, 1975) and how areas selected for 'special' treatment can become stigmatised. In addition there is the danger of assuming that concentrations of disadvantage in neighbourhoods necessarily means the families living in deprived areas suffer from an accumulation of deprivations (the 'ecological fallacy').

ACQUIRING RESOURCES

The codes of acquisition governing the ways in which resources are secured by the state before redistribution are, of course, fundamental to any study of the gains in 'welfare' achieved by state intervention. Taxation has been defined as a 'compulsory levy made by public authorities for which nothing is received *directly* in return' (James and Nobbs, 1998: 100, emphasis added). It can take a variety of forms.

Direct or indirect?   Although the distinction is opaque it has become conventional to classify taxes according to their incidence, that is, who actually pays the tax. Income Tax, for example, is usually paid directly by the individual and is labelled a direct tax whereas Value Added Tax, formally levied on businesses, is labelled an indirect tax because it is usually passed on to the consumer in the form of higher prices. If taxation is imposed directly on income then, depending on the marginal rates of tax levied, it may have an impact on work incentives. Taxes on expenditure – 'paid imperceptibly' according to Adam Smith (1776) – are less likely to have an impact on work incentives and allow the state to discourage the consumption of 'de-merit' goods such as tobacco. However, the incidence of such taxes will fall disproportionately on the poor unless a range of 'essential' goods and services are exempt.

'Merit' or 'demerit' goods?   Some items of consumption may be regarded as so important to the individual or the state that it is deemed inappropriate to tax these goods. Indeed, a tax allowance may be given to encourage consumption. Home ownership, subsidised until April 2000 by tax relief on mortgage interest, is an example of such a 'merit' good. During the twentieth century an extensive system of 'fiscal welfare' evolved and, in 1997/8, various forms of tax allowances cost the Inland Revenue £21 billion (Inland Revenue, 1997). This 'hidden welfare state' (Howard, 1997) also extends to virtuous behaviour. In 1999 New Labour introduced a Working Families Tax Credit (WFTC), unavailable to households where no-one is in work, whereby the Inland Revenue makes a positive payment to low income families. In certain presentations of expenditure figures the cost of WFTC is represented as part of the tax system and its cost is deducted from gross tax revenues (Twigger, 2000: 10).

'Earned' or 'unearned' income?   In the early twentieth century the distinction between 'earned' and 'unearned' income formed an important and contentious new principle of taxation (Whiting, 2000). The term 'unearned income' was used to refer to income from investments especially from land. In the past, special rates of taxation were levied on increases in land values and until the 1980s, investment income was subject to higher rates of tax than 'earned income'. Moreover between 1920 and 1973, the Inland Revenue allowed 'earned income relief' of two-ninths of the income not derived from investments to be deducted from the assessment of taxable income. The earned/unearned distinction fell out of use in the 1980s but was revived, in a modest form, by New Labour with its 'windfall' tax on the 'unearned' profits of the privatised monopoly utilities and the increases in Stamp Duty on the sale of homes.

Central or local taxation   In the UK the central state has allowed local government to raise a specific tax to finance local services. Traditionally this has taken the form of a levy on the value of immovable property (the rate) but in 1990 (1989 in Scotland) the rate levied on business premises became the responsibility of the central state. At the same time the domestic rate was replaced by a community charge (poll tax) imposed, with few exceptions, on all the electors in an area. In 1993 the community charge was abolished and the council tax, based on bands of property value but with discounts for single-adult households, was introduced.

Progressive, proportional or regressive taxation?   The incidence of a tax is regressive if people with the lowest resources pay a higher proportion of their income. It is proportional if all people pay the same percentage of their income and it is progressive if the proportion of income taken in tax grows as income increases (Kay and King, 1986: 217).

Earmarked or general taxation?   Since the second half of the nineteenth century the Treasury has upheld the definition of taxation as a compulsory levy made by public authorities 'for which nothing is received directly in return'. It has insisted on a single 'Treasury pool' and has been reluctant to allow the hypothecation of specific taxes to specific purposes. However, in 2000/1 extra taxation on cigarettes was earmarked for spending on the National Health Service and local authorities were allowed to charge 'congestion' taxes provided they spend the income on improvements in public transport. Some authorities have advocated an extension of the principle of hypothecation because public opinion surveys have identified a willingness to pay higher tax rates provided the extra resources are linked to a 'public service pledge' to improve a particular service (Fabian Society 2000: 173).

THE ART OF THE POSSIBLE

> ... it also needs to be borne in mind that political machinery does not act of itself. As it is first made, so it has to be worked by men, and even by ordinary men.
>
> J.S. Mill, 1996 [1861]: 191

'Welfare' is concerned with what ought to be but, to borrow the title of Lord Butler's memoirs, politics is 'the art of the possible' (Butler, 1971). In a pluralist, democratic system, the outcomes of 'grand narratives' on social distribution – the 'big ideas' of politics – are often the result of the compromises made as an 'old' order moves towards the 'new' and sometimes back again. The establishment of the National Health Service illustrates this point. Between the wars the Labour Party devised a blueprint for the delivery of health care. Medical services would be free at the point of consumption and delivered by the state through salaried employees organised in a system of 'primary' and 'secondary' health centres. However, the politics involved in gaining the agreement of all the parties with an interest in health care resulted in a fragmented service, the retention of a small but significant sector of 'for profit' medicine and considerable autonomy for the medical profession in determining the distribution of health care.

Implementation

The achievement of some desired change in distributive outcomes depends on its interpretation by the various participants in the implementation process and on the reactions of the 'subjects' of the desired change. In the UK the delivery of a policy – 'the stated intention of the government' (Levin, 1997: 15–27) – often relies on quasi-autonomous agencies such as local government, housing associations and health authorities. Even when the central government has direct control of the administration of a particular service, the degree of commitment from professionals and the interpretation of policy by 'street-level' and 'high office' officials can influence the outcomes of a policy initiative. In addition, policy 'subjects' are not mere pawns responding in predictable and manageable ways to levers pulled from above. Policy initiatives can produce unintended outcomes. Three examples illustrate the point.

The allocation of local authority housing   In 1969 the Housing Management Sub-Committee of the Central Housing Advisory Committee recommended 'need' as the principle on which local authority housing should be allocated. In 1973 Pat Niner examined the formal allocation policies of six local authorities in the Midlands. She found considerable differences in the formal allocation policy statements adopted by the six authorities to the extent that a family ranked top priority in one authority would receive a very low priority in another (Niner, 1975: 28). However, having examined the actual outcomes of the allocation processes in the six authorities, Niner discovered 'the formal allocation policy had little effect on the degree of selectivity of the allocation process'. She concluded that 'some other powerful force must be at work which can make a date order allocation scheme as selective as a points order scheme designed specifically to favour … items of housing need' (1975: 52). This 'powerful force' was the combined impact of the discretion exercised by officers in the authorities plus 'the pattern of refusals of the offer of tenancy; and the accommodation available for allocation' (1975: 57). In other words, formal allocation systems were undermined by 'street level bureaucrats' interacting with potential tenants anxious to be allocated a tenancy in the most desirable areas.

The RAWP formula   In 1976 a new formula was introduced to distribute central resources to regional and area health authorities with the Government promising that, in time, each region and area would receive a level of funding relative to its need for health care. The formula, known as the RAWP formula after its creator, the Resource Allocation Working Party (1976), initially worked well as additional funds made 'levelling up' possible. However, in the mid-1980s spending restraints meant that some regions and areas in the South received less than in previous years and had to reduce their service provision. The political backlash arising from these service cuts led to inertia in the future implementation of the RAWP formula, especially at sub-regional level, and hence the initial aims of the policy were undermined (Mohan, 1998; Glennerster et al., 2000).

Tenant's choice and housing action trusts   In 1980 local authority tenants were given a legal right to buy their homes. This right generated over 800,000 sales but by the mid-1980s it was beginning to lose momentum. In combination with the decline of the private landlord sector, the right to buy had helped to produce a shortage of family accommodation for rent in many areas. The Conservative Party's 1987 manifesto declared that the shortage of rented accommodation:

> restricts housing choice and hinders the economy. People looking for work cannot easily move to a different area to do so. Those who find work may not be able to find rented accommodation nearby ... [And] the economy as a whole is damaged when workers cannot move to fill jobs because there are no homes to rent in the neighbourhood. (Conservative Party, 1987)

To promote the supply of rented accommodation by the 'independent' sector and reduce the role of local government in supplying housing, the Conservatives announced they would abolish rent regulation and take steps to ensure that local authorities transferred their stock to new landlords. Nicholas Ridley, the then Secretary of State for the Environment, believed that council tenants 'received a rotten service – repairs and maintenance and improvements were minimal – yet they were trapped in their houses by the lack of availability of alternative accommodation to rent' (Ridley, 1991: 87). This thinking led him to introduce 'Tenants' Choice' and Housing Action Trusts in the 1988 Housing Act. Under 'Tenants' Choice' the Housing Corporation would introduce tenants to an 'alternative' landlord and a ballot would be held to determine whether or not tenants wished to transfer their tenancy to this new landlord. Housing Action Trusts, according to Margaret Thatcher, were set up 'to take over bad estates, renovate them and pass them on to different tenures and ownership' (Thatcher, 1993: 571).

Tenants' Choice had little impact. Only two tenant groups took up Tenants' Choice and Housing Action Trusts languished until special deals were negotiated allowing residents to return to local authority tenancies when the refurbishment of the estate was complete. The distributive consequences of this policy failure are difficult to assess. It is clear that the Conservative Government was prepared to commit substantial resources to removing rented accommodation from local government control. Tenant resistance meant that the millions of pounds devoted to the project remained unspent. As Mrs Thatcher said, 'one would never have guessed that we were offering huge sums of taxpayer's money' (Thatcher, 1993: 601). On the other hand transfer to a new landlord would have meant paying higher rents in the future so, in the long-term, opposition to transfer might have produced real gains for tenants. Whatever the distributive consequences they were not those intended by the Government when the policy was formed.

CONCLUSION

The 2001 edition of *Social Trends* (Office for National Statistics, 2001) gives a statistical snapshot of the distribution of wealth in the UK in the late 1990s. The figures relate only to 'marketable' wealth (wealth that can be sold for cash). In 1998 the wealthiest 10 per cent of adults held 56 per cent of all the marketable wealth whereas the least wealthy 50 per cent held only 6 per cent. In 1997/8 30 per cent of the adult population reported that they had no savings and 50 per cent had savings of less than £1500 (Office for National Statistics, 2000: 97).

Income is more evenly distributed than wealth. In 1999/2000, the fifth of households with the highest incomes obtained an average of £54,400 per year from 'market-related' activities. In contrast, the poorest fifth acquired £2840 (Lakin, 2001: 41). Adding in the value of all benefits in cash and kind and deducting indirect and direct taxation gave the top fifth £38,300 per year, compared to the £8870 obtained by the fifth of households with the lowest incomes. The impact of state activity was to reduce inequality from the nineteen-fold difference produced by the operations of 'primary' distributive systems (the structured market and the family) to a four-fold difference in 'final income'. But what mechanisms have shaped the distributive outcomes of the 'primary' systems of income distribution and what role has the state played in generating and sustaining these mechanisms? In what circumstances did the extensive state involvement in the distribution of 'final' income arise? What principles have been applied by the state in its acquisition of resources and to their subsequent redistribution? Have these principles enhanced 'social justice' and reduced 'social exclusion'?

2

The 'Invisible Hand' and the Emerging State

THE MARKET

It is, of course, an error to construct the nineteenth century as the era of doctrinaire prohibition of government intervention. Nonetheless, as Hoppen (1998: 92) has argued, 'the ideology which spoke most powerfully to the condition of the new industrial society was that which had first sprung from the so-called classical economists and then been filtered down through the utilitarianism of Jeremy Bentham and his disciples'.

Adam Smith (1723–1790)

A critique of mercantilist ideas was at the heart of Adam Smith's *Inquiry into the Nature and Causes of the Wealth of Nations* (1776). Mercantilism, a loose collection of maxims derived from the doctrine of the absolute rights of kings, asserted that, because the wealth in the world is finite, any increase in trade by one nation must be at the expense of its competitors. Mercantilists exhorted each sovereign to aim for a favourable balance of trade to supply the bullion for 'the defence of the realm'. Moreover, 'the task of the wise administration of the nation was to maintain all its objects (persons, things) in their rightful place' (Dean, 1991: 30). The state's human assets – its 'loyal subjects' – had to be regulated both at home and abroad. Welfare measures formed an important part of this social control apparatus (Krieger, 1974: 557). Parishes were required to levy a rate to set the poor to work, labour mobility was discouraged by the severe punishment of 'sturdy vagabonds' and regulations governing wage levels were issued to 'yield to the hired person ... a convenient proportion of wages' (Statute of Artificers, 1563). The Navigation Acts (1651–1849) managed overseas trade, restrictions were placed on the export of coal, machinery and wool (Checkland, 1983: 18) and men with mechanical skills were not allowed to emigrate (Floud, 1997: 160).

Adam Smith attacked mercantilism with the argument that a nation's wealth resided, not in the accumulation of bullion, but in the effective use of its stock of labour skills. He claimed the division and specialisation of labour expanded wealth by increasing the dexterity of the labour force and facilitating the use of mechanical devices. Individuals and nations need not be self-sufficient for they could meet their wants 'by treaty, by barter and by purchase' of goods produced by others (Smith, 1776, Book 1: 119). Consumption being 'the sole end and purpose of all production' then 'all are obliged by self-interest to bring the results of their efforts 'into a common stock, where every man may purchase whatever part of the produce of other men's talents he has occasion for' (Smith, 1776, Book 2: 155). The market performs the task of distributing the 'common stock' efficiently. Each person, on entering the market is

> led by an invisible hand to promote an end which was no part of his intention ... By pursuing his own interest he frequently promotes that of society more effectually than when he really intends to promote it. (Smith, 1776, Book 1: 400)

Thomas Robert Malthus (1766–1834) and David Ricardo (1772–1823)

Thomas Robert Malthus' various essays on the *Principle of Population*, published between 1798 and 1826, supported Smith's thesis that intervention in markets produced undesirable consequences. Population, Malthus argued, increases in a geometrical ratio, whereas 'the subsistence for man which the earth affords' grows only in an arithmetic ratio. This proposition led to the dismal conclusion that 'positive checks' of famine, infanticide and plague on population growth were inevitable. State intervention to assist the poor to meet their subsistence requirements would not prevent the day of reckoning. On the contrary, by discouraging the 'negative checks' of forgoing marriage and abstaining from sex, it would bring the doomsday forward.

David Ricardo reached a similar conclusion on the futility of state intervention to assist the poor. His *Principles of Political Economy and Taxation* (1971 [1817]: 1) was 'the inquiry into the laws which determine the division of the product of industry among the classes who concur in its formation'. Ricardo identified three elements in 'the product of industry'; land, for which rent was paid, labour, remunerated by wages and capital, whose reward was interest. He believed there was little scope for increasing the 'product of industry' through increases in 'rent'. 'A rent is paid because corn is high', he said, not because rent determines the price of 'corn' (the product of the land). Wages were determined by the 'iron law' identified by Malthus and hence there was a national 'wage fund' – the amount necessary to keep the number of labourers constant. Economic progress could come only through augmenting the propensity of capitalists to invest by increasing the interest paid on their investments.

Jeremy Bentham (1748–1832)

Support for 'laissez-faire' from the domain of political theory came from Utilitarianism. Jeremy Bentham, the most influential promoter of the theory, recognised a political response was necessary to the forces of industrialisation that were starting to dissolve the bonds of custom, tradition and religion. In *A Fragment of Government* (1776) and *An Introduction to the Principles of Morals and Legislation* (1781) he defined happiness as the 'felicific calculus' of that which reduces individual pain and enhances personal pleasure. Because the 'utility' of a good is 'that property in any object whereby it tends to produce benefit, advantage, good or happiness ... to the party whose interest is considered', it followed that no activity has a value above the calculus of individual pleasure and pain. Each person knows what makes him happy so 'Pushpin is as good as poetry'. The objective of government is to promote 'the greatest happiness of the greatest number', an aim best achieved by laissez-faire, but not in every case. When it could be shown beyond reasonable doubt that laissez-faire did not produce 'the greatest happiness of the greatest number' then state intervention was justifiable, but only if such intervention was efficient. Bentham's enthusiasm for efficiency was demonstrated in his *Pauper Management Improved* (1798) where he presented proposals to convert the 'dross' of society into 'sterling'. A National Charity Company was to be set up to erect 'industry houses', each with 5000 paupers, to which all those without visible means of support would be sent (Jacobs, 1976: 94). Each 'industry house' could be made to yield a profit by 'the unremitting supervision and discipline, the ingenious economics of diet, dress and lodging, the prolonged hours of labour and the enforced stay of apprentices during their years of greatest productivity' (Himmelfarb, 1984: 81).

EXTERNALITIES

Take my word for it, Sammy, the poor in a loomp is bad.

Alfred Lord Tennyson, *The Northern Farmer - New Style*, 1856

The notion that the state should 'leave to be' helped to restrict the forms of state intervention developed under mercantilist influence. Assistance to the destitute was curtailed (the Poor Law Amendment Act 1834), agriculture was exposed to foreign competition (the repeal of the Corn Laws 1846) and paternalistic relationships between employer and employee were undermined when the Truck Act of 1831 prevented the payment of wages in kind. The main reason the dominance of 'laissez-faire' did not empty the statute books was the recognition that, in an industrial, urban economy, no man is an island. In the middle years of the nineteenth century, a type of politician/administrator began to emerge who adopted the basic tenets of 'laissez-faire', but supported limited forms of state intervention. A notion of 'the community interest' was an integral part of Utilitarianism (Barry, 1990: 21, Searle, 1998: 27) and, through 'scientific investigation', utility experts discovered what economists in the twentieth century came to call 'externalities'. 'Externalities' occur when there are gains (a positive externality) or losses (a negative externality) 'sustained by others as a result of actions initiated by producers or consumers or both ...' (Hardwick et al., 1994: 209).

The urbanisation of the nineteenth century generated massive externalities such as human dunghills, polluted rivers and the keeping of cattle in the backyards of terraced property. Most important were the deaths from cholera and typhoid that, unlike other major killers such as typhus and tuberculosis, spread rapidly to the middle class (Laybourn, 1995: 84). When cholera deaths were traced to houses supplied with water contaminated by human excrement, the need for an efficient sewerage system, available to *all* households, became clear. Experts in 'utility maximisation' regarded 'externality' as a sufficient reason to justify state intervention in the form of regulation and, if necessary, the use of collective revenues to provide 'public' services. Nonetheless, this 'expert' recognition of 'externalities' did not automatically lead to intervention. The plea for 'economy', buttressed by a demand for local autonomy, remained strong. As James Hole said of the local boards of health established in many urban areas under the Public Health Act 1848:

> They and those that elect them, are ... the owners, generally speaking, of the very property which requires improvement ... Every pound they vote for drainage, or other sanitary improvement is something taken out of their own pocket ... to the ratepayers themselves a little claptrap about centralisation, and still more appeal to their own pockets ... is sufficient cause for the rejection of the most useful measures. (Hole, 1866, cited in Wohl, 1983: 170)

Hence the path to public health was twisted and troublesome, which meant the administrative machinery necessary to supply the infrastructure for public health – sewerage and water supply – was not in place until the late 1880s.

The notion of 'externality' helps to explain the movement for public health but politicians/administrators such as Edwin Chadwick, Nassau Senior, James Kay and John Simon interpreted the notion of 'harm to others' in very broad terms equating it with a strong notion of 'national morality'. Their investigations into the 'state of the nation' led them to conclude the 'slum' produced harm to society going well beyond its contribution to the spread of disease. The term 'slum' was applied to an entire area of social pathology as well as to a single dwelling deemed unfit for human habitation. As Mellor (1977: 42) has explained, 'the slum was the locale of vice, crime, delinquency and disease, a disorderly gathering of people beyond society and without community'. It spawned a number of undesirable consequences. Moral degradation, associated with overcrowding, was thought to be endemic in slum areas. John Montgomery told the Social Science Association 'If human beings are crowded together then moral corruption takes place, as certainly as fermentation or putrefaction in a heap of organic matter' (Montgomery, 1862, cited in Wohl, 1983: 287). The high death rate in the slums led to the substitution of young and inexperienced labour for skilled hands and added to the poor rate by the premature death of the main breadwinner (Chadwick, 1842). Conditions in the slums so depressed the human spirit that 'the temptation to drown care in intoxicating liquors … is seldom permanently resisted' (Chadwick, 1842). Mearns summarised the problem in *The Bitter Cry of Outcast London*:

> seething in the very centre of our great cities, concealed by the thinnest crust of civilisation and decency, is a vast mass of moral corruption, of heartbreaking misery and absolute godlessness … The terrible flood of sin and misery is gaining upon us. (Mearns, 1883: 1,56)

The perceived connection between cleanliness and godliness helped to promote local authority provision of public baths and washhouses (Parry, 1993: 207). Relief from 'narrow courts and confined streets' was promoted by The Towns Improvement Act 1847, which granted powers to local authorities to acquire land and maintain parks (Cherry, 1988: 46). The immorality associated with overcrowding was tackled by the Common Lodging-Houses Act of 1851 that required the registration of all common lodging houses, gave local authorities the right to determine how many people could reside in a lodging house and allowed the authorities to evict those above the prescribed maximum. The 1875 Public Health Act declared 'any house or part of a house so overcrowded as to be dangerous or injurious to the health of the inmates' to be a 'statutory nuisance' and liable to closure. The 1875 Artisans' and Labourers' Dwellings Improvement Act (the Cross Act) made provision for the eradication of the slum area. Its aim was to create a 'virtuous circle' whereby state finance, in the form of cheap loans, was used to clear the slums with the enhanced value of the sites providing future resources for clearance. The 'virtuous circle' did not develop. The Cross Act placed a duty on local authorities to arrange for new dwellings to be built on or near the cleared site, sufficient to rehouse the displaced persons (in 1882 this duty was reduced to 50 per cent of displaced persons). However, when local authorities attempted to meet this duty, they found land costs were far greater than housing suppliers could afford so the promise to clear all the slums in London, at a cost to the rates of two million pounds, was not fulfilled (Yelling, 1986). Sometimes the rehousing of former slum dwellers in an 'improvement scheme' was ignored. Joseph Chamberlain – convinced 'the horrible, shameful houses in which many of the poor are expected to live' caused intemperance (Chamberlain, 1874, cited in Watts, 1992: 58) – introduced a 'grand town improvement' scheme to redevelop 93 acres of central Birmingham. However, he left the provision of replacement homes to the private sector on the argument there was adequate dwelling-house accommodation for the artisan and labouring classes within the borough (Powell, 1972: 27). The death rate declined from 53.2 to 21.3 per thousand but the redeveloped area contained very few houses for the working class. As a local newspaper commented at the time:

New Birmingham recipe for lowering the death rate of an insanitary area. Pull down nearly all the houses and make the inhabitants live somewhere else. 'Tis an excellent plan and I'll tell you for why. Where there's no person living, no person can die. (cited in Watts, 1992: 53)

PHILANTHROPY

Adam Smith held the 'beneficent virtues' in high regard but he did not believe charitable giving was essential to a stable society. 'Society may subsist among different men, as among different merchants', he explained, 'from a sense of utility, without any mutual love or affection' (quoted in Mencher, 1967: 66). Nonetheless, the heyday of laissez-faire was also the heyday of philanthropy. Driven by Evangelical Christianity there was a remarkable increase in the number of charities between 1850 and 1900 (Heasman, 1962: 8).

Religious motivations underpinned charitable activity because magnanimity was the passport to salvation and a good in itself. Moreover, because suffering was linked to sin, if the needy could be attracted into virtuous belief by the example of the donor, then the quality of charity was twice blessed. Benevolence was expressed in a variety of contexts. The Churches were deeply involved in education because children needed to be taught their letters to read the Bible and education was considered inseparable from the teaching of Christian morality. Religious rivalry fuelled the drive to offer schooling for, if taught correctly, the children of today would become the 'true believers' of tomorrow. The National Society for Promoting the Education of the Poor in the Principles of the Established Church supervised the provision of education linked to the Church of England and its rival, the British and Foreign Schools Society, performed a similar task for dissenters.

Health care was also a major arena for philanthropic activity (Abel-Smith, 1964: 41). Hospitals established in earlier times were extended and new 'specialist' hospitals were set up to enable doctors with a particular interest to develop their expertise. Donations to hospitals were encouraged by the 'ticket' system whereby, in return for a donation, the benefactor was entitled to nominate patients for treatment. However, by the late nineteenth century, many voluntary hospitals were in financial difficulties and, in an attempt to raise revenue, they started to introduce pay-wards for the middle class and charge nurses for their training (Waddington, 1996: 189–90). What are now called the 'personal social services', financed today mainly by local authority social services departments, formed a third domain of charitable activity. Special local interest groups, often linked to a national organisation, were created for almost every contingency with 144 new charitable agencies established in London alone in the 1850s (Owen, 1965: 169).

Altruism, arising from religious beliefs, played an important role in the development of voluntary organisations, but philanthropy also served more self-regarding purposes. In his *Reflections on the Revolution in France* (1790), Edmund Burke emphasised the need for an ordered, hierarchical society – one that promoted social inclusion via reciprocal obligations. The exercise of social control, via the demand for obligations in return for charity, was deeply rooted in the voluntary welfare system. Hannah Moore, the founder of several charitable schools, put the matter bluntly. In a year of severe depression, when labourers had been relieved by charitable organisations, she told the people in her area:

> We trust the poor in general … have received what has been done for them as a matter of favour, not of right – if so, the same kindness will, I doubt not, always be extended to them, whenever it shall please God so to afflict the land. (Hannah Moore, 1801, cited in Jones, 1952: 158)

Subtler forms of social control can be found in the activities of the Charity Organisation Society and the voluntary housing movement.

The Charity Organisation Society

Character is the key to circumstances. He therefore that would permanently mend circumstances must aim at character. All that can be done externally to remove obstacles and improve circumstances should be done, but there will be no lasting betterment without the internal change. (23rd Report of the Charity Organisation Society, 1894, cited in Kirkman Gray, 1908: 112)

The proliferation of charities caused concern about the impact of indiscriminate largesse on the moral fibre of its recipients. In 1869 the Society for Organising Charitable Relief and Repressing Mendicity, to become known simply as the Charity Organisation Society (COS), was formed to tackle the problem in London and similar organisations developed in the provinces. The COS's philosophy was based on the notion that charity, 'unwisely administered', was 'capable of doing incalculable harm' by attracting 'the individual from the wise and natural toilsomeness of life' (COS, cited in Humphreys, 1995: 53). By encouraging co-operation between charities and the Poor Law authorities the COS hoped to establish distributive principles for assistance and apply these principles to reward self-help and repress begging. Charles Stewart Loch, the first Secretary of the COS, set out the 'principles of charity' as the person benefiting should be restored to self-dependence, all forms of pressure should be used to promote self-reliance and consideration must be given to the whole family when assessing requests for assistance (Woodroofe, 1962: 33). Restoration to independence was to be achieved through a relationship between the caseworker and the receiver of relief – a relationship intended to restore the personal connection between the classes believed to have been severed by urbanisation. 'In a great city' said Loch 'the larger proportion of applicants for relief are made from strangers to strangers' hence 'the element of obligation inherent in the gift had gone' (Loch, 1895: 61–2). The 'casework' relationship also served as the mechanism for separating genuine 'needs' from artificial 'wants' and for controlling misfeasance. COS volunteers were to 'visit those who have been helped and exercise a personal influence over them, so as to insure that the aid given is really beneficial' (COS, 1893, cited in Fido, 1977: 209). Loch also claimed the voluntary sector and the state had discrete clientele; charitable aid should be restricted to the 'deserving poor' and state relief should be concentrated on the 'undeserving' poor. The COS mounted numerous campaigns against out-relief, favoured by some Guardians because it was economical (Humphreys, 1995: 52). It wished to see the 'undeserving' poor 'treated in the workhouse, with gentleness and human care but under strict regulation and not a high scale of comfort' (Bosanquet, 1893: 329). Begging was to be strictly deterred and the COS recommended 'all who, by begging, proclaim themselves destitute, must be taken at their word. They must be taken up and kept at penal work not for one morning, as now, but for a month or two' (COS, cited in Jones, 1984: 273).

The distinction between 'deserving' and 'undeserving' poor and the associated exclusion of the 'undeserving poor' was at the core of COS philosophy. Whether or not a supplicant for aid was classified as 'deserving' depended on the judgement of the 'caseworkers' employed by the COS. These social workers were responsible for ensuring that material aid formed part of a plan to restore the recipient to independence and, in the absence of other forms of help in times of distress, a needy person was at the mercy of the caseworker. In return for help the applicant had to submit to detailed enquiries into her personal circumstances, receive regular home visits and accept 'simple recipes' on how to manage on a low income from someone whose superior social status was supposed to make her befitting to deliver such lectures (Humphreys, 1995: 145). This process of separating the 'deserving' from the 'undeserving', by the courteous yet patronising dispensers of relief, was resented by the 'dis-respectable' and 'respectable' poor alike. Emerging socialist ideas fuelled this resentment. When George Landsbury was told by Lord Swaythling that he gave one-tenth of his income to the poor, he retorted 'we Socialists want to prevent you from getting the nine-tenths' (cited in Finlayson, 1994: 157). J.A. Hobson accused the COS of hypocrisy because of its belief that cash for the poor, without obligations, was 'undeserved' whereas the 'unearned' income of the rich from land was a legitimate entitlement (Hobson, 1891). Mrs Townshend (1910: 12) added the charge that the COS neglected the influence of social conditions on behaviour. The COS responded to this criticism and, according to a leading figure in the COS, the deserving/undeserving distinction was 'largely passing out of use' by the end of the nineteenth century (Bosanquet, 1917: 112) being replaced by the less censorious terms 'helpable' and 'unhelpable' (Lewis, 1995: 58). Nevertheless, although only alcoholics were routinely denied help, patro-nising attitudes persisted and the COS remained firmly opposed to any state assistance to the poor outside a stern Poor Law.

The voluntary housing movement

The provision of accommodation by the voluntary sector contained three elements. Some wealthy manufacturers built 'model villages', usually linked to their factories. Often established from the purest of motives – many of the industrial philanthropists had connections with the Society of Friends – these 'model villages' offered a pervasive form of social control. Loss of a job could also mean eviction from home and exclusion from recreation. The mainstream voluntary housing movement was involved in erecting 'model' dwellings, often in clearance areas. Some associations derived their resources entirely from charitable endowments, but most set out to demonstrate that 'wholesome' dwellings could be provided for the working class if financiers limited their investment return to five per cent rather than the normal seven to ten per cent. The demonstration was not successful. The houses, built to sanitary standards, had to be let at rents beyond the means of the poorer sections of the working class. Letting to skilled workers rather than to the poor was defended with the argument that new dwellings, occupied by 'artisans', would release existing houses where poorer people could live. In *The Homes of the Working Classes* (1866) James Hole claimed '...by increasing the number of first class houses for mechanics the vacated tenements increase the supply for the second and third classes and thus all classes are befitted (quoted in Boddy and Gray, 1979: 43). But 'trickle down' failed. The rapid urban population growth at the time and the limited replacement of demolished dwellings meant the housing needs of the poor were submerged by new household formation. As the Charity Organisation Society noted:

> there is a constant influx and migration of people and an annual increase of the population of about 60,000; the vacuum, such as it is, is immediately filled up, and there is no reason for believing that, when 'Dwellings' are erected, houses occupied formerly by better class tenants, are occupied by the next and lower grades. (Charity Organisation Society, 1881: 123–4)

The COS recognised the fundamental housing problem of the urban poor was their inability to afford to live in properties built to 'sufficient' standards (Jones, 1984: 197). However, it rejected subsidies because '...not only would the profits of commercial investment be impaired, but the principle of self dependence would be attacked, habits of self-indulgence would be encouraged, and even the wages of unskilled labour might be reduced' (Charity Organisation Society, 1881: 11). Octavia Hill's solution was to provide accommodation for labourers in irregular work by purchasing dilapidated properties, improving them to basic standards – some of her dwellings were declared unfit for human habitation – and offering rooms to tenants at a low rent (Darley, 1990: 135). She believed 'if the property required 'reconditioning' then 'so sometimes did the occupants' (Curtis, 1956: 58). 'If the loving kindness of the friend', she said, is united 'to the control of the landlord ... you will rule a little kingdom in righteousness' (Hill, 1889: 459). In the belief that a great deal of the degradation of the poor could be attributed to the absence of middle-class influence in poor areas (Lewis, 1991: 35), Octavia Hill employed 'governing and guiding' women to improve the character of her tenants. These attempts at moral improvement often failed and, in accordance with Octavia Hill's strict rules on the payment of rent, the tenant was evicted.

THE FAMILY

The Elizabethan Poor Law required 'liable relatives' to repay the authorities for the upkeep of their kin; the communal duty to assist the destitute was accompanied by a community right to demand recompense from the 'extended' family of the pauper.

> The father and grandfather, mother and grandmother and children of every poor, old, blind, lame and impotent person or other poor person not able to work, being of sufficient ability, shall at their own charge relieve and maintain every such poor person. (43 Elizabeth 1 c.2 cited in Bruce, 1973: 39)

This obligation to support members of the extended family was not complemented by rights vested in children, women and elderly people to claim maintenance directly from the male head of the household. English common law 'did not recognize any enforceable duty on a parent (unless he had made a contract to do so) to support his child or pay his debts or to educate it' (Department of Health and Social Security, 1974b: 100). Until 1870 a man owned the property of his wife and had a common law duty to maintain her. A man owed this duty to maintain to the community not to his spouse and, until the 1886 Maintenance of Wives Act, a wife could not sue for maintenance in a magistrate's court even when she left her husband (Land, 1995: 85). Elderly people had no legal rights to claim maintenance directly from their children and most Boards of Guardians appeared to have ignored their duty to claim the cost of maintaining elderly people from liable relatives (Hoppen, 1998: 317).

In the early nineteenth century illegitimate children had more legal rights than legitimate children. Under the bastardy laws a single woman could declare a man to be the father of her child and the overseers of the poor could apply to a justice of the peace for a warrant requiring the putative father to pay maintenance. The Poor Law Commissioners believed this right to maintenance was an incentive to female immorality and deception. They expressed concern that 'innocent' men could be made responsible for illegitimate children (Checkland and Checkland, 1974: 259–72) and declared:

> what Providence appears to have ordained that it should be, a burthen on its mother, and, where she cannot maintain it, on her parents. The shame of the offence will not be destroyed by its being the means of income and marriage, and we must thrust that as soon as it has become both burdensome and disgraceful, it will become as rare as it is among those classes in this who are above parish relief … (Poor Law Commissioners, 1834, cited in Department of Health and Social Security, 1974: 115)

The bastardy clauses of the 1834 Poor Law Amendment Act reflected the Commissioners' view that females were responsible for illegitimacy.

Maintenance orders could not be for an amount greater than parish relief and they lasted only until the child was seven.

Systematic thinking on the nature of the family as a secular, social institution was rare even at the end of the nineteenth century. However, in 1906, Helen Bosanquet, an influential member of the COS, provided a succinct justification of the prevailing orthodoxy. She summed up the family in a sentence:

> What is a Family, and what is its purpose? No one will feel himself at a loss in answering the question; man, woman, and child, the 'practical syllogism', two premises and their conclusion, these in their combination form the Family, and the purpose of the combination is the mutual convenience and protection of all the members belonging to it. (Bosanquet, 1906: 16)

Bosanquet regarded the father as the source of authority in the family. This authority was derived 'not only by natural disposition, but also and mainly by the natural and necessary division of labour between the two chief members of the partnership' (Bosanquet, 1906: 272). The wife was assigned the functions of family income manager and carer of home and children, while the husband and adult children assumed responsibility to provide income. Men, according to Bosanquet, were 'incapable of the more domestic duties incident upon the rearing of children' and it was 'largely this incapacity which gives him the power both of concentration and of width of view' (1906: 272–73). 'If the husband is the head of the family', she continued, 'the wife is the centre. It is she who is primarily responsible for the care of the children; to the utmost extent of which the family means will allow, it is her duty to see they are well cared for, both physically and morally; and it is generally agreed that this duty can be properly fulfilled only by personal attention' (1906: 279). Bosanquet recognised that sometimes women, 'neglected their primary duty' and worked outside the home. Nonetheless she asserted that 'nothing could so well emphasise the importance of the woman in the Family as the miserable condition of home and children when she is not in the Family but in the mill' (1906: 294).

Bosanquet's account captures the dominant view of the relationships involved in the 'ideal' family. The civil and political citizenship of men derived from their rational, abstract, disembodied minds enabled them to apply dispassionate reason and standards of justice (Lister, 1997: 68). The citizenship of the male was enhanced by his role in 'protecting, subsuming and even owning others' (Fraser and Gordon, 1994: 88). Women's concerns were with the particular, the private, the creation of the home as a 'moral haven' and as 'the chancellor of the domestic exchequer' (Select Committee on the Married Women's Property Bill, cited in Lewis,

1999: 254). This did not preclude women from entering the public sphere, indeed Bosanquet was a powerful advocate of their inclusion, but their role was in the civic dimensions of domestic life not in the domains of economic or foreign policy. The dearth of evidence makes it difficult to assess the extent to which reality of the family matched Bosanquet's rhetoric. Recorded illegitimacy per 1000 births was 42 at the turn of the century (Bliss, 1909: 594) but 'premarital pregnancy was far more common, as high as 40–50 per cent in some parishes early in the century, although far lower later' (Himmelfarb, 1995: 42). In 1901 about 13 per cent of married women were engaged in paid labour outside the home (Bourke, 1994: 100).

THE STATE AS PROVIDER

> To shift the responsibility of maintenance from the individual to the State is to sterilise the productive power of the community as a whole, and also to impose on the State ... so heavy a liability ... as may greatly hamper, if not almost ruin, it. (Charles Loch, 1895)

Education

The economists who promoted the market as the most efficient distributive mechanism agreed that education was the most important exception to the general prohibition against state intervention. Adam Smith recognised the idea of 'externalities'. He claimed 'the expense of the institutions for education and religious instruction is ... beneficial to the whole society, and may, therefore, without injustice, be defrayed by the general contribution of the whole society' (cited in Copley and Sutherland, 1995: 88). Smith promoted state involvement in education because, with the division of labour, 'the minds of men are contracted and rendered incapable of elevation' and hence, without education, 'corruption and degeneracy' of labouring people were likely (Smith 1776: 734). He recommended that the state should establish a school in every area that would charge a modest fee. Whereas attendance would not be compulsory, Smith believed that making an examination in the 'three Rs' a condition of entering a guild or trade would encourage education. Despite the endorsement of state involvement in education by liberal economists, the idea encountered strong opposition. Provision of education removed children from the labour force thereby infringing the principle of laissez-faire and it was argued that, because religion and education were synonymous, then education must be provided by the churches. Others believed any education would be 'prejudicial to the morals and happiness of the labouring classes' teaching them 'to despise their lot in life' and making them 'insolent to their superiors'

(Davies Giddy, 1807, cited in McCoy, 1998: 110). Initially the supply of education was left to the voluntary and commercial sectors. When, in 1834, the Manchester Statistical Society conducted a survey of education in Manchester, it classified the schools into seven types:

1   Endowed schools, financed by wealthy benefactors, providing educa-
    tion entirely free of charge. They ranged from the Manchester
    Grammar School to schools for workhouse children who made pins in
    the morning and were taught by older paupers in the afternoon.
2   Infant schools financed by the churches and small payments from the
    parents of the pupils.
3   'Dame' schools – entirely commercial and little more than child-minding
    establishments but catering for over half the children under five.
4   Common day-schools – commercial schools for older children charg-
    ing from 2 pence to 7.5 pence per week.
5   'Superior' private and boarding schools.
6   Evening schools catering for students between 14 and 18 years of age.
7   Sunday schools, which instructed children in religion, reading and
    writing without interfering with weekday industry.

In Manchester only 56 per cent of children between five and 15 were receiving any form of instruction and, of this number, more than half were receiving only Sunday school lessons (Simon, 1938: 121).

State intervention in education started in 1833 when, following Althorp's Factory Act, which stipulated that children should be schooled for at least two hours per week, grants were made to religious bodies to enable them to develop educational establishments. The annual grant – extended to Roman Catholic schools in England in 1847 – was modest. By the early 1860s, central government provided only 23 pence in every pound of the revenue received by Anglican schools and 26 pence in the pound to non-conformist schools (Hurt, 1971: 64). State involvement in the direct provision of education has been explained by a variety of factors. Changes in the franchise produced the need to 'compel our future masters to learn their letters' (Lowe, 1867). Non-conformists wanted a system of education that would not perpetuate the influence of the Church of England (Bebbington, 1982: 127). Compulsory education in Prussia was perceived as producing an efficient labour force and it was necessary to occupy children who were being progressively excluded from the labour force (Musgrove, 1964: 76). According to West (1965: 167) '93 per cent of school leavers were already literate when the 1870 school boards first began to operate'. This evidence has been used to support the argument that it was the absence of 'public' education (schooling controlled by 'fit and proper persons' and not by parents) that was critical in the demand for state education.

In 1870 W.E. Forster, the Vice President of the Committee of the Privy Council on Education, told the House of Commons:

Upon the speedy provision of elementary education depends our industrial prosperity. It is no use trying to give technical education to our artisans without elementary education; uneducated labourers ... are for the most part, unskilled labourers ... Upon this speedy provision of education depends also, I fully believe, ... the safeguarding of our constitutional system ... Upon this speedy provision of education depends also our political power ... if we are to hold our position among men of our own race or among the nations of the world we must make up for the smallness of our numbers by increasing the intellectual force of the individual. (W.E. Forster, 1870)

'Of those children aged between six and ten', he informed the House, 'we have helped about 700,000 more or less, but we have left unhelped 1,000,000; while of those between ten and twelve, we have helped 250,000, and left unhelped at least 500,000'. The first problem was therefore to 'cover the country with good schools'. The educational condition of each district would be assessed. 'If, in any one of these districts we find the elementary education to be sufficient, efficient, and suitable', said Forster, 'we leave that district alone but, if insufficiency is ascertained, then it is by public provision that need must be supplied'. The mechanism of public supply would be an elected School Board and the finance would come from rates and central grants with local management subject to central inspection and control. The 1870 Education Act did not make elementary education compulsory but School Boards could require attendance by passing by-laws. Most did not make such by-laws until the Compulsory By-Laws Act 1880 required all education authorities to legislate on school attendance. The impact of the 1870 and 1880 Acts is revealed in the experience of Reading where, in 1872, 4884 places were available in private, voluntary and church schools. By 1902, 14,010 places were available of which 9552 were supplied by local government (Alexander, 1985: 142).

Poor relief

'An Act for the Relief of the Poor' 1601, a consolidation of earlier legislation, placed an obligation on 'the churchwardens of every parish' to appoint 'overseers of the poor'. The rationale of the parish – an ecclesiastical unit – as the local administrative unit was that it would produce sufficient voluntary donations for the relief of the poor. However, voluntary donations proved inadequate (Ashley, 1925: 111) and, by 1601, overseers had gained the power to raise 'competent sums of money' by a compulsory rate. The duties of the overseers included provision of 'convenient houses of dwelling for the impotent poor', 'putting children out to be apprentices' and the purchase of 'a convenient stock of flax, hemp, wool, thread, iron, and other ware and stuff, to set the poor on work' (An Act for the Relief of the Poor, 1601, cited in Bruce, 1973: 39).

The cost of relief raised the issue of which parish should support a supplicant for assistance. The Law of Settlement, 1662, set out the basic conditions governing this obligation. A person acquired 'settlement' in a particular parish by occupying a property worth more than ten pounds per year, by serving an apprenticeship in the parish, by marriage and by being hired for more than a year. Without such settlement rights 'outsiders' could be removed from the parish within 40 days of arrival. This settlement law reflected concern about the potential disruption of the social order caused by labour mobility and was accompanied by strong measures to deter 'sturdy vagabonds'. A series of statutes in the early sixteenth century produced a Tudor version of the 'three strikes and you're out' approach to criminal justice produced in the USA in the 1990s. A first offence of vagrancy was punished by 'whipping with rods', a second offence by the 'stigmatic amputation' of an ear, a third offence by execution (Humphreys, 1999: 44–5).

A myriad of aid systems developed under the 1601 Act. Some were austere (including workhouse provision), others have been regarded as 'generous' according to the standards of the time (King, 2000: 54; Thane, 2000: 147–59). Daunton (1995: 452) claims the dominant ethos was that the parish had a duty to provide 'appropriate' assistance to deal with 'life cycle' indigence. It has even been claimed the standard of relief in rural areas for the elderly poor was more generous in relative terms than provision in the post-war welfare state (Thomson, 1984). In many areas 'country gentlemen' were prepared to defend the parish assistance as a 'natural' right of the poor and appeals against decisions by the overseers could be made to the county courts.

By the early nineteenth century the operation of the Elizabethan Poor Law was perceived by liberal economists to be an anachronistic remnant of mercantilist principles (Mencher, 1967). This view gained purchase as concern mounted about the rising cost of relief, the 'ingratitude' of the poor and the failure of the system to prevent social unrest (Burnett, 1994: 38). The 1824 Vagrancy Act was an attempt to revise earlier vagrancy legislation, perceived as 'extremely loose in its definitions and enactments' (House of Commons Select Committee, 1821, cited in Humphreys, 1999: 81). It classified vagrants into three types – 'idle and disorderly', 'rogues and vagabonds' and 'incorrigible rogues' and allowed justices of the peace to punish any 'suspicious' vagrant, on the evidence of one 'credible witness' with imprisonment of up to 12 months or a public flogging for 'incorrigible rogues'.

In 1832 a Royal Commission on the Poor Law was appointed. Its report, published in 1834, identified the variety of practices in the 15,000 parishes and declared many of them to be unacceptable. At the heart of the polemic against the Poor Law was the notion that it encouraged the labouring classes to believe that they had a right to relief and thereby promoted unruly behaviour if this 'right' was denied (Burnett, 1994: 31). The 1832 report was replete with stories of the recipients of relief brazenly asserting their rights. Asked by the clerk to the magistrates at Swaffham, Suffolk about the burdens to the parish caused by her seven illegitimate children, the accused woman responded that 'I am not going to be disappointed in my company with men to save the parish' (Checkland and Checkland, 1974: 265). This 'comfort' of the belief in a right to subsistence, financed by a levy on assets, was condemned as likely to annihilate all property and worsen the condition of the poor. According to David Ricardo:

> Instead of making the poor rich, they [the Poor Laws] are calculated to make the rich poor, and whilst the present laws are in force, it is quite in the natural order of things that the fund for the maintenance of the poor should progressively increase, till it has absorbed all the net revenue of the country, or at least so much of it as the state shall leave to us, after satisfying its own never failing demands for the public expenditure. (Ricardo, 1817: 36)

The system was believed to abet idleness and penalise industriousness. Parish relief encouraged 'pauperism' – a loathsome, contagious moral disease (Rose, 1988: 57; Driver, 1993: 18). Thrifty workers with savings were debarred from relief and the wages of independent labourers were forced down by competition from those 'on the parish'. According to the wage-fund theory, popular at the time, only a fixed sum was available for the labouring class, and so the cost of relief must inevitably fall on the 'independent' labourer. Hence, according to Malthus, a labourer who marries without being able to support a family 'may in some respects be considered as an enemy to all his fellow-labourers' (cited in Englander, 1998: 8).

The Speenhamland system attracted particular criticism. 'Gilbert's Act' of 1782 sanctioned the supplementation of wages by the parish. In 1795, the justices in Berkshire, meeting at Speenhamland, declared that 'every poor and industrious man' would receive an allowance from the poor rates when his income fell below a given standard depending on the price of bread and size of family. It subsidised both those in work with very low wages and those totally without work and was condemned as 'breaking the bond of mutual dependence between the master and his servant' by allowing the community to subsidise the employer.

The Poor Law Commissioners digested all the invective against the Poor Law current at the time. They blamed the Poor Law for creating indolence by its 'perverse incentives' (to use the 1980s terminology of the New Right) and reached this conclusion:

> It appears to the pauper that the Government has undertaken to repeal the ordinary laws of nature: to enact, in short, that the penalty which after all must be paid by someone for idleness and improvidence is to fall, not on the guilty

person or on his family, but on the proprietors of lands and houses incumbered by his settlement. Can we wonder if the uneducated are seduced by a system which offers marriage to the young, security to the anxious, ease to the lazy, and impunity to the profligate. (Poor Law Commissioners, 1834, cited in Edsell, 1971: 5)

They believed clear distinctions between the independent labourer, those with a tendency to idleness and the 'impotent' poor were necessary. Thus

except as to medical attendance ... all relief whatever to able-bodied persons or to their families, otherwise than in well-regulated workhouses (i.e. places where they may be set to work according to the spirit and intention of the 43rd of Elizabeth) shall be declared unlawful, and shall cease. Conditions in the workhouse should not be really or apparently so eligible as the situation of the independent labourer of the lowest class. (Checkland and Checkland, 1974: 375)

As Barry (1990: 27–8) has pointed out the 'less eligibility' of the workhouse was 'an ideal adjunct to laissez-faire economics, because, while dealing with a problem that the market apparently could not handle, the phenomenon of avoidable indigence, it operated through the same mechanisms, the irresistible pull push of pleasure and pain'. The offer of the 'less eligible' workhouse

served as a 'self-acting test' for the able-bodied applicant for relief. It would require no magistrate, no government official, no 'means test' ('merit test', as it was called at the time), to determine the neediness of the applicant; if he was willing to receive relief on condition of entering the house, that would be evidence enough of his need. (Himmelfarb, 1995: 131)

Thus, from 1834, it was to be all or nothing for the able-bodied worker. He either earned enough to support his family or he and his family were obliged to enter the workhouse where they may be separated and accommodated in different wards (Davidof, 1990: 201). To encourage efficiency, the Commissioners also recommended poor relief should be administered through unions of parishes and that the new 'guardians of the poor' should be elected by local ratepayers rather than appointed by JPs. The influence of utilitarianism was also apparent in the condemnation of the general mixed workhouse found in some parishes. Prior to 1834 a typical general mixed workhouse was:

occupied by sixty or eighty paupers, made up of a dozen or more neglected children (under the care, perhaps of a pauper), about twenty or thirty able-bodied adult paupers of both sexes, and probably an equal number of aged and impotent persons, proper objects of relief. Amidst these, the mothers of bastard children and prostitutes live without shame ... To these might often be added a solitary blind person, one or two idiots, and not infrequently are heard, from among the rest, the incessant ravings of some neglected lunatic. In such receptacles the sick poor are often immured. (Checkland and Checkland, 1974: 378)

According to the Commissioners the various categories of paupers should be housed in different buildings under separate management and be dealt with under regimes adapted to their different circumstances.

The Poor Law Amendment Act 1834, made provision for the amalgamation of parishes and the election of guardians but the principle of the 'less eligible' workhouse was not embodied in the law. Instead central Poor Law Commissioners were to be appointed under whose 'direction and control' the local system of relief would operate. Edwin Chadwick, the first Secretary of the Poor Law Commissioners, drew up lists of regulations for implementation by the localities. As a preliminary to the total abolition of 'out-relief' for the 'able-bodied' the regulations stated that no assistance should be given for the costs of accommodation and half of the assistance granted should be in kind (Rose, 1971: 103). The regulations also covered the admission of paupers to workhouses and their classification, discipline and diet. The system of poor relief was to be administered according to the rationalist, efficient principles of utilitarianism. When admitted, people were to be placed in a probationary ward where the pauper would be thoroughly 'cleaned' and 'clothed in the workhouse dress'. Paupers would be classified into seven classes and each class assigned to 'an apartment or separate building, without communication' except for 'special reasons'. With 'the approval of the Commissioners the aged and the infirm', if married, could reside in the same apartment. No person would be allowed to visit any pauper 'except by permission of the master and provided that the interview shall always take place in the presence of the master or matron'. Workhouses were to be erected according to the model plans supplied by the Commissioners and were based on Bentham's principle of constant surveillance. Observation and discipline were to be the major mechanisms for establishing 'less eligibility'.

Cajoling the localities into implementing these regulations proved difficult especially in the North (Laybourn, 1995: 26). Fifteen thousand parishes were quickly grouped into 700 unions and, by 1839, about 44 per cent of these unions either had built or had started to build a workhouse. However, in the North, there was strong resistance to the imposition of the workhouse system from the working class. Chartism, a working class political movement flourishing between 1838 and 1850, demanded political change as a means to secure a fairer society (Jones, 1985). Chartists wanted universal male suffrage and other electoral reforms to end the 'couch opulence' of the rich and 'the individual ownership of the soil'. They bitterly opposed the Poor Law Amendment Act because, by almost denying the working man a right to existence, it forced him to accept any wage offered by the employer. Chartist opposition to the workhouse system found some support from manufacturers. 'Model' workhouses were expensive and, in areas where industries were subject to the booms and busts of the trade cycle, it made no sense to throw families out of their homes and into a workhouse during short periods of recession. The Poor Law Commissioners had no power to disallow outdoor relief, merely to 'regulate' it. Thus, despite periodic crusades against outdoor relief, many unions continued to make it available to able-bodied men. Indeed some commentators have claimed 'the humdrum workings of the [old and new poor laws] were fairly similar' (Midwinter, 1967: 106). Nonetheless, although the 'principles of 1834' were often modified in practice, they made a lasting impression on working-class consciousness. The margin between poverty and indigence was thin and to depend on the state involved acquiring the socially excluded status of 'pauper' – a status involving potential incarceration in a workhouse with a harsh and, according to rumour, brutal regime. The ultimate stigma was the pauper funeral when the deceased was carried through the back streets to a grave with the mark of 'P' for pauper.

The 1834 Poor Law Amendment Act was based on separating the able-bodied from 'the impotent' on the principle 'work for those who can, security for those who cannot'. This distinction proved difficult to establish and initially:

> ... the authorities' definition of 'able-bodied' lacked both consistency and usefulness. Amongst those so classified were men and women in all states of physical health, the blind, lame and infirm; the only category never included were the 'lunatics'. (Beenstock and Brasse, 1986: 22)

However, towards the end of the nineteenth century, the Guardians were making firmer distinctions between different categories of pauper. Attempts were made to discriminate between the 'respectable aged' and those 'whose destitution is distinctly the consequence of their own misconduct' (Royal Commission on the Aged Poor, 1893, cited in Thane 2000: 192). In 1896 the Local Government Board recommended the 'respectable' elderly people be given higher outdoor relief (Slater, 1930: 224) and the aged poor, destitute through no fault of their own, were encouraged to apply for out-relief rather than enter the workhouse

(Webb, 1907a: 1). The 'offer of the house' to elderly people remained in use in some areas as a means of encouraging support from relatives and friends but the 'less eligibility' of the workhouse was often modified by 'indulgences' such as tobacco, books and newspapers (McBriar, 1987: 46) and by allowing married couples to share the same bedroom (P. Murray, 1999: 52).

Although women formed the majority of paupers (Digby, 1996: 68), the Poor Law regulations concentrated on men as the family 'bread-winners'. Younger women were a difficult group to classify; should they be treated as 'able-bodied' if they were independent of a man or given a special status as potential mothers? Eventually a clear policy emerged. Women were to be regarded in the same way as men: if able-bodied they were considered as available for work and subject to the full requirements of less-eligibility (Englander, 1998: 23). There was little dissent from the view that unmarried mothers should be treated harshly – 'there was no question of out-relief and the only help to be had was by entering the workhouse' (Middleton, 1971: 271). Irish migrants were also singled out for special treatment. According to Lees (1998: 217) 'dislike of the Irish, especially destitute ones, ran rampant in England'. It was a common belief that … even the meagre relief of the Poor Law would enable the Irish to indulge their 'vicious appetites' (Cornwall Lewis, 1836, cited in Lees, 1998: 217) so it was thought necessary to apply all the powers of 'removal' available to prevent the establishment of eligibility for relief.

The Commission on the Poor Laws had attempted to make a clear distinction between the able-bodied and the 'impotent' poor. The strict deterrence principle was to be applied only to the able-bodied; if 'in-house' provision was necessary for the 'impotent poor' then it was to be provided in special buildings or at least in special wards. In practice the application of this principle was haphazard but, towards the end of the nineteenth century, there was a trend towards a more sophisticated classification of paupers accompanied by greater reliance on institutional provision. The sick began to receive special treatment. The importance of individual health for the health of the nation had been recognised as early as 1841 when it was announced that smallpox vaccinations paid for by the Poor Law would not carry the pauper stigma. Following the abolition of the central Poor Law Board and the transfer of its duties to the Local Government Board – responsible for public health (Hardy, 2001: 19) – new infirmaries were built which were often under management separate from the workhouse. Some of the wards in the new infirmaries were of a high standard with 'all reasonable and proper appliances for the treatment of diseases of every kind' (Bosanquet, 1909: 209). However the Boards of Guardians were not authorised to seek out persons who needed treatment and could not treat people unless they were destitute (Webb and Webb, 1929: 760).

At the end of the nineteenth century poor relief began to be seen as an arena for the prevention of future destitution through the 'dispauperisation' of poor children. A determined effort was made to move children from the general mixed workhouse into 'certified' charitable schools, district pauper schools, grouped cottage homes and 'scattered homes' (McBriar, 1987: 46) and 'boarding out' and adoption were increasingly in use by the end of the century (Hopkins, 1994: 184).

State housing

State housing played a minor role in the social programmes of the late nineteenth century. Lord Shaftesbury's Labouring Classes Lodgings Houses Act 1851 granted local authorities the power to erect 'separate houses or cottages for the working class' and in 1866 the Treasury agreed to make loans to local government to build houses. These measures were rarely used and, in 1885, Shaftesbury remarked that he believed he was the only living Englishman to know of the existence of the local authority power to erect houses (Bowmaker, 1895: 28). The Artisans' and Labourers' Dwellings Improvement Act 1875, which allowed local authorities to demolish slums, stated 'the local authority shall not themselves, without the express approval of the confirming authority, undertake the rebuilding of the houses'. Any consent to build was conditional on the local authority selling the houses within ten years. Only in 1890, under the Housing of the Working Classes Act, did local authorities obtain a clear and firm power to erect dwellings outside clearance areas. This legislation was the outcome of Andrew Mearns's pamphlet, *The Bitter Cry of Outcast London*, published in 1883 and the conclusions of the Royal Commission on the Housing of the Working Classes (1885). Mearns claimed that, in overcrowded dwellings, 'the vilest practices', including incest, 'are looked upon with the most matter of fact indifference' and the Royal Commission concluded that over-crowding had replaced sanitation as *the* housing problem (Himmelfarb, 1991: 66). The 1890 Act enabled the medical officer to draw up an official report on housing and present it to the local authority which was bound to take action if it possessed sufficient resources for the purpose (Kaufman, 1975 [1907]: 36). It permitted local authorities to build houses, inside or outside 'improvement areas' as an example to private developers that 'model dwellings' could be erected at a reasonable profit for the investor (Morton, 1991: 2). Local authorities had built 20,000 dwellings by 1914 and many of these were subsidised by 'creative accounting'. Local authorities bought land at market value and by 'charging it to its housing schemes at its value for working class dwellings (a pure figment), the ratepayer made up the difference between this and the real market value' (Shaw, 1908: 72).

MUTUAL AID

How had this class, without administrative training or literary culture, managed to initiate and maintain the network of nonconformist chapels, the far flung friendly societies, the much abused trade unions, and that queer type of shop, the co-operative store. (Webb, 1979: 59)

Friendly societies

The absence of rights in the 'social' product to help families in times of need provided a spur to the development of commercial insurance and self-help movements (Gorsky, 1999: 308). Commercial companies such as the Prudential and the Pearl specialised in death insurance and provided an expensive weekly door-to-door collection service (Mackay, 1889: 246). Mutual-aid societies were not based on the profit motive or charitable notion that one group should provide aid to another but on an association of people pledged to offer *reciprocal* assistance.

For certain benefits in sickness ... [we] subscribe to one fund. That fund is our Bank – and to draw therefrom is the independent and manly right of every Member, whenever the contingency for which the funds are sub-scribed may arise, as freely as if the fund was in the hand of their own banker, and they had but to issue a cheque for the amount. These are not BENEVOLENCES – they are rights. (Ancient Order of Foresters, 1879, cited in Green, 1999: 22)

Mutual-aid organisations assumed a variety of forms with Friendly Societies being the most important in terms of membership. On joining a Friendly Society a contribution was made to a 'common fund' for use in providing funeral grants, sick pay and benefits to widows and their children. Many societies also supplied medical care and ran convalescent homes. They were fraternal, self-governing associations, often organised into 'lodges' and affiliated to national organisations such as the Manchester Unity of Oddfellows, the Ancient Order of Foresters and the Rechabites. 'Brotherhood', indeed 'sisterhood', for there were a few all-women societies, was a vital element of Friendly Society activity. Provision for conviviality, in the form of a beer fund and a 'club night', was often made and solidarity was expressed in processions, usually in Whitsun weeks (Hopkins, 1995: 14).

Some authors have seen the Friendly Societies as a demonstration that 'the instinct of groups of people to provide independently for their welfare where a need exists and the means are available is amazingly strong' (Hanson, 1972: 138). Green (1985: 1) has estimated the societies 'had attracted at least three-quarters of manual workers well before the end of the nineteenth century'. He regards the societies as a maturing form of 'welfare without politics', drowned by the advancing tide of state welfare in the twentieth century. However, an important factor in the growth of Friendly Societies was dread of the Poor Law, which was seen as pauperising 'the flower of the working classes' (Royal Commission on Friendly Societies, 1874, cited in Gosden, 1961: 12). Moreover, the membership and activities of the societies, though impressive, is a misleading guide to the potential of mutual aid as a form of welfare provision. Seebohm Rowntree noted how some workers were members of several societies and 'the very poor are but seldom members of Friendly Societies. Even if they can be induced to join, they soon allow their membership to lapse' (Rowntree, 1901: 356). Many of the Friendly Societies excluded the 'bad lives', imposed upper age limits on membership and insisted on a minimum income as a condition of membership. Strict control was exercised over claims from potential malingers (home visits from fellow members were the norm) and those considered to be responsible for their illnesses were not allowed to claim benefits (Hopkins, 1995: 18–20).

Trade unions

In the early nineteenth century trade union welfare activity consisted mainly of 'helping jobless workers through the so-called tramping system, granting them a meal, a pint of beer and a night's lodging in each town as they searched for work' (Southall, 1999: 351). However, as membership increased, the major 'artisan' unions introduced weekly payments for their unemployed as an incentive to join a union and to prevent skilled work-men undercutting wage rates when in need. At the turn of the century trade unions were mainly benefit societies. According to Clough

> the annual expenditure of 100 leading unions on strike pay or lock-out benefit only once exceeded 13 per cent of income between 1899 and 1909; during this period expenditure on unemployment and friendly benefits averaged 60 to 70 per cent. (1992: 20)

Unions specialised in unemployment benefits being 'particularly fitted to cover such a risk, since their members could keep a check on malingering, help each other to find jobs and – in the event of a deficit – subscribe to a general levy' (Harris, 1972: 296). By 1899, 980,000 workers were eligible for some form of out-of-work assistance from their union.

Co-operatives

Between 300,000 and 400,000 people were members of the co-operative societies in the 1870s (Finlayson, 1994: 30). Friendly Societies made provision for unexpected contingencies whereas co-operators wanted to ensure the surplus made from retailing remained in the hands of the working class. Anyone who joined a co-op and bought goods from the co-operative store was entitled to a dividend on the value of the goods purchased.

Building societies and building clubs

Some co-operatives expanded their activities into providing homes for rent but, by the 1840s, a separate building society movement had developed. A number of workers formed a 'terminating' society and agreed to pay into a fund that would be used to build houses. When sufficient finance had been raised to buy a house lots were drawn to determine which member of the society should move into the new dwelling. Payments into the fund continued until every member was able to become a homeowner and then the society was terminated. In order to speed up the housing of its members some societies allowed people who did not require homes to join the association paying them interest on their investment. These societies were called 'permanent' and had become the most common form of building society by the start of the twentieth century. Permanent societies attracted savers from all classes and, towards the end of the nineteenth century, their management had become middle-class. Despite the occasional collapse of a society the movement was very successful in attracting the savings of working people. They offered good security to investors, opened the opportunity to obtain a mortgage and the society offices were accessible. In 1869 there were 1500 societies with a membership of 300,000 (Finlayson, 1994: 32) and, by 1891, 2333 building societies existed with 605,000 members (Hopkins, 1995: 56). Building clubs were similar to terminating building societies but allowed local solicitors and accountants to participate in the activities of the club to add the respectability necessary to secure loans from local banks (Fisk, 1996: 48–9).

Friends, neighbours and the extended family

The extent and nature of 'informal' assistance from friends and neighbours is unknown. Many of the poorest people lived a nomadic life, constantly on the move to find employment and lodgings (Davin, 1996: 26–43), and so, in the early part of the century, the opportunity to develop networks of informal support was limited. Nonetheless shared hatred and fear of the workhouse and the developing opportunities to 'put down roots' encouraged neighbourhood assistance. The journalist George Sims noted in his 1883 report *How The Poor Live*:

> The poor are kinder to each other than the rich; they are bound by stronger ties of sympathy; their hearts respond more readily to generous impulses. They have greater opportunities of helping each other, and there are no barriers of pride between them. They live their lives before each others' eyes, and their joys and sorrows are the common property of the entire community. (Sims, 1883, cited in P. Murray, 1999: 74)

It was commonplace for neighbours to 'take in' the children of parents facing hard times and the 'extended' family had a significant role in providing assistance in finding a job or accommodation for kin migrating to cities.

> ... depending on the housing supply, newly married couples, frequently co-resided with parents, and sometimes where mothers worked outside the home there was a co-residing grandmother or other relative to provide child care. At the same time considerable numbers of children resided with grand-parents. (Dupree, 2000: 356)

NATIONALISM AND SOCIAL EXCLUSION

Smellie (1937: 171) notes how, during the nineteenth century, nationalism changed from 'a spiritual tradition to a self-conscious pose ... a creed to be taught ... a business to be developed'. Nation-states, being 'imagined communities', require the construction of the 'ideal citizen', a 'John Bull', against which aspiring members can gauge the extent of their inclusion. The idealised citizen of the Victorian era was the 'freeborn Englishman' – Protestant, property-owning and of independent, 'manly' character. Political inclusion reflected the nature and degree of economic and social inclusion. The 1867 Reform Act enfranchised male householders and thereby incorporated the 'respectable' working class whereas selected women could vote in county, borough and Poor Law elections (Harris, 1993: 190) – a reflection of the 'domestic sphere' as the female domain. Catholic, civil and political disabilities were removed in 1829. Later, the Roman Catholic Church was allowed limited funding to establish schools but, according to some commentators, this enhanced inclusion was acquired by forsaking other identities – in the case of Irish Catholics, their 'Irishness' (Hickman, 1998: 169).

While awaiting incorporation the 'populace' was encouraged to confirm its affinity to the nation by expressing its loyalty, a strategy deployed by the Tories in their calculated creation of a mass party of supporters via the Conservative Registration Association and the Primrose League (McWilliam, 1998: 92, 95). Other demonstrations of 'belonging' came from parades, applause for 'jingoism' in the music halls plus hostility to, and mockery of, 'outsiders'. The Irish community was regarded almost as an 'externality' in itself. Thomas Carlyle denounced the Irish labourer as reducing the wages of the 'Saxon' man because 'the Irishman ... lodges in any pig hutch or dog hutch, roosts in out-houses and wears a suit of tatters' (Carlyle, 1839, cited in MacRaild, 1999: 158). James Kay agreed: 'The contagious example which the Irish have exhibited of barbarous habits and wont of economy', he said, 'have demoralised the people' (Kay, 1970 [1832]: 27).

TAXATION AND LOCAL GOVERNMENT

In the nineteenth century, the raising of state revenue was governed by the maxim that the purpose of taxation was to supply the state with its necessary resources and not to redistribute income. In the early 1850s Gladstone commented that 'the most dangerous of propositions that could be made in a country like this would be an attempt, upon abstract principles, to devise a graduated tax on incomes, arriving at an adjustment of different rates of assessment according to the means of the taxpayer' (Gladstone, cited in Field, Meacher and Pond, 1977: 12). Graduated taxation, he said, 'tended to communism'. Progressiveness in taxation was also opposed because, by penalising hard work, it would limit economic growth. Herbert Spencer, anticipating the arguments made in favour of the Poll Tax in the 1980s, claimed that everybody, however poor, should pay a share in the cost of government because government benefited everyone (cited in Jones, 1914: 132). Some commentators conceded the case for limited tax allowances to reflect ability to pay. 'In a community where indigence is relieved from public funds', said Sidgwick (1883: 55) 'consistency requires that the Government should not endeavour to take by taxation from the poor, who remain independent, a part of what it would have to give them if they sought its aid'. However, 'a small, uniformly applied, proportionate tax was the most that was considered legitimate, and the lower the tax the better because this 'realised the Gladstonian ideal of leaving money, to fructify in the pockets of the people' (Collini, 1979: 116).

Income tax, first introduced in 1799, became an enduring element of the tax system when the repeal of the Corn Laws deprived the state of some of its tariff revenues (Cronin, 1991: 21). It was charged at 3 per cent for most of the second part of the nineteenth century (Kay and King, 1986: 20). Various forms of indirect taxation were levied and, even in the period of free trade, a number of import duties were retained. Jevons estimated that, in the late nineteenth century, the proportion of income paid in taxes by families spending £40, £85 and £500 per year was 9 per cent, 7.6 per cent and 7.7 per cent respectively.

About 73 per cent of 'social welfare' spending came from the rates (Peacock and Wiseman, 1961). These levies on the value of property in a locality were progressive in incidence but all householders paid rates, with the inhabitants of rented property paying as an addition to their weekly rent. As the public health and education responsibilities imposed on local government increased and local government began to spend substantial sums of money on roads (Millward and Sheard, 1995) the unfair incidence of rates on individuals and localities became 'high politics'. Service charges helped to reduce the 'rate burden'. Elementary education, for example, did not become free until 1891 when the Free Education Act empowered School Boards to admit children without charge. Even after the passing of this Act, some schools continued to impose charges (Simon, 1965: 132).

'Grants in aid' from central government were one solution to the problem of the different rateable values in different areas. They were awarded with reluctance because 'financial orthodoxy held that local authorities should be disciplined by the establishment of a direct connection between local expenditure and rates' (Bellamy, 1988: 24). In the late nineteenth century assistance from the central state formed only a small proportion of local expenditure – less than 8 per cent in 1888 (Burgess and Travers, 1980: 30). This lack of central assistance allowed the doctrine of laissez faire to be maintained on the argument that local services, locally financed, reflected civic autonomy not 'state' intervention. When made, central grants were linked to a specific purpose that the central government wished to promote. Grants assumed a number of complex and ever-changing forms with Robert Lowe's 'payment by results' perhaps the most interesting. 'Payment by results' was based on attendance and the results of an examination, conducted by a government inspector, of each child in reading, writing, arithmetic 'needlework for girls, drawing for boys' and recitation of 80 lines of poetry, the meanings and allusions being properly understood (Curriculum guidelines, 1890, cited in Himmelfarb, 1991: 137). Lowe's system became one of the principal targets of local authority teachers and educational administrators who wanted to be free from central control. Robert Lowe's claim that 'if it is not cheap it shall be efficient; if it is not efficient it shall be cheap' was ridiculed and the system was condemned as encouraging the rote learning of a severely limited range of information. In 1895 Lowe's system was replaced by a system of specific percentage grants plus a grant 'in aid of necessitous areas where the produce of the rates fell short of a fixed sum per scholar' (Clarke, 1937: 577) but this 'dole' – as a Treasury official called it (Peden, 2000: 6) – constituted only a tiny proportion of the total spending. After education, the Poor Law represented the major 'personal service' burden on the rates. Central government provided limited assistance to local Boards of Guardians in the form of a specific percentage grant supplemented by a payment for each pauper lunatic removed from the workhouse to a separate institution.

CONCLUSION

The statistics available at the end of the nineteenth century tell us little about the respective roles of self-help, the market and inheritance in determining the standard of living of different social groupings. They are insufficient even to form robust conclusions on general trends in the standard of living (Williamson, 1985: 53; Hoppen, 1998: 78).

In the nineteenth century the market became more influential as a distributive mechanism but it operated within a structure set in earlier times. Social mobility was extremely limited with less than 5 per cent of men with working class fathers moving into the middle/upper classes (Savage and Miles, 1994: 32). Inherited land formed 25 per cent of national wealth in 1878. The findings of the *Return of Owners of Lands and Heritages* (1872), ordered by the Prime Minister, Lord Derby, to quell the 'wildest and most reckless exaggerations' of land agitators, revealed a pattern of land ownership 'apparently untouched by a century of industrialisation and half a century of market economics' (Harris, 1993: 100). Although over one million landowners were identified most owned one acre or less and 7000 people owned 80 per cent of the entire country (Scott, 1994: 40; Hunter, 1997: 21). Land may have been in decline as an element in national wealth but it provided the passport to other forms of assets in the form of commercial, residential and industrial property plus the growing category of 'income from abroad' (Wasson, 2000).

Money's comprehensive review of the evidence contained in Estate Duty statistics, published in 1905, revealed 'in an average year 27,500 persons die worth £57,000,000 while 686,500 persons die worth only £29,000,000' (Money, 1910: 53). Atkinson (1972: 45) estimates the top 5 per cent of wealth owners in 1911 held 87 per cent of the total personal wealth in England and Wales. Money explored the distribution of income by dividing the population into three categories. The 'rich', with a household income of more than £700 per annum, formed 2 per cent of the population but held 34.2 per cent of the national income. The 'comfortable', with an income between £160 and £700 per annum, formed 8.7 per cent of the population and held 14.3 per cent of national income. The 'poor', with an income below the income tax threshold of £160, held 51.5 per cent of national income but formed 88.4 per cent of the population (Scott, 1994: 42). Manual workers made up the majority of those receiving less than

£160 per annum but Money estimated about 3 million people – 'petty tradesman, civil servants, clerks, shopmen, travellers, canvassers, agents, teachers, farmers inn-keepers, lodging-house keepers, pensioners and so forth' (Money, 1910: 16) – also earned less than the tax threshold. The system of taxation made little impact on the distribution of wealth and income. Figures presented in *Riches and Poverty* indicate that schedule A tax (land and houses) took only 3 per cent of the annual income produced, schedule B ('the farmers tax') 1.5 per cent, schedule C (tax on profits from securities) 6 per cent and schedule D (profits from trades, professions, overseas investments, etc.) 3.7 per cent. (Money, 1910: 283–305).

Money made no allowance for the value of state social services. Had he done so, his results would not have changed. The role of the state in the redistribution of income was strictly limited and the notion that people might have rights to an income outside that received from inheritance, work and the patriarchal relationships within the family had hardly reached the mainstream political agenda. Real wages increased by about 70 per cent between 1850 and 1900 (Hunt, 1981: 73) and this was used to refute arguments in favour of redistribution by the state. W.H. Mallocks's *Classes and Masses, Wealth, Wages and Welfare in the United Kingdom. A Handbook of Social Facts for Political Thinkers and Speakers* (1896) alleged that the improvement in the condition of the working class since 1850 had been a result of the increase in national wealth and that the 'working class of 1880 were in a better pecuniary position than their fathers would have been had they plundered and divided all the wealth of the richer classes at the time of the Great Exhibition' (cited in Shannon, 1996: 64).

3

The Rise of Collectivism

SOCIALISM

Following the decline of Chartism there was no organised movement in Britain, other than perhaps the Christian Socialists, identifiable as 'socialist' (Francis and Morrow, 1994: 293). Nonetheless, local republican and radical societies continued to function and supplied a basis for the socialist movements that emerged in the 1880s when a new account of 'socialism' and how it might be achieved became available in Britain (Harris, 1993: 227; Wheen, 1999: 124).

Karl Marx (1818–1883)

According to Marx the value of any manufactured object is related to the labour power consumed in its production. Labour is the worker's only saleable commodity hence all the owners of the means of production have to offer to secure a worker's labour is an amount sufficient to meet his immediate 'subsistence' requirements plus the reproduction costs of the next generation of labour. Capitalists purloin all the additional 'use' value produced by the working class so class conflict is the inevitable consequence of this 'exploitative' mode of production. This conflict would lead to the revolutionary overthrow of the capitalist system. 'Social reformers, economists, philanthropists, humanitarians, improvers of the condition of the working class, organisers of charity ... hole in the corner reformers of every possible kind' (Marx, 1968 [1875]: 58) merely delay the process by temporarily mitigating the consequences of capitalism.

Marx rejected as 'utopian' any contemplation on the nature of society following the displacement of capitalism. 'It is not the consciousness of men that determines their existence', he said, 'but their social existence that determines their consciousness ...' (Marx, 1875, cited in Tucker, 1972: 425). New forms of social organisation could emerge only when economic relationships had been transformed but, despite this refusal to sanction utopian blueprints, it is possible, from signposts scattered in Marx's writings, to indicate how he conceived post-capitalist society. A 'socialist' phase would follow the collapse of capitalism when the capture of the means of production by the proletariat would lead to its conscious organisation on a planned basis. In this 'socialist' phase – the transition between capitalism and communism – distribution would be based on the principle 'from each according to his ability; to each according to his work' after allowances had been made for

> replacement of the means of production used up; an additional portion for expansion of production; a reserve or insurance funds to provide against misadventures, disturbances through natural events, etc; the general costs of administration not belonging to production; that which is destined for the communal satisfaction of needs, such as schools, health services, etc. and funds for those unable to work, etc. (Marx, 1875, cited in Tucker, 1972: 388)

Gradually socialism would give way to a communist society that would apply the distributive principle 'from each according to his ability, to each according to his need' (Marx, cited in Johnston, 2000: 89). Marx offered only a sketchy account of the mechanisms required for distribution according to need. He believed the rationing problem would be mitigated by the higher production derived from technological progress and the elimination of 'the general cost of administration not belonging to production' that, under capitalism, sprang from the role of the state in the control of the working class (Marx, 1968 [1875]: 318). Most important of all, work would be done to satisfy a human need. Freed from the alienation caused by the requirement to work to maximise the capitalist's profits and, with the mental and manual division of labour abolished, men and women would work to master nature and so satisfy human needs:

> ... in communist society, where nobody has one exclusive sphere of activity but each can become accomplished in any branch he wishes, production as a whole is regulated by society, thus making it possible for me to do one thing today and another tomorrow, to hunt in the morning, fish in the afternoon, rear cattle in the evening, criticise after dinner, in accordance with my inclination, without ever becoming hunter, fisherman, shepherd, or critic. (Marx, 1845/6, cited in Bottomore and Rubel, 1990: 110–11)

Thus, by assuming scarcity diminishes under communism and indicating people would produce willingly to satisfy human needs, Marx eliminated any pressing requirement for a theory of social justice to establish principles of fairness in distribution (Kymlicka, 1990: 164). Production, when fastened to human needs, meant a separate *re*distributive mechanism – a social welfare system – was unnecessary.

Fabian socialism

Whereas Marx denounced capitalists for taking all 'surplus value' produced by workers, the Fabian Society, formed in 1884, chastised only those who relied on 'rent'. To the Fabians 'rent' meant 'the differential advantageousness of any factor of production over and above the worst in economic use' (Webb and Webb, 1913). It took the form of:

- economic rent – the supplementary product created by advantages of site;
- rent of ability – the additional product created by superior skill relative to unskilled workers;
- economic interest – the use of superior quality capital;
- rent of opportunity – the additional product generated by the existence of contingent advantages such as temporary monopolies due to possession of the means of production in a certain form, place or time.

So, according to Fabian theory, the exploitation of the working class was not as total as Marx had alleged. Capitalists did not purloin *all* the value produced by the working class and the capitalist, as the organiser of investment, deserved some reward for his efforts (Macfarlane, 1998: 129). This belief justified a gradual approach to the achievement of socialism with a huge step towards social justice made possible by the appropriation of 'rent' to finance public services.

> An increase in the death duties, the steady rise of local rates, the special taxation of urban ground values, the graduation and differentiation of the income-tax, the simple appropriation of the unearned increment and the gradual acquirement of land and other monopolies by public authorities, will in due course suffice to 'collectivise' the bulk of the tribute of rent. (Sidney Webb, 1908, cited in Greenleaf, 1983: 374)

Nonetheless, even when the social surplus attributed to rent was harvested, the inefficiency of uncoordinated capitalist activity would remain. In contrast to Marx's belief in a diminishing state, the socialism advocated by the Fabian Society was 'state socialism exclusively' (George Bernard Shaw, cited in Sullivan, 1998: 111). Fabians regarded the state as the quintessence of rationality. They believed it was possible to discover rules, divorced from political activity, capable of providing society with a sense of direction. Moreover, if rational thought could discover laws for the construction of a 'good' society, then the main instruments for assembling that society must be the 'intellectual aristo-cracy' – the 'modern efficients' or the 'new samurai' to quote H.G. Wells' terminology. Expert knowledge of the 'facts' of each situation, together with inductive reasoning, would produce a solution to each social problem. The rationality inherent in the approach would lead, in an 'irresistible glide' (Webb, 1962 [1913]: 56) to an integrated, harmonious, socialist society. Sydney Webb put the matter succinctly when he asserted government must become 'more and more the business of elaborately trained experts, and less and less the immediate outcome of popular feeling' (Webb, 1908, cited in Greenleaf, 1983: 359–60). Thus, whereas Marx believed the transformation of society would come through working-class action, perhaps of a violent nature, Fabians put their trust in 'the inevitability of gradualness'. Society would be permeated by 'rational', hence inevitable, Fabian principles.

The formation of the labour party

The Fabian Society, the Marxist Social Democratic Federation and the Socialist League all promoted socialist ideas but the impetus for radical change came from a variety of 'grassroots' working class movements. The so-called 'new' Unionism of unskilled workers was more militant and class-conscious than the 'old' unionism created by the 'aristocracy of labour'. In addition associations of workers developed in the West Riding of Yorkshire and in parts of Lancashire. The great majority of the workers who joined these associations were ignorant of socialist doctrine but their grievances about social conditions offered a fertile ground for radicals. In 1893 a meeting of labour organisations was held in Bradford and the Independent Labour Party was formed with the aim of securing 'the collective ownership of the means of production, distribu-tion and exchange'. Initially the Independent Labour Party gained little support from the trade unions. However, the idea of a party dedicated to ensuring that 'labour' was independently represented in Parliament gradually gained ground as trade unions felt assailed by the impact of new technology, adverse legal decisions and more aggressive employ-ers. In 1900 the Labour Representation Committee was formed with the aim of establishing a voice in Parliament for the working class. In some constituencies arrangements were made between the Labour Represen-tation Committee and the Liberals – sometimes called the 'Progressive Alliance' – to prevent a division of the anti-Tory vote. These arrange-ments helped to secure the return of 30 'Labour' members in 1906. They formed their own party in Parliament and called themselves 'The Labour Party'.

THE 'NEW' LIBERALISM

The emergence of the Parliamentary Labour Party presented a clear threat to the Liberals. Would not the working class become, in Marx's terms, a 'class for itself' and support the party claiming to represent organised labour? This situation 'lent itself to those who offered rational humanistic panaceas which were radical and theoretically grounded but which posed no fundamental threat to the operations of the capitalist economy' (Bowpitt 2000: 24). A new brand of Liberalism emerged in response to the renaissance of 'socialist ideas' and the threat from Labour. This 'new', sometimes called 'social', Liberalism contained many shades of opinion and, at its most radical, shaded into Fabian Socialism.

Henry George (1839–1897)

The distinction between 'deserved' and 'undeserved' income – with undeserved income available for redistribution to secure social justice – was at the heart of the 'new' Liberalism. Agitation over the land issue was at the centre of the fragmented working-class movements that survived the demise of Chartism (Finn, 1993) but the publication of Henry George's *Progress and Poverty* (1879) projected land reform to the forefront of radical politics. George asked, 'Why is it that the introduction of improved processes and labour-saving machinery ... has multiplied enormously the effectiveness of labour yet poverty with all its concomitants shows itself in communities just as they develop the conditions to which material progress tends?' (George, 1979 [1879]: 4–5). He found the answer in the system of land ownership. Following Ricardo, George defined rent as 'consideration for the use of land' (George, 1979: 66). 'Rent' increased with expanding population and the consequent inflation in land values reduced the proportion of the social product going to capital and labour. High land prices created a situation in which 'in the new settlements, where land is cheap, you will find no beggars' whereas in 'great cities where land is so valuable that it is measured by the foot, you will find the extremes of poverty and luxury' (George, 1979: 111). The remedy was 'to substitute for the individual ownership of land a common ownership' (George, 1979: 128) but, as this would produce 'bitter antagonism', then rent should be appropriated by the taxation of land at site value. Such a tax would represent 'the taking by the community, for the use of the community, of the value that is the creation of the community' (George, 1979: 139). George's 'single land tax' was intended to replace all other forms of taxation. By abolishing 'rent' it would 'raise wages, increase the earnings of capital, extirpate pauperism, abolish poverty, give remunerative employment to whoever wishes it ... and carry civilisation to yet nobler heights' (George, 1879, cited in Heilbroner, 1955: 170).

George's ideas had a major impact on radical thinking at the end of the nineteenth century (Hall and Ward, 1998: 9). His simple and plausible theory contained the potential to remedy industrial poverty without the total transformation of society advocated by Marxist socialists. Its influence was manifest in the 'Radical Programme', launched by Joseph Chamberlain in 1885. Chamberlain, then a member of the Liberal Party, proposed a number of reforms including some based on the proposition that 'the expense of making towns habitable for the toilers who dwell in them must be thrown on the land which their toil makes valuable without any effort on the part of its owners' (Chamberlain, 1885: 87). Ebenezer Howard used George's theory to promote the Garden City idea. In *Garden Cities of Tomorrow* (1902) he argued that the benefits of living in the town and the country could be combined if citizens lived in a planned garden city surrounded by a 'green belt'. An essential element of Howard's scheme was the quasi-public ownership of the land. Although he never worked out the correct relationship between those who provided the initial capital for the garden city and its future residents, Howard envisaged a substantial surplus arising from development gain (Hall and Ward, 1998: 25). As the town grew, its land value would increase and this community gain could be used to supply facilities for local residents and to stimulate co-operative housing ventures.

Thomas Hill Green (1836–1882)

Green was a tutor at Balliol College, Oxford and an active member of the Liberal Party. His influence on the early development of state welfare has been described as 'enormous' (Plant et al., 1980: 80) because he offered an interpretation of liberty 'which gave the state a particular moral significance' (Vincent and Plant, 1984: 2).

For Green, self-realisation was the means by which the spiritual progress of mankind was maintained. He was critical of Utilitarianism because, in treating all actions as arising from pain and pleasure, it ignored man's *purposeful* behaviour. The capacity for self-reflection and for moral action in choosing to do what is good was essential for self-development. Green believed personal identity was derived from social roles and relationships 'just as language of some sort is necessary to the real existence of thought' (Green, 1988 [1895]: 114). 'Purpose' gave meaning to the life of the individual and thus a society based only on market transactions stunted the growth of a purposeful community. 'To be actuated by a desire for pleasure', he said, 'is to be actuated by a desire for some specific pleasure to be enjoyed by oneself. No two or more persons whose desires were only of this kind could really desire anything in common' (Green, 1883: sec. 282). Thus, according to Green, 'when we speak of freedom as something to be so highly prized, we mean a positive power or capacity of doing or enjoying something worth doing or enjoying, and that, too, something that we do or enjoy in common with others' (Green, 1881: 9).

Contrary to some interpretations of his work, Green did not award the main role in character development to the state (Richter, 1996: 268). The primary responsibility for character building rested with the individual in free association with the 'institutions of society'. 'No one can convey a good character to another', said Green, 'everyone must make his character for himself'. He noted how certain legal institutions 'take away the occasion for the exercise of moral virtues e.g. the Poor Law, which takes away the occasion for the exercise of parental forethought, filial reverence and neighbourly kindness' (Green, 1988 [1895]: 21). Thus he placed great stress on mutual obligations; the elite should 'hinder hinderences' to character formation and, in return, working people, when free from debilitating influences, should attend to 'the affections and recognised obligations of family' (Green, 1895, cited in Nicholson, 1990: 57). Green urged the common good not 'as the rationale of collectivism' (Clarke, 1978: 15) but 'as an ethical criterion to spur on a more strenuous individualism'. The state should limit itself to regulatory activity and control 'only those actions which are better done from a bad motive than not done at all' (Green, quoted in Mabbott, 1948: 66). Education was the exception to this general prohibition against state services because the public provision of free elementary education and compulsory school attendance would remove the barrier of 'the dead weight of ignorance' from moral improvement.

Leonard Trelawney Hobhouse (1864–1929)

Green's philosophy was used both to defend the forms of voluntary provision advocated by the Charity Organisation Society and to promote enhanced regulatory activity by the state. However, his 'idealist' notion of the state as a 'community acting through law' (Green, 1988 [1895]: sec. 209) opened the door for a 'liberal' rationale of a more extensive state devoted to promoting social justice.

Hobhouse moved 'new Liberalism' a step closer to collectivism. He regarded society as an organism constantly in a process of evolution. However, in contrast to the 'organic social darwinism' advanced by Herbert Spencer in *The Man 'Versus' the State* (1884b), Hobhouse claimed the evolution of human consciousness was towards a higher moral order based on ethical reasoning, not on the survival of the fittest. He believed 'the rational self-direction of society through mind was part of the natural evolutionary process' (Freeden, 1978: 69). This rationality was itself ethical because it embodied the sentiment of mutuality – 'a feeling for the common good, a readiness to forego personal advantage for the general gain, a recognition of mutual dependence' (Hobhouse, 1893: 4–5). The underlying logic of his organic theory took Hobhouse towards the notion of the state as the complete embodiment of the will of society but he recoiled from this totalitarian conclusion. He regarded citizens of a political democracy 'as simply members of a large co-operative society' (Dennis and Halsey, 1988: 80). Respect for the values of tolerance, open-mindedness, fraternity and free association, together with the belief that freedom ultimately comes from within, led him to reject the label of 'socialist'. He was prepared to accept the title 'liberal socialist' but declared his opposition to 'mechanical' (economic) and 'official' (state) socialism. 'Mechanical' socialism constructed a total system on the single determinant of class conflict. The 'official' version of socialism was bureaucratic and elitist dictating to each individual how he should conduct his life.

Hobhouse claimed real freedom came through the self-realisation achieved by the fulfilment of obligations, but he accepted that social rights were vital if these obligations were to be met. He recognised a right to work and a right to receive an adequate income for the fulfilment of the obligations of fatherhood and motherhood (Page, 1996: 38). The resources to pay for this 'living wage' would come from the redistribution of the 'undeserved' income derived from land and inheritance. 'We cannot afford to pay £500,000,000 a year', he asserted, 'to a number of individuals for wealth that is due partly to nature and partly to efforts of their fathers' (Hobhouse 1893: 78). If the resources for the 'living wage' were to be taken from the 'collective social surplus' produced by the community then the state, acting on behalf of this community, had a right to enforce the obligations of citizenship. It could legitimately act as 'over-parent' securing 'the physical, mental and moral welfare of children, partly by imposing definite responsibilities on the parents and punishing them for neglect, partly by elaborating a public system of education and hygiene' (Hobhouse, 1911: 25).

John Atkinson Hobson (1858–1940)

Hobson's work took 'new' liberalism a step closer to socialism. He believed 'the growth of reason enabled humans to economise in their energies devoted to basic survival' (Townshend, 1990: 28). Reason, when applied to production, led to the creation of a surplus for use in 'civilisation'. 'Civilisation' involved greater intellectual interaction and co-operation with others and this co-operation eventually developed to form an 'organic unity' with an existence outside individuals and with 'needs' of its own. Hobson developed the biological analogy by referring to the 'sensorium' and the 'cells' of society. The sensorium was society's 'brain' giving it 'organic purpose'. It was represented by a government staffed by an 'expert governing class' dedicated to meeting physical needs. The 'cells' would concern themselves with the detailed implementation of policy.

Prescriptions for society flowed from Hobson's conception of its 'organic unity'. His focus on 'the whole' enabled him to pinpoint the cause of unemployment as 'underconsumption'. In *The Evolution of Modern Capitalism* (Hobson [1926] 1894) he asserted that the lack of demand for goods was the result of maldistribution of income with some 'satiated' and others 'starved' of purchasing power. If the surplus of the 'satiated' was redistributed then the correct saving–spending ratio would be restored and unemployment would be reduced (Skidelsky, 1967: 31). Hobson also argued for social reform to promote national productivity via the creation of a more efficient workforce. He believed that distribution according to need must improve efficiency because 'larger output of energy requires a larger replacement through consumption' (Hobson, 1901: 64). Sources of finance for welfare services were located in Hobson's distinction between the 'productive' and 'unproductive' surplus of capitalism. Capitalists were entitled to the rewards necessary to persuade them to use their capital, but many capitalists were able to appropriate 'interest' above 'the saving needed to supply the requisite amount of new capital for industrial progress' (Hobson, 1910: 80). This 'unearned income', was seen by Hobson as 'the only properly taxable body, for any tax which falls upon that income which is either cost of production or productive surplus encroaches on the fund for maintenance and progress, thus reducing the future efficiency of industry'. It was, 'therefore, of paramount importance to the state to discover the forms and the magnitude of the unproductive surplus' so that this 'unearned income' could be taken by the state for use in promoting its own needs (Hobson, 1910: viii).

Hobson's ideas were similar to the Fabian Socialists' but differed in important ways from the Fabianism promoted at the time. Hobson did not aspire to total common ownership of the means of production. He believed the main purpose of the state was to ensure 'lower order' (physical) needs were met. Community ownership of the industries necessary to supply the basic necessities of life and the provision of social welfare services was justified but 'higher order' needs were dependent on the functions that individuals performed in society. They varied in a myriad of ways and should be left to the individual to satisfy through market transactions.

POVERTY AND NATIONAL EFFICIENCY

The rise of collectivism promoted 'scientific' investigations into the nature and extent of 'need'. Charles Booth's house-by-house survey of the poorer districts of London was aimed at refuting Marxist claims that a third of the population lived in chronic want. Booth discovered 1.3 million (nearly one-third) living in poverty (Booth, 1902–3) but his poverty line was vague and his arithmetic of woe imprecise. Seebohm Rowntree's study of York was more systematic. In *Poverty: A Study of Town Life* (1901)

Rowntree – 'throughout his life a new Liberal' (Briggs, 1969: 38) – used the notion of 'physical efficiency' to link the 'wants' of the individual to the 'needs' of society for an efficient labour force.

Rowntree's food requirement was sufficient to maintain men involved in a 'moderately active day's work' (stone-breaking for eight hours). Women received 80 per cent of the man's ration and children from 30 per cent, depending on age. Fuel, light and the replacement of household items were added to the food requirement. The clothing standard was assessed by interviews with working people who were asked 'What in your opinion is the very lowest sum upon which a man can keep himself in clothing for a year? The clothing should be adequate to keep the man in health, and should not be so shabby as to injure his chances of obtaining respectable employment' (Rowntree, 1901: 107–8). On Rowntree's definition 9.9 per cent of the people of York lived in 'primary' poverty and a further 18 per cent in 'secondary' poverty. 'Secondary' poverty was defined as:

> Families whose total earnings would be sufficient for the maintenance of merely physical efficiency were it not that some portion of it is absorbed by other expenditure, either useful or wasteful. (Rowntree, 1901: 87)

Rowntree attributed secondary poverty mainly to wasteful expenditure on alcholic drink (Gillie, 2000: 97).

If a situation is to become a 'social problem' then a feasible solution must be available. By identifying a 'cycle of poverty' Rowntree indicated such a solution. He claimed:

> The life of a labourer is marked by five alternating periods of want and comparative plenty. During his early childhood … he will probably be in poverty; this will last until he or some of his brothers or sisters, begin to earn money and thus augment their father's wage sufficiently to raise the family above the poverty line. There then follows a period during which he is earning money and living under his parents' roof; … this is his chance to save some money and pay for furnishing a cottage. This period of prosperity may continue after marriage until he has two or three children when poverty will overtake him. This period of poverty will last perhaps for ten years until the first child is fourteen years old and begins to earn wages … The man enjoys another period of prosperity only to sink back again into poverty when his children have married and left him and he himself is too old to work … (Rowntree, 1901: 170–1).

Thus, on Rowntree's diagnosis, income redistribution was necessary to overcome poverty but most of the necessary redistribution could be over the lifetime of the individual by means of compulsory savings to cover social contingencies. Such 'lifetime' redistribution minimised the requirement for 'vertical' redistribution from rich to poor.

THE CONSERVATIVE RESPONSE

A.J. Balfour, Conservative Prime Minister from 1902 to 1905, summarised the Conservative approach to social reform when he said:

> Social legislation, as I conceive it, is not merely to be distinguished from Socialist legislation, but is its direct opposite and its most effective antidote. Socialism will never get possession of the great body of public opinion in this country, among the working classes or among any other classes, if those who wield the collective forces of the community show themselves desirous, in any way in their power, of using those forces, so far as they can be used to benefit of the people concerned, to ameliorate every legitimate grievance and to put society upon a more solid basis. (Balfour, 1895, cited in Evans, 1978: 136)

By 'social legislation' Balfour meant any legislation designed for 'the amelioration of the lot of the great classes of society' (Balfour, 1892, cited in Shannon, 1996: 246) without interfering with established property rights. The Conservative Party recoiled at the ideas of Henry George, correctly recognising them as a new and dangerous dimension of the long-standing radical hostility to the land-owning class. Organisations to defend the interests of landowners such as the Liberty and Property Defence League and the Land Union were established quickly and a system of central government assistance to local government through 'assigned' indirect tax revenues was introduced. This formed part of a Conservative strategy to ensure that the potential burden of social reform was shared by all classes and thereby rebuff the demand for social measures. In Ireland the existing pattern of land ownership was protected by state funds for relief work in distressed areas, by giving seed potatoes to the very poor, by the promotion of migration and by the supply of funds for the purchase of land to resell as small farms.

Social initiatives from the Conservative administrations of 1886 to 1905 were pragmatic, cautious and rare. Lord Salisbury's 'credentials as an economic libertarian were impeccable' (Roberts, 1999: 279). Nonetheless he justified state intervention in housing because 'loathsome' dwellings led to poor education, the attraction of the public house, the 'plague of intemperance' and thus a danger to the middle class. (Taylor, 1975: 85). Under the Housing of the Working Class Act 1890 local authorities obtained a clear and firm power to erect dwellings outside clearance areas but, as Morton (1991: 2) commented, 'There was no question at this point of any agency operating on other than restrained commercial terms. Authorities were expected to act like the Trusts and companies and seek a return not exceeding 5 per cent'. The Employers' Liability Act of 1897 laid a duty on an employer to pay a man half his wages if totally incapacitated in an accident arising out of the course of his employment. Condemned as a 'collectivist' measure because it interfered with freedom of contract between employer and employee (Dicey, 1981 [1914]: 282) its collectivism was modest indeed. Only particularly hazardous industries were covered and the Act permitted contracting out by employers subject to the provision of satisfactory independent arrangements. The 1905 Unemployed Workman's Act, like the 1886 circular allowing local authorities to provide temporary work without the stigma of pauperism, was designed as a temporary expedient to cope with the social unrest generated by cyclical unemployment. The Act allowed the use of rates to establish Distress Committees in the major urban areas to create work to alleviate temporary unemployment and to establish farm colonies to relocate urban workers (Bernstein, 1986: 124). Even this limited measure was regarded by many Conservatives as 'too akin to Socialism' and was justified by Government on the argument that if nothing was done to counter unemployment then the demand for more radical measures would be greatly strengthened (Fforde, 1990: 79).

The Education Act 1902 was the most important social measure passed by the Conservatives. It owed a great deal to the national efficiency dimension of Imperialism that developed in the Conservative Party following Joseph Chamberlain's defection from the Liberals over the issue of Home Rule for Ireland. In the period up to 1900 the local Boards, established under the Education Act 1870, had tackled their duties enthusiastically and some Boards offered instruction beyond 'elementary' education. In 1899 the district auditor declared spending on 'advanced instruction' in Science and Art by the London School Board to be beyond the scope of the Elementary School Code. Chamberlain surcharged the members of the Board for thereby creating a hiatus in the development of 'secondary' education in state schools.

The provisions of the 1902 Education Act were aimed at correcting the perceived deficiencies of the 1870 legislation, imposing order on the development of post-elementary education and consolidating the position of the Church of England in education. Introducing the Education Bill, Balfour noted 'two unforeseen consequences' of the 1870 legislation and 'three considerable omissions'. The unforeseen consequences were the rivalry between the voluntary schools and the Board schools and the strain the expansion of the 'rate-aided' system had put upon local finances. The omissions were 'no organisation for voluntary schools', no sufficient provision for education of teachers and 'our primary system was put in no kind of rational or organic connection with our system of secondary education'.

The 1902 Education Act absorbed the powers of ad hoc school boards into the mainstream system of local government with 315 local authorities (non-county boroughs and districts with populations over 20,000) assuming responsibility for elementary education. This ensured the agency responsible for collecting the rates also determined levels of expenditure on education. Voluntary schools became eligible for support from the local rates in addition to central grants and county borough authorities were granted the power to supply 'secondary' education.

The Regulations for Secondary Schools, 1904, effectively ensured the 'new county secondary schools ... should follow closely the conventional pattern of the old public and grammar schools'. To receive central grants secondary schools had to provide 'general instruction', offer a complete course to 'carry on the scholars to such a point as they may be reasonably be expected to reach at the age of 16' and teach 'English, History, Languages (ancient and modern), Mathematics and Science' (Regulations for Secondary Schools, cited in Maclure, 1973: 156). Fees were charged in secondary schools but, from 1907, to qualify for state assistance secondary schools had to admit up to a quarter of their pupils from the elementary schools without charges. The Elementary Code placed emphasis on the formation and development of character and in assisting 'both girls and boys, according to their different needs, to fit themselves practically as well as intellectually, for the work of life'. (Elementary Code, 1904 cited in Holland, 1904: 4).

The most controversial element of the 1902 Education Act was the award of assistance from the rates to church schools. This offended Nonconformists – Methodists, Baptists and Congregationalists – who were bitterly opposed to entrenchment of the Church of England in educational provision. It even annoyed some Anglicans because Roman Catholic schools also qualified for rate assistance. This 'religion on the rates' had a serious impact on the electoral fortunes of the Conservative Party. The 1902 Act united all the factions of the Liberal Party after the divisions over the Boer War and was attacked on the grounds that 'public money will be used to teach doctrines which the vast majority do not believe in' (Lloyd George, cited in Wrigley, 1976: 20).

THE LIBERAL REFORMS 1906–1914

The Liberal Party won the 1906 General Election with a majority of 130 seats over all the other parties combined. The national Liberal election campaign concentrated on free trade, the ending of 'religion on the rates', Irish government and licensing (Bernstein, 1986: 79). However, some Liberal candidates included social reform measures in their election programmes and, after a modest start, the pressure for social improvement as a route to social justice gathered momentum (Hennock, 1987: 2).

School meals

The 1906 Education (Provision of Meals) Act illustrates the pragmatic nature of the initial reform process. The high rejection rate of potential recruits for the Boer War highlighted the problem of child malnutrition and this led to the appointment of an Inter-departmental Committee on Physical Deterioration. Its report, published in 1904, recommended feeding 'necessitous' schoolchildren, teaching child care to mothers, instructing girls in cookery, the medical inspection of children and the imposition of restrictions on juvenile smoking. The Conservatives responded by issuing the Relief (School Children) Order in 1905 allowing schools to provide meals for poor children with the cost met by Poor Law authorities. This order imposed the legal liabilities of pauperism on parents whose children were fed by the state. The 'take-up' of such school meals was extremely low demonstrating that services associated with the Poor Law were not acceptable even to the poorest of the working class. The Labour Party took the lead in demanding all children in need should be fed and legislation was introduced by a Labour member, as a private member's bill, which attracted support from the Liberals. The bill 'became the centre of violent controversy' (Gilbert, 1966: 103) being attacked by some MPs as 'rank socialism' and defended by others as 'first-rate Imperialism' (Gilbert, 1966: 124). The 1906 Act gave local education authorities powers to 'take such steps as they think fit for the provision of meals for children at any elementary school in their area'. Local authorities could assist in defraying the cost of providing meals for any elementary school-children who were 'unable by reason of lack of food to take full advantage of the education provided for them'. Charges had to be made for the meals which LEAs could recover from parents 'unless they are satisfied that the parent is unable by reasons of circumstances other than his own default to pay the amount'. In fact few payments were made for meals; in 1909–10 £62,200 was spent on school meals in London, while the repayments by parents amounted to only £28 (Hurry, 1910: 239).

The state supply of school meals established an important beachhead for the subsequent development of welfare programmes. Despite the permissive nature of the initial legislation – only 131 of 322 LEAs had established schemes by 1911–12 – Parliament had recognised that members of a family could receive a 'personal' service from the state without the taint of pauperism. Some found such largesse offensive. Dicey, the noted Conservative lawyer, asked 'Why a man who first neglects his duty as a father and then defrauds the state should retain his full political rights is a question easier to ask than to answer' (cited in Hay, 1975: 43), while the Charity Organisation Society claimed such measures 'teach him [the child] to look to outside help for the things he has a right to expect from his parents, a lesson he will not be slow to remember when he himself is a parent' (cited in Pope et al., 1986: 66). Bosanquet expressed the view that it was better 'to allow in such cases the sins of the parents to be visited on their children than to impair the solidarity of the family and run the risk of permanently demoralising large numbers of the population by the offer of free meals to their children' (cited in Davin, 1996: 210).

School medical inspection

The Education (Administrative Provisions) Act 1907 placed a duty on local education authorities to 'provide for the medical inspection of children' on their admission to a public elementary school. Inspection was compulsory, but treatment permissive until the Education Act 1918 (Frazer, 1950: 401). The 1907 Act also allowed local authorities to provide vocational advice and 'vacation schools, vacation classes, play-centres, or other means of recreation during their holidays...'

Old age pensions

The Old Age Pensions Act 1908 granted a maximum pension of 25 pence each week to people over the age of 70. Comparisons of real incomes over time are fraught with difficulties due to changes in patterns of consumption and changes in the relative prices of items in the 'shopping basket'. At the turn of the nineteenth century a Mars bar cost £4 in 1998 terms whereas watching Arsenal play football cost the equivalent of 50 pence! However, based on calculations produced by the Government Statistical Service on the purchasing power of the pound, the single person's pension was worth about £16 at 1998 prices. [Henceforth values in 1998 terms are presented in squared brackets.] The first pension payments, financed from general taxation, were subject to a test of means and 'character'. Elderly people with an income over £31.50 per year [£2016] were not entitled to a pension and pensions were reduced for those with a yearly income between £21 [£1344] and £31.50 [£2016].

State pension plans had been in circulation for many years. Gladstone, for example, in an attempt to undermine the growing influence of the Friendly Societies, then regarded as potentially seditious working class organisations, introduced a bill to Parliament in 1854 to permit the working class to purchase annuities from the Post Office Savings Bank (Quandagno, 1982: 177). Macnicol (1998) attributes the developing support for state pensions to the increasing displacement of older workers from the labour force and the desire to remove 'respectable' elderly people from the Poor Law to strengthen its deterrent impact on younger workers. Disagreements between those in favour of state involvement to assist old people centred on the contributory principle. Canon William Blackley argued in favour of compulsory contributions as necessary to equalise the burden between the provident and the improvident (Parrott, 1984: 103). He was concerned about 'young labourers by the dozen without a change of decent clothes, continually and brutally drinking, and living almost like savages, while earning fully a pound a week' (Blackley, 1879, cited in Macnicol, 1998: 62). The leaders of organised labour regarded pensions as a reward for service to the nation – an 'endowment for old age'. They believed pensions should be financed from general taxation with the bonus that taxing the 'unproductive surplus' would boost consumption and lower unemployment (Freeden, 1978: 203). Eventually the issue was settled on political and pragmatic grounds. A contributory system would have aroused opposition from Friendly Societies who were suspicious of any competition for the limited savings of working people. Nonetheless, the Friendly Societies recognised that their own sickness schemes were in jeopardy because of claims from elderly people (Quandagno, 1982: 178) and, in 1902, they accepted the idea of a non-contributory pension (Grimes, 1991: 12). Pensions based on contributions also carried the problem that, if the respectability of an 'annuity' for old age was to be achieved, the first pensions would have to be delayed until a fund had accumulated – bad politics for a Liberal Party intent on stunting the growth of the Labour Party. Financial concerns – the cost of the Boer War was frequently cited – ruled out payments to all elderly people and the test of means plus the age limit helped to reduce the cost of a non-contributory scheme to the Exchequer. The Charity Organisation Society was totally opposed to pensions of any kind believing there was nothing special about the age of 70 as a marker for 'an estate of life in which state subsidy should begin' (Charity Organisation Review, 1894, cited in Macnicol, 1998: 83). The COS mounted a vigourous campaign against state pensions and, although it failed to prevent the introduction of a scheme, the character tests, added to the bill under COS pressure, met some of the objections of those who felt that 'doles' from the state would undermine self-reliance. Past pauperism, a conviction under the Inebriates Act, 1892, a term of imprisonment and failure 'to work according to his ability, opportunity and need, for the maintenance of himself and those legally dependent on him' (Section 111b Old Age Pensions Act, 1908) meant disqualification from entitlement for 515,000 elderly people (Webb, 1907b: 2).

The state pension was extremely popular and in 1911 the pauper disqualification was withdrawn. The payment was not sufficient to live on without additional income but the contribution elderly people could now make to household finances was welcomed. It certainly had an impact on the receipt of Poor Relief with a 26 per cent reduction in out-relief payments recorded in 1911 (Webb and Webb, 1929: 805). The novel method of administration contributed to the acceptability of the scheme. Customs and Excise administered the means test, issues of eligibility were decided by a special local committee and, in a masterstroke of social administration, pensioners were allowed to collect their weekly payment at the Post Office thereby disconnecting the state pension from the Poor Law.

A minimum wage?

The notion of a 'living wage' was in wide circulation towards the end of the nineteenth century. The Fabians concentrated on achieving a 'minimum standard of living' rather than a minimum wage and included the state 'social' wage as part of their notion of a 'living wage'. In contrast the Labour Party wanted a minimum wage from the employer of £1.50 [£96] a week. The Liberal Party rejected this demand claiming it would jeopardise industrial productivity but was prepared to 'uphold the principle while leaving the details to be adjusted to individual circumstances by wage boards and tribunals' (Freeden, 1978: 238). The Trade Boards Act 1909 established machinery to negotiate minimum wages in the female-dominated trades of tailoring, box-making and lace-making and in 1912 the miners secured what amounted to a minimum wage.

Labour exchanges

In *Unemployment: A Problem of Industry* (1909) William Beveridge provided the rationale for the 'nationwide' Labour Exchanges established under the 1909 Labour Exchanges Act after pilot schemes in London (King, 1995: 21). Beveridge argued that the demand for labour fluctuated and hence a reserve of labourers was desirable. However, when needed, these reserve workers had to be brought quickly into the labour force, a task that could be efficiently carried out by Labour Exchanges. Such exchanges would also be helpful in separating the 'workshy' from the 'deserving' poor.

> If all the jobs offering in a trade or a district are registered at a single office, then it is clear that any man who cannot get work through that office is unemployed against his will. He may be relieved without deterrence ... (Beveridge, 1909: 215–16)

Organised labour did not welcome the Labour Exchanges fearing that they would be used to supply cheap labour from distressed districts to undermine wage rates in more affluent areas (Evans, 1978: 292).

Health insurance

The insurance principle, as a means of meeting social needs, provoked powerful resistance. This opposition came from Socialists, Fabian Socialists, Trade Unions, Friendly Societies and even from some of the 'new' Liberals. Concern stemmed from doubts that 'compulsory thrift' could promote good character and from the idea that the 'unproductive' surplus of capitalism, not the worker's wage, was the appropriate source of finance for social security. The Socialist newspaper, *The Clarion* condemned contributions as 'a poll-tax levied irrespective of ability to pay' (cited in Evans, 1978: 278). Even Lloyd George was concerned about the impact of compulsory contributions on the low paid (Bunbury, 1957: 48). However, the insurance principle also had some powerful advocates. Winston Churchill believed that it was not enough 'to meet the socialist with a negative' and that the English progressive should take a leaf from Bismark 'who dealt the heaviest blow against socialism ... by the great system of state insurance...' (cited in Gilbert, 1966: 257). Insurance provided the mechanism to meet the contingencies of industrialisation by 'horizontal redistribution' within the working class and to cement the appeal of thrift as a mark of character. In its final form the health insurance scheme embodied the following principles.

Benefits in return for contributions   The principal argument in favour of insurance – the contractual nature of insurance gave a right to benefit – concealed a more fundamental question. Should the contractual right be based on the contributions necessary to ensure that annual income met annual expenditure (dividing out) or should the scheme be 'funded' and hence 'true insurance founded on actuarial principles' (Bunbury, 1957: 27)? In a properly 'funded' scheme, the rate of contribution ought to have been fixed at a level sufficient, with interest, to cover sickness claims over the long term and older workers, on entry to the scheme, should have paid more because age is related to health. After long discussions the Government used an Exchequer contribution as the reserve fund. This device enabled benefits to be paid following only 26 weeks of contribution. The basic benefits on offer were:

- sickness benefit of 50 pence [£32] per week for men and 37.5 pence [£24] for women lasting 26 weeks followed by a disablement benefit of 25 pence [£16] for as long as the disablement lasted;
- medical benefit, consisting of medical treatment and attendance, including 'proper and sufficient medicines' from a general practitioner;
- sanatorium benefit for the treatment of tuberculosis;
- maternity benefit paid on the husband's insurance record and, if insured, that of his wife.

Administration through quasi-autonomous agencies The involvement of Friendly Societies in the administration of health insurance was part of the scheme at its creation but the commercial insurance companies, fearful of losing their funeral expenses business, insisted on being included as 'approved' societies. The 'approved' societies had a significant role in the administration of cash benefits being charged with policing the cash benefits parts of the legislation with regard to

> manner and time of paying or distributing, and mode of calculating, benefits, suspension of benefits, notice and proof of disease or disablement, behaviour during disease or disablement, and the visiting of a sick or disabled person, and for the infliction and enforcement of penalties. (National Insurance Act, 1911: section 14)

Also, the original intention had been to allow Friendly Societies to oversee the medical practitioner services, as they had done in their own schemes (Cherry, 1996: 42) but opposition from the doctors led to the creation of special Insurance Committees, with substantial medical representation, to administer this service.

Pooling the risks of the working class Health Insurance covered the majority of working class men. People earning more than £160 [£8000] per year were excluded as were married women not in work. The exclusion of married women provoked significant opposition. The Women's Industrial Council condemned the exclusion 'as considering the work of a wife and mother in her home of no money value' (cited in Digby and Stewart, 1996: 13) and the Labour Party pressed for the inclusion of married women with the argument:

> When the wife is sick it is nearly always necessary to pay for outside help which has to be brought in. The married woman requires nursing, the housework requires to be done, young children require to be looked after, and it entails extra expenditure, which the wages of the husband makes it impossible for him to adequately meet. As a result the poor woman suffers, the children suffer, and a great deal of discomfort is added to the life of the husband which might easily be obviated. (Keir Hardy, 1911, cited in Pope et al., 1986: 57)

Lloyd George rejected Labour's proposal claiming the married woman's contribution would have to be paid by her husband and the majority of working class families could not afford a higher payment. Nonetheless, the Woman's Co-operative Guild continued to press for the independent role of women to be recognised and won a limited victory when, in 1913, Parliament voted in favour of making the maternity grant payable directly to the woman. Many Labour Party MPs voted against this change arguing that it was a slur on working-class husbands to claim they would not spend the maternity grant properly and that direct payment to the woman breached the contractual relationship between the worker and his 'approved' society (Pederson, 1993: 56).

'Corporate' responsibility   The 'tripartite' contributory system, with the employer, employee and Exchequer all making payments, enabled Lloyd George to sell the scheme as ' ninepence for threepence'. The specific employer contribution also helped to satisfy the 'organic' ideas of society held by the intellectual 'new' Liberals because the employer contribution opened the possibility of using the insurance mechanism as a preventative measure; variations in employer payments would reflect the efforts made by employers to reduce the ill-health of their employees. This idea was included in the scheme but was not implemented.

Work creation

Unemployment was a critical issue for the Labour movement and, in 1907, the Labour Party introduced its first 'right to work' measure to Parliament proposing to create a central unemployment committee to organise committees to develop local projects. Each local committee would be responsible for finding a job for all the unemployed people in the area, but, to confirm the Labour Party's respectability, 'loafers and shirkers' would be excluded (Walters, 2000: 38). If no work could be found then maintenance 'for the necessities of life' was to be provided (Brown, 1971: 85). The bill was opposed by the Liberals with the argument that a right to work or maintenance would impair industrial efficiency by destroying 'the character, the self-reliance and the moral fibre of the men of the country' (Vivian, 1908, cited in Bernstein, 1986: 125). Nonetheless, the Liberals investigated methods of work creation. In 1906 the *Royal Commission on Coast Erosion and Afforestation* was appointed to consider the possibility of 'using the labour of unemployed persons upon such work of reclamation' (cited in Harris, 1972: 337). It concluded afforestation was especially suitable for public investment to absorb surplus labour because it was unattractive to the private investor (the returns being long term) and used a high proportion of unskilled labour. Despite Treasury opposition on the grounds that work creation stopped private sector investment (Peden, 2000: 66) the Development and Road Improvement Funds Act became law in 1909. It established a Development Commission with powers of compulsory purchase and the authority to give financial assistance to specified activities such as forestry and land reclamation.

Unemployment insurance

Unemployment insurance, included in Part Two of the 1911 National Insurance Act, was more limited than health insurance. It covered only about 2.25 million workers out of a labour force of 19 million and pooling the risks only of occupations with a similar likelihood of unemployment. Contributions were tripartite with the employer's contribution subject to a refund if the worker was retained for at least 45 weeks per year. One week of benefit was paid for every five contributions subject to a maximum of 15 weeks' benefit. Benefit was withheld if an unemployed worker was sacked for misconduct or involved in a trade dispute, but the growing influence of organised labour was reflected in the requirement that a man would only be expected to take employment 'in his own employment or trade and under conditions to which he was accustomed' (Walters, 2000: 64). Unemployment insurance was designed to deal only with the consequences of 'cyclical' unemployment in certain trades. It attracted opposition from a section of the Labour movement as demanding flat-rate contributions in return for a meagre benefit – less than a quarter of the average wage. Nevertheless, it was an important testing ground for the social engineering advocated by the Fabians and 'new' Liberals. It provided a mechanism for encouraging the ending of casual labour by charging higher contributions to employers hiring such labour (Beenstock and Brasse, 1986: 3) and helped to divide the 'unemployed sheep from the unemployable goats' (Whiteside, 1991: 63). Those in regular employment would be helped in short periods of frictional unemployment but the remainder – surplus to normal requirements – formed a 'residuum' to be dealt with by different methods.

SOCIAL EXCLUSION

> We have allowed to grow up amongst us the conception of ... [a] class to which we apply a great variety of names, all tending to the degradation of those concerned. We call it the Residuum, the Poor, the Submerged, the Proletariat, the Abyss; and we call its homes Slums, and Ghettos, and Mean Streets....
> (Bosanquet, 1902: 331)

Historians have identified the idea of the 'residuum' as 'one of the key concepts in late Victorian social science' (Harris, 1993: 67). All the radical movements active in the late nineteenth century believed in the existence of a 'residual' stratum in society although they disagreed about its causes. The 'residuum' idea set standards to cement membership of the social order and established benchmarks for those aspiring to inclusion. It helped to fix limits to the 'subjects' of social justice by identifying those either lacking in moral character and hence redeemable or as incapable of developing a moral character and hence candidates for total exclusion from the civic order.

Marx referred to the 'lumpen-proletariat' as 'a passive putrefaction of the lowest strata of the old society' (Marx, 1848, cited in Bovenkerk, 1984 pp. 20). Its existence, which Engels attributed to 'environmental factors' (Mann, 1992: 131), aroused the antagonism of revolutionaries because its 'local inter-connection' meant it could not form the basis of radical class action. (Marx and Engels 1969: 278). The 'lumpen-proletariat' had no revolutionary potential and its members could 'but die out, leaving, it is hoped, no progeny as a burden on a better state of things' (Hyndman, 1887: 129).

Fabians were concerned that the behaviour of the 'residuum' would undermine the case for social reform by tarnishing the reputation of the public services. The partial inclusion of the respectable working class male into civic society had to be accompanied by the identification of those unworthy of citizenship. In 1889 they declared their objective as providing 'generously, and without stigma, for the aged, the sick and those destitute through temporary want of employment, without relaxing the "tests" against the endowment of able-bodied idleness' (Webb, 1962: 86). 'Malingers' caused a great deal of disquiet. Braithwaite records that, on the first reading of the National Insurance Bill, the civil servants 'were all going through a panic about malingering' being concerned with 'weaklings' wanting a 'pension for a headache' (Braithwaite, 1957: 97, 115). Sidney Webb thought that the German health insurance scheme had greatly increased 'shirking'. He wanted to classify paupers and arm an assortment of 'expert' public officials with 'sweeping and compulsory powers of detention over anyone who fell below the minimum of mental and physical fitness recognised by society' (Searle, 1976: 242). Illness, being a 'public nuisance' had to be 'suppressed in the interests of the community' by the compulsory treatment of all sick people (Webb, 1906, cited in Radice, 1984: 164). The able-bodied unemployed would be sent to 'human sorting houses' where they would be tested and trained. Those designated 'idle' would be given 'training in character, under the beneficent influence of continuous order and discipline'. The most obstinate cases would be committed to a Detention Colony (Royal Commission on the Poor Law, Minority Report, 1909, cited in Pierson, 1979: 318).

Women did not escape association with fecklessness. Legislation was passed prohibiting children from entering public houses, imposing stiffer penalties on parents found guilty of 'overlaying' while under the influence of drink and making parents responsible for the death of a child caused by the lack of fireguards in the home (Kent, 1999: 239). Young (1989: 107–8) notes:

Working people … resented this new interference in their lives. Some of the working women's objections were explained by Anna Martin: The Bill will put a stop to our chief bit of pleasure. Our husbands often take us out on the trams or out into the country in the summer evenings, and we go and sit with them in a respectable public-house for half an hour … but it will be different if the men have to go in by themselves and we have to stand outside with the children.

In the early twentieth century there was growing concern about working-class mothers being unskilled in 'mothercraft' and the Charity Organisation Society argued that the provision of school meals and sterilised milk had hindered the development of 'the arts of housekeeping'. 'The true policy', said Bosanquet, 'lies in the better training of women and girls in the arts of housekeeping and child rearing: and more especially in some knowledge of proper feeding' (cited in Dwork, 1987: 133). The appointment of health visitors, started as a voluntary movement activity in 1862, began to spread to local government and, by 1905, about 50 towns had paid visitors (Hendrick, 1994: 97). These intrusions were resented by many working class women because the demands for higher standards were difficult to meet on a low income (Minor, 1979: 121).

The continuance of the 'residuum' was linked to the notion that human attributes were genetically determined. The Eugenics Education Society, founded in 1907, 'spoke on behalf of the educated middle class' who wanted to work with 'better human material' (Mazumder, 1992: 8,27). Its leading figures believed that

the class structure of Britain reflected in large part a hierarchy of innate ability, at the top of which was the elite of the professional middle class and at the bottom of which were the poor, unemployed and 'criminal' … the professional middle class should be encouraged to have more children, and the 'unfit' should be discouraged (and perhaps ultimately prevented) from propagating. (MacKenzie, 1999: 56)

One dimension of this concern for human stockbreeding was the identification of a new 'urban type': 'stunted, narrow-chested, easily wearied; yet voluble, excitable, with little ballast, stamina or endurance – seeking stimulus in drink, in betting, in any unaccustomed conflicts at home and abroad' (Masterman 1909: 8). The pauper was also 'made of inferior material'.

It is a mistake to suppose that the typical pauper is merely an ordinary person who has fallen into distress through adverse circumstances. As a rule he is not an ordinary person, but one who is constitutionally a pauper, a pauper in his blood and bones. He is made of inferior material, and therefore cannot be improved up to the level of the ordinary person. The hereditary nature of this incapacity … emphasises the necessity of protecting the community against them, and, in particular, against the perpetuation of the degenerate stocks which they represent. On this ground alone the proper authorities should be vested with the power of segregating and detaining – permanently, if necessary – those who burden the present and imperil the future of our race. (Pearson, 1911: 917)

Many 'new' Liberals fell under the influence of the new 'science of the mind'. As Thomson (1998) has said:

Because New Liberals placed so much emphasis on the importance of character, they could adopt surprisingly draconian policies towards mental defectives, who, by definition, had a biological lack of character, and who threatened to disrupt social policies which were designed for those citizens who did. (Thomson, 1998: 41)

J.A. Hobson recommended 'sternly repressing the anti-social conduct which produces the physically unfit' because 'selection of the fittest, or at least, rejection of the unfittest, is essential to all progress in life and character' (cited in Freeden, 1978: 178). William Beveridge, a believer in eugenics throughout his life, commented:

… those men who through general defects are unable to fill such a whole place in industry, are to be recognised as unemployable. They must become the acknowledged dependents of the state, removed from free industry and maintained adequately in public institutions, but with a complete and permanent loss of all citizen rights including not only the franchise, but civil freedom and fatherhood. (Beveridge, 1906: 327)

Hobhouse adopted a more cautious approach. In *Social Evolution and Political Theory* (1911) he recognised that 'the case of the feeble-minded becomes perhaps the strongest case for the application of eugenic methods' (Hobhouse, 1974 [1911]: 45). However, he refused to generalise from the feeble-minded, 'a type which is becoming possible to identify with fair precision', to other members of the residuum. He could not accept pauperism as 'in the main a hereditary trait' (Hobhouse, 1974 [1911]: 74) and, like many social reformers of his time, he tended to favour 'environmental' explanations of the existence of a 'residuum' (Harris, 1993: 243). However, this did not modify his policy prescription.

It is his right and his duty to make the best use of his opportunity, and if he fails he may fairly suffer the penalty of being treated as a pauper or even, in an extreme case, as a criminal. (Hobhouse, 1911: 165)

Hobhouse followed Booth closely on the issue (Dennis and Halsey 1988: 89). In his social survey of London, Charles Booth identified eight 'classes'. Class A were 'the lowest class of occasional labourers, loafers and semi-criminals' (Booth, 1969 [1892]: 33). Comprising only 0.9 per cent of the population they were 'a disgrace but not a danger' to society (Booth, 1969 [1892]: 40). Class B, being more numerous were more dangerous. They made up 7.5 per cent of the population, existed on casual earnings and were 'the material from which paupers were made' (Booth, 1969 [1892]: 176). They could be distinguished from Classes C and D (the Poor) in that they were 'ill-nourished and poorly clad' and were 'from mental, moral and physical reasons incapable of better work' (Booth, 1969 [1892]: 43–4). Booth claimed Classes A and B were a 'crushing load' on the poor because of their competition in the labour market. They

should be allowed to live as families in industrial groups, planted wherever land and building materials were cheap – being well-housed, well-fed and well-warmed. They would be employed from morning to night, trained, and if they showed a willingness to work hard, would be allowed to return to open society. (Booth, 1969 [1892]: 167)

Jones (1960: 47) notes how 'social issues connected with feeble-mindedness became hotly debated' in the late nineteenth century. Robert L. Dugdale's study (1877) of an American family, with five mentally defective sisters whose descendants had produced 128 prostitutes, 142 habitual paupers, 64 workhouse inmates and 72 habitual criminals was frequently quoted. Its message was reinforced by Goddard's study (1912), of Martin Kallikak who, in four generations of descendants, had produced 36 illegitimate children, 24 alcoholics and 33 'sexually immoral' offspring. Evidence from Britain was advanced to support the notion that 'feeble-mindedness' caused social pathology. Mr Baldwin Fleming, General Inspector to the Local Government Board, claimed 'every Board of Guardians was familiar with the problem of the mentally defective girl who came to the workhouse, perhaps five or six times, to bear her illegitimate children. The children were nearly always defective' (cited in Jones, 1960: 53).

The Eugenics Society promoted 'positive' and 'negative' measures to improve the 'national stock'. Positive measures included changes in the income tax system to assist married couples to rear children, which had the appeal of encouraging only the middle class to breed because only the middle class paid income tax at the time (Searle, 1976: 88; Mazumbar, 1992: 49). The 'negative' measures included the 'sterilisation of the unfit' and the prohibition of marriage between partners judged of poor stock (King, 1999: 53). In 1908 the Royal Commission into the Care and Control of the Feeble-Minded, set up in response to growing concern about the deterioration in intelligence of the nation, published its report. It found considerable evidence to demonstrate that mental deficiency was a major factor in pauperism, crime, illegitimacy and alcoholism. Because mental defectives were unfit to 'take part in the struggle of life' it recommended they should be segregated to protect them from their own 'instinctual responses' and exploitation by others. A pressure group, an amalgamation of the National Association for the Care of the Feeble-Minded and the Eugenics Education Society, was formed. It demanded every candidate for Parliament should 'support measures ... that tend to discourage parenthood on the part of the feeble-minded and other degenerate types' (cited in Kevles, 1986: 98).

In 1913 Parliament passed the Mental Deficiency Act that granted powers to a Board of Control to supervise, protect and control all defectives as defined in the Act. Defectives could be certified and either placed under a guardianship order or in an institution. Only three Members of Parliament opposed the legislation on the grounds that it infringed civil liberties (Kelves, 1986: 99).

TAXATION

The 'new' Liberalism made an explicit connection between the establishment of state services and the taxation necessary to pay for them. Certain forms of income were 'undeserved' because they flowed from the 'social' creation of value. It followed that public services – if financed from 'unmerited excess' – were not 'doles' but a 'deserved' share in wealth created by the community. The Labour Party also made a distinction between 'earned' and 'unearned' income with Ramsey McDonald summing up Labour's 'fundamental principle of finance' as wanting 'to divide the non-producing parasite dependent upon society from the producer and service giver' (McDonald, 1909, cited in Whiting, 2000: 10).

Henry George had produced a compelling argument for the taxation of land and, by 1907, 130 Members of Parliament were members of the Land Nationalisation Society (Gilbert, 1987: 374). George's ideas were reflected in Lloyd George's 1909 'People's Budget' that included a 20 per cent levy on the 'unearned increments' from land sales and an annual tax on the capital value of 'undeveloped' land. (Peden, 2000: 46). Lloyd George defended these taxes by pointing out:

land that not so many years ago was a 'sodden marsh' selling at £3 an acre was now, as result of the commerce that comes through the docks and the consequent demand for accommodation, selling at £8,000 an acre. 'Who created those increments? Who made the golden swamp? Was it the landlord? Was it his energy? His brains? His forethought?' he asked giving the answer ' Purely the combined efforts of all the people engaged in the trade and commerce of the Port of London – trader, merchant, shipowner, dock labourer, workmen – everybody except the landlord'. (Lloyd George, 1909: 43)

Harcourt's 1894 reform of death duties had 'ended the discrimination in favour of land and brought all forms of property left at death into a uniform and somewhat higher rate of tax' (Jenkins, 1998: 63). However, Harcourt's reform did not attempt to impose higher rates of tax on land or to attack the 'unearned increment' (Daunton, 1995: 139). In contrast Lloyd George wanted the Treasury to become 'a weapon of social policy' (Evy, 1971: 67) by forcing the landed interest to pay for a larger share of state spending. Therefore, in addition to the new land taxes, he increased estate duties to 25 per cent on estates worth over £1million (Jenkins, 1998: 166).

Lloyd George's taxes on land and inherited wealth could be vindicated on the 'unmerited income' argument but his 'supertax' of 2.5p in the pound on incomes in excess of £5000 per annum was more difficult to justify. Why should large incomes be penalised by 'supertax' if acquired, not through 'social' processes, but by personal effort? The answer was a mixture of expediency and principle. Revenue was necessary to finance the Liberal social programme and additional spending on defence (Gilbert, 1987: 368–9). If free trade was to be maintained, it could not be found from the tariffs. Utilitarian theory suggested that marginal utility diminished in inverse ratio to increments in income so J.S. Mill's 'equality of sacrifice' could be taken to mean that graduated taxation was necessary (Shehab, 1953: 200). Moreover the notion of 'unearned income' could be extended beyond land to include 'rents' in the Fabian sense of the term. Some calculations had estimated 'unearned' income at 66 per cent of total national income (Bowley, 1919).

CONCLUSION

David Miller (1999: 4) attributes first use of the term 'social justice' as a book title, to Wessel Willoughby writing in 1900. Its use reflects the growing influence of 'social democratic' thinking that attempted to incorporate the organised working class into the established order by a redistribution of the 'social surplus' to those who showed 'good character' by participating in voluntary and state insurance schemes. Nonetheless, despite the brouhaha surrounding the 1909 budget, the Liberal Reforms had little impact on the distribution of income. State expenditure as a proportion of the GNP (excluding military spending) increased by only 1.2 per cent between 1900 and 1913 (Davis, 1998: 26). Much of this spending went on the 'sanitary police' who patrolled the 'externalities' of public health (Mallet, 1913: 470) and on social insurance with its horizontal (within classes according to contingency) rather than vertical ('rich' to 'poor') redistribution. Nonetheless, the notion of an 'undeserved social surplus', developed by the 'new' Liberals, offered the potential for more radical social and economic change in the direction of social justice. In introducing his National Insurance Bill to Parliament Lloyd George had recognised the limitations of social insurance in mitigating the social evils of the day. He believed insurance 'was merely a contribution to that end' and that

> In both town and country the land system hinders everything now – hinders smallholdings, hinders allotments, hinders workmen's dwellings, hinders every attempt at social amelioration. It thwarts every enterprise, commercial, industrial, social and economic, including municipal enterprise. You will do no good until you recast the system. (Lloyd George, 1911, cited in Wrigley, 1976: 40)

Lloyd George launched his land campaign in October 1913 and thereby put land reform at the centre of Liberal Party politics (Fforde, 1990: 126). Henry George's ideas permeated Lloyd George's proposals. A 'Ministry of Land' would be established with appointed land commissioners to implement its policies. These commissioners would have extensive powers to ensure that the land was utilised 'in the best interests of the community'. In the country the commissioners would determine rents, fix rates of compensation for improvement, intervene in evictions, set minimum wages, establish maximum hours and distribute central grants for the provision of houses. In urban areas commissioners would control leases and supervise the building of homes on land whose value would be fixed at 1910 levels. Central grants and additional revenue from the local taxation of land values would help to finance low-cost housing in rural areas.

4

Collectivism Contained

In a buoyant post-war economy, when the absorption of 'residual' labour into the war effort had silenced the advocates of the 'residuum' thesis, the principles underlying the Liberal reforms continued to be applied. A confident, assertive working class managed to secure gains in wages, lower working hours and welfare provision (Waites, 1987: 87). However, after 1921, when financial orthodoxy asserted that cuts in public expenditure were the necessary condition of recovery from the recession, these 'progressive' principles were contained. Over the period state welfare spending expanded but much of the increase was concerned with alleviating the consequences of the recession, maintaining the nation's 'human stock' and containing the working class in urban areas.

Unemployment insurance

The prosperity of the period 1912 to 1914 and the low rate of unemployment during and immediately after the First World War meant the Unemployment Insurance Fund showed a healthy surplus. State unemployment insurance was deemed a success so the scheme was extended to those covered by health insurance, despite opposition from some of the 'beneficiaries' who regarded their contributions as poor value for money in a time of high employment (Whiteside, 1991: 73). However, soon after coverage was enlarged the post-war boom ended, unemployment trebled and many of those newly included in the unemployment scheme had paid insufficient contributions to claim benefit. They had to be granted 'exceptional' benefit unjustified by contributions – the first of many departures from strict insurance principles. In 1921, following a period of high inflation, benefit entitlement was extended to 26 weeks and the Unemployed Workers Dependants (Temporary Provisions) Act allowed 25 pence [£7.50] for the wife of an unemployed man and 5 pence [£1.50] for each child. These dependants' additions again breached the actuarial principles but political expediency, not actuarial soundness, was paramount at the time as was demonstrated in a report presented to the Cabinet in 1921. 'A very large proportion of the unemployed today are not the usual type of unskilled or work-shy men ... these men fought in the war and they are not prepared to see their families endure misery and want without a serious struggle and even disorder' (PRO Cab. 23/27, 6 October 1921 cited in Gilbert, 1966: 72). An earlier report had pointed out how, 'in the event of rioting, for the first time in history, the rioters will be better trained than the troops' (cited in Gilbert, 1970: 75).

Unemployment, having increased to 16.9 per cent of the insured workforce in 1921 remained at over 10 per cent until 1927. Unemployment was concentrated in particular areas and the average period of worklessness was increasing. What was to happen to the unemployed when their benefit entitlement expired? Benefits, unjustified by contributions, might be excused as a necessary expedient arising from wartime disruption but, with the return to 'normalcy', could payments to the 'able-bodied' outside the Poor Law be justified? If not, what of the danger of social unrest as thousands of 'respectable' men were thrown onto the stigmatised, feared and detested Poor Law? A compromise emerged: insurance benefits were divided into 'standard' (strict entitlement under the insurance scheme) and additional payments called 'uncovenanted' (1921), 'extended' (1924) and 'transitional' (1927) benefits. These 'additional' payments were not means tested, but initially they were subject to more rigorous eligibility tests than the standard benefit with claimants having to prove they were genuinely seeking work. Their cost continued to be attributed to the National Insurance Fund 'to be made good when the recession abated'. But the recession did not abate – by 1932 unemployment had reached 22.1 per cent of the insured workforce and 16 per cent had been out of work for more than 12 months (Constantine, 1983: 10). As unemployment soared so did the National Insurance Fund deficit with the Government having to find about £80 million a year in addition to its contribution to the main insurance scheme (Glynn and Oxborrow, 1976: 254). The Conservatives attributed the growth in the unemployment register to the abolition, in 1929, of the 'genuinely seeking work test', under which unemployed claimants had to prove, to the satisfaction of a local official, that they were looking for work. Despite its replacement by a requirement on claimants to take up any offer of 'suitable' work, the abolition of 'genuinely seeking work test', it was alleged, 'enabled "cute" men and women to claim benefits to which they were not entitled' (Skidelsky, 1967: 232). William Beveridge joined the chorus of disapproval asserting that the availability of 'unearned' benefits without conditions encouraged 'voluntary' unemployment. 'There would be little sense in trying to find an actuarial basis for fire insurance' ... in a country with no fire engines and no penalties for arson (Beveridge, 1931, cited in Birch, 1974: 105). In 1930 the Government made the deficit on the Unemployment Insurance Fund a charge on the Consolidated Fund (general government income) but the shortfall remained clearly identifiable. Such an open recognition that unemployment benefit was 'unfunded' made it a conspicuous target for cuts in public expenditure.

When borrowing became necessary to finance a currency outflow, the international bankers demanded reductions in public expenditure as a condition of a loan, a demand totally in accord with the Treasury belief in a 'balanced budget'. The Committee on National Expenditure (May Committee, Cmd 3902) recommended a £97 million cut in government spending with 60 per cent to fall on unemployment benefit. The standard rate of benefit was to be reduced by 20 per cent and the 'transitional' benefit was to be means tested. It fell to a minority Labour Government, led by Ramsay MacDonald, to handle the crisis but the Cabinet refused to accept the full range of the May proposals on unemployment benefits (Skidelsky, 1967: 376). The Government resigned and a 'national' administration took office drawing almost all its support from Conservatives and Liberals, but with Ramsay MacDonald as Prime Minister. A reduction in unemployment benefit by 10 per cent was introduced immediately, justified on the argument that the cost of living had declined since 1929. Married women, with entitlements to insurance benefits through contributions before marriage, had their entitlement extinguished by the Anomalies Regulations – it being deemed an 'anomaly' that a woman could rely on both the state and her husband as sources of income. Eligibility for a transitional payment was made conditional on a household means test administered by the Public Assistance Committees of local government – the agencies that had taken over responsibility for poor relief from the Boards of Guardians in 1929. These Public Assistance Committees had considerable discretion in deciding how household resources should be treated but, in the case of workers entitled to 'transitional' payments, the National Exchequer financed the allowances. Some local authorities were generous in interpreting the regulations and, in Durham and Rotherham, the Government appointed special commissioners to administer transitional payments because of the alleged laxity of the local administration. Twelve other authorities were warned about their conduct (Millett, 1940: 27). Unemployed workers, not covered by the unemployment insurance scheme and therefore not entitled to 'transitional' benefits, created an additional problem (Webb and Webb, 1929: 676). They were the full responsibility of local government and their maintenance costs fell on the rates – a severe burden in depressed areas with low rateable values and a strong disincentive to industrialists looking for sites to establish new factories (Williams, 1943: 227).

In 1934, a national Unemployment Assistance Board was created to eliminate the problems of local discretion and the uneven rate burden. It was responsible for establishing scales of maintenance for all unemployed people without entitlement to insurance benefits and for administering these maintenance scales. Henceforth, levels of assistance to the long-term unemployed became a central government responsibility. Although the Unemployment Assistance Board was set up to take 'relief out of politics', its recommendations on maintenance scales had to be approved by the Minister of Labour and Parliament (Millett, 1940: 119).

Health insurance

The Health Insurance legislation of 1911 ensured that 'approved' societies paid benefits at a minimum level, but a society could award additional benefits if it generated a surplus. By 1936, some 13.1 million people were entitled to dental benefit, 11.3 million to optical benefit to purchase spectacles and 1.9 million to optical care (Herbert, 1939: 206). Health insurance attracted criticism on a number of grounds. It was often alleged that the general practitioner, available under the medical services part of the scheme, did not devote the same care to his 'panel' patients as to his private patients (Digby, 1996: 217). The restriction on membership to those earning less than £260 per year [£8800] caused difficulties for those marginally above the threshold but the major criticism was the exclusion of children and married women (without paid work) from free care. Local government attempted to fill the gap by providing services aimed at improving the 'national stock'. The Boards of Guardians (Public Assistance Committees after 1929) appointed GPs on a part-time basis to provide medical care to those claiming 'out-relief'. Many local authorities also provided antenatal care and in 1937 nearly all the welfare authorities in England and Wales were supplying milk to expectant and nursing mothers. Under the Milk Act, 1934, a measure to assist farmers to sell surplus milk, local authorities could supply one third of a pint of milk to children either free or at cost price. By 1939 56.6 per cent of elementary school children were receiving milk (Hendrick, 1994: 140). The appointment of health visitors and the establishment of child welfare centres, assisted by central government grants, developed rapidly in the 1930s although the availability of these services remained patchy. Every child had to be medically inspected three times while at school and the local authority had to provide treatment in elementary schools. Children under school age were not covered and Herbert (1939: 140) noted '16 per cent of the children who entered public elementary schools in 1937 were found to have defects requiring treatment'. The Midwives Act, 1936, established the machinery for the creation of a full-time salaried midwifery service to be organised by local government. Midwifery was not free but the lump sum maternity grant, paid on the husband's insurance record, helped to meet some of the cost.

The basic cash benefits paid through the health insurance scheme were meagre, only 75 pence [£25] for a man and 60 pence [£20] per week for a woman with her own contributory record. After six months a disablement benefit, at half the sickness benefit rate, was paid. Unlike unemployment benefit, there were no allowances for dependants so, for a family with one child, sickness benefit was only half the rate of unemployment benefit. Most 'approved' societies paid more than the minimum but the ability of a society to offer additional benefits varied according to the industry covered and, in the case of societies based on geographical areas, the environment of the local population. Thus, members of 'approved' societies obtained different benefits from the same compulsory contribution – a situation attacked on the grounds that 'inequality at the level of necessity is intolerable' (Levy, 1944: 253). The variations in payments were justified with the argument that Friendly Societies were mutual, democratic and participatory organisations and thus 'uniformity' of benefits should not be expected. The health insurance scheme remained solvent throughout the 1920s despite the problems encountered in the recession. As unemployment increased so too did claims for sickness benefit. This was attributed to the channelling of the needs arising from unemployment through the 'easier' channel of a claim for sickness.

Widows', orphans' and old age pensions

During the war the old age pension was increased and the Rylands Adkins Committee was appointed 'to consider what alteration, if any, as regards rates of pensions should be made in the existing statutory scheme'. The committee noted that 'the amount of pension is not designed to be adequate itself for complete support' but recommended an increase to 50 pence [£16] to restore the pension's value to its 1908 level. The Old Age Pensions Amending Act of 1919 implemented this recommendation and abolished the character tests introduced in 1908. In 1921 a boost was given to the provision of occupational pensions by the introduction of tax relief on pension contributions.

The introduction of contributory pensions was prompted by the alleged failures of the 1908 scheme, deep concern within the Treasury about the future implications of tax-financed social security and the determination of Neville Chamberlain to promote a 'New Conservatism' of social concern fused with financial rectitude. Not only did the contributory pension nullify the threat of finance by progressive taxation it also reduced the cost to the Exchequer of the non-contributory pension. According to Field et al., (1977: 75–6) 'the government of the day estimated that by 1956 workers ... would pay not only for the entire cost of their own pension, but also the pensions of those still drawing the 1908 benefit'. Under legislation passed in 1925, in return for at least three years additional contributions, a pension was paid without a test of means at the age of 65. A married woman received a pension, on her husband's contributions, if she and her husband were both over 65. The pension lasted until the age of 70 when elderly people covered by the contributory scheme were transferred to the non-contributory pension, paid without a means test. In addition the widow of an insured person with children under 14 became entitled to allowances for herself and additions for her children with the child allowances converted into an orphan's pension if the widow died. In 1929, following active campaigning by women's groups, the Labour government awarded pensions to childless widows over 55. The contributory old age pension was 50 pence [£17.50] per week for the insured person and 50 pence for his wife, the same level that had been set for the means-tested pension.

IN CASH OR IN KIND?

The issue of allocations in cash or in kind was rarely debated in the inter-war years. It was assumed only a contributory record justified payments in cash and even this principle was questioned on the argument that cash payments did nothing to promote desirable behaviour. In regard to the maternity grant, the Minority Report of the Royal Commission on National Insurance (1926) argued:

> The interest of the Approved Society in the child-bearing woman begins and ends with the handing over to her a lump sum of money ... much more could be done for child-bearing women who need other services directed to safeguarding the health of mothers and infants by Local Authorities, who already administer such services, than by Approved Societies who have nothing to do with them.

Local authority housing

The Minority Report of the Royal Commission on Housing in Scotland (1917) had suggested the payment of a rent allowance to

> men with three children or more, equal to the difference between the average rent of a two-roomed dwelling and 'the higher rent of which would be requisite for the proper housing of the family on the higher standard to be enforced in the near future'. (Holmans, 1987: 44)

Such proposals for cash allowances to allow working people to rent a home of their choice received scant support: the working class simply could not be trusted to spend state-provided cash in a 'responsible' manner and state aid had to promote moral improvement. So, when it was deemed necessary to create 'a land fit for heroes to live in', by adding homes to those supplied in a market crippled in the war years, local authorities were chosen as the main providers. Between 1919 and 1933 local government was allocated 'producer' subsidies from central government, of varying amounts, to encourage them to supply dwellings at below cost price (Merrett, 1979). State provision of homes allowed physical forms of housing to be designed to promote acceptable behaviour. Raymond Unwin, the principal architect of local authority housing, set out his design ideas in *Cottage Plans and Common Sense* (1902). He condemned the

> little walled-in back yard ... somewhat firmly established in the public affection because 'entrenched behind the feelings of pride and shame, it appeals alike to those who are too proud to be seen keeping their houses clean and tidy, and to those who are ashamed to have it seen how unclean and untidy they are'. (Unwin, 1902: 3)

A housing manual was issued by the Local Government Board containing advice – based on the Tudor Walters Report – on the design of the new houses. In order to be eligible for subsidy houses had to be built at no more than 12 per acre and could be either parlour (type A) or non-parlour (type B). Homes were to contain amenities such as an inside toilet, a garden, electricity and a bath, but an appeal from feminist socialists for the new estates to include communal restaurants and laundries was ignored (Sanderson-Furniss and Phillips, 1920: 51). The moral improvement of the working class was the dominant theme in the design of council housing in the inter-war period with the provision of a garden regarded as a path to character improvement. The absence of legal rights for council tenants – it was assumed that citizens required no protection from democratically accountable 'public' bodies – meant that tenants could be evicted almost at will; a powerful deterrent to 'uncivil' behaviour.

The poor law

The process of reducing reliance on the Poor Law continued throughout the inter-war period. Unemployment benefits and the non-contributory old age pension (blind persons over 50 received a pension in 1920) helped to prevent large numbers of people from having to apply for poor relief. In addition, specialist forms of provision for people with a physical handicap or a mental disorder developed in both the statutory and vol-untary sectors. Nonetheless, despite the radical cry to 'Smash Up the Workhouse', it remained an important element of the welfare system between the wars. Receipt of relief, 'in kind' in the workhouse (officially renamed 'poor law institution' in 1913), became the fate of 'men without a settled way of living', unmarried mothers, elderly people, plus people with learning and physical disabilities who slipped through the ragged net of voluntary and specific statutory provision.

HEALTH CARE

When the Boards of Guardians were abolished the Public Health Committees of the county councils and county borough councils were encouraged to appropriate the former Poor Law infirmaries (Powell, 1997a). The elected members of these committees wanted to expand their infirmaries into a general hospital service for those with an acute illness and to match the standard provided by the voluntary hospitals. The Annual Report of the Medical Officer of Health for Oldham illustrates the spirit in which some Health Committees approached the task of developing a municipal hospital service:

> ... on 1st April, 1930, the Board of Guardians ceased to exist and their hospital services passed to the Health Committee. This date is indeed a milestone in our history .... From a Workhouse Infirmary the Boundary Park Hospital rapidly became a most efficient general hospital held in the highest esteem by the public and the medical profession. (Oldham Borough Council, 1949: 31)

In many areas there was fierce rivalry between the voluntary hospitals and the developing municipal service. This rivalry encouraged the development of improved services for those with an acute illness but fostered the exclusion of elderly people. The chronically sick, especially elderly people, were excluded from hospitals provided by the Public Health Committee. Hence the same document that expressed pride in the creation of a general hospital in Oldham noted that the numbers in the chronic sick wards, still administered by the Public Assistance Committee had increased greatly (Oldham Borough Council, 1949: 134).

The abolition of Boards of Guardians was intended to promote the development of specialisation by adding momentum to the 'process known for the last twenty years as the break up of the Poor Law' (Local Government Act, 1929: 2). In some areas the change did accelerate the trend towards the creation of specialist services, often in co-operation with the voluntary sector (Middleton, 1971: 282). Specialisation was also evident in the services provided for those with a mental disorder. In 1918 some county councils and boroughs pooled their resources to build mental hospitals and institutions for people with a mental handicap (Crowther, 1978: 37). In 1929 a joint committee of the Board of Control and the Board of Education investigated the issue of 'mental defectives'. It held that the number of mental defectives had increased and that the majority owed their defect to 'bad racial inheritance, being the more extreme cases of the subnormal tenth of the population, which also provides lunatics, prostitutes, criminals (especially recidivists) and unemployables in great abundance' (cited in Slater, 1930: 317). The joint committee recommended that marriage of mental defectives should be illegal and that each new Mental Deficiency Authority should maintain a village colony for industrial training in 'useful arts'. The general trend in the 1930s was for the Public Assistance Committees to become the supervisors of a 'safety net' for those who failed to qualify for 'mainstream' or specialist forms of help. They were responsible for a range of 'residual functions': the care of elderly people, providing temporary accommodation for homeless families, the care of 'children deprived of a normal home life', the supervision of unmarried mothers and the provision of support at home or in residence to people with a physical disability or a mental disorder.

EDUCATION

The 1918 Education Act ended the exemptions from compulsory schooling up to age 14, abolished all remaining fees in elementary education and, in an unimplemented clause, made provision for compulsory part-time 'continuation classes' up to the age of 16. The 1921 Education Act consolidated earlier legislation and set out the powers available to local authority Education Committees. Local government was no longer thought of as merely filling in the gaps left by the voluntary sector. Its role was to

> maintain and keep efficient all public elementary schools in the area ... adapt the teaching in the higher classes of the public elementary schools to the requirements of older children and to take such steps as seem desirable, after consultation with the Board of Education, to supply or aid the supply of higher education (secondary, technical, commercial and adult). (Clarke, 1937: 455)

Nursery schools

The 1870 Education Act did not specify a minimum age for attendance at primary school and, in 1901, about 43 per cent of three and four year olds attended 'baby classes' at elementary school (Blackstone, 1971: 28). In 1908, the Board of Education pronounced the learning methods employed in elementary schools – 'military rather than maternal' according to one inspector – inappropriate for very young children. It recommended excluding the very young from elementary schools and the development of nursery schools for all children whose parental care was unsatisfactory. Local authorities acted on the first recommendation but not the second with the result that by 1912 the number of children under five attending schools was cut by half (Blackstone, 1971: 32). However, growing concern about the competence of many working-class mothers in child care provided the backdrop to the inclusion of clauses in the 1918 Education Act allowing public funds to be spent by local education authorities on the development of nursery schools. The 1918 Maternity and Child Welfare Act empowering local health authorities to establish day nurseries for the care rather than the education of very young children thereby created a divided responsibility for pre-school care and education that still exists today. The growth of education and care for the under fives was stunted by the financial crises of the inter-war period. By 1936 only 6000 children under five were receiving education in nursery schools with a further 159,600 on the registers of elementary schools – about 14 per cent of the total number of children under five (Blackstone, 1971: 57).

Elementary and secondary education

The educational system between the wars was dominated by the distinction between 'elementary' and 'secondary', often called 'higher', education. This division was generally conceived as relating to different types of education rather than to the progressive stages in educational advancement as incorporated into the 1944 Education Act. It was the duty of the parent only 'to cause a child to receive efficient elementary instruction in reading, writing and arithmetic' (Clarke, 1937: 450). The 'three Rs' formed the core of the elementary school curriculum but the question remained as to what additional education should be offered to children who had acquired the necessary basic skills.

The Hadow Committee, set up to explore this issue, noted that of the 2.9 million children between 11 and 15, 1.8 million were receiving no form of 'advanced instruction'. It recommended education be thought of as successive stages rather than as parallel systems. At the age of 11 pupils from 'primary' schools should be transferred to a different school, or if this was not possible, to a different type of education, to be known as 'secondary'. Two main types of secondary schools were identified: 'grammar' schools pursuing 'in the main a predominantly literary or scientific curriculum' and 'modern' schools giving 'at least a four years' course from the age of 11, with a "realistic" or practical trend in the last two years'. Given that only 25 per cent of children at elementary schools were in 'higher grade' classes or schools in the late 1920s, Hadow's recommendations reflected 'progressive' thinking on education at the time. However, education experienced a high proportion of the central government cuts that followed the financial crisis in 1931 so, despite the large increase in local authority rates during the inter-war period, insufficient resources were available to expand the system on the lines suggested by the Hadow Committee. The available resources were concentrated on the grammar schools with places expanding from 300,000 in 1926 to 460,000 in 1937 (Rubinstein, 1984: 11). Fees had to be paid but, in return for grants, the grammar schools had to allocate a minimum of 25 per cent of their school places to the local education authority. In some areas education authorities offered more than the minimum number of places and, in a few areas, all grammar school education controlled by the local authority was free. Free places were awarded on the outcome of an examination popularly known as 'the scholarship' and, by 1930, 50 per cent of secondary school places were available free. The financial stringency of the early 1930s led to a modification of this system; places won by 'scholarships' were provided without charge only following a test of means. Parents of children who obtained a 'scholarship' had to sign an undertaking that the child would complete the full secondary course leading to matriculation and could be fined if they failed to keep their word. Many parents did not take up the offer of a free place.

In the late 1930s the educational system was organised on principles reflecting the British class structure. The overwhelming majority of children left school at 14 almost half having been educated in an 'all-through' elementary school in which the official class size standard was 50 pupils (Stevenson, 1984: 238; Barber, 1994: 1). About 14 per cent received 'secondary' education in a grammar school and, of these, about 4 per cent went on to university (Branson and Heinemann, 1973: 189). One in a hundred children received a university education. The 6 per cent of children educated privately in 'public' schools acquired a high proportion of university places, especially at Oxford and Cambridge. Only 20 per cent of total university places were taken by children who had received a free place at a secondary school (Branson and Heinemann, 1973: 189).

THE VOLUNTARY SECTOR

Hospitals

In the 1930s 'secondary' health care was provided by both voluntary and municipal hospitals. The voluntary hospitals were extremely suspicious of state aid. They supplemented their endowments from wealthy benefactors from a variety of sources including payments for treatment in the public wards assessed on a means-tested basis and flag days, when nurses collected donations from the public. The most important source of additional revenue came from pay beds and contributory systems whereby a weekly payment entitled the contributor to a hospital bed when needed.

According to the official historian of the National Health Service 'Voluntary hospitals were an extraordinary collection of heterogeneous institutions, ranging from teaching hospitals with an average of over 500 beds in 1938, to minute cottage hospitals' (Webster, 1988: 3). A number of attempts were made to bring order to this capricious accumulation of voluntary hospital services. The Dawson Report commented:

> that the [voluntary] hospitals have fallen on evil days is known to all. The reason is two-fold. One is that the prices of all the commodities a hospital has to buy – its coal, food, linen, etc., as well as the salaries and wages it has to pay, have increased. The other reason is that the investigation and treatment of disease are becoming increasingly complex. (Ministry of Health 1920: 6)

It suggested that all the services, curative and preventive, should be brought together in close co-ordination under a single Health Authority for each area. Voluntary hospital provision would have to conform to the plans of the single health authority and in return would receive 'grants in aid for work carried out'. The Cave Committee (Ministry of Health, 1921) noted the lack of co-operation between the voluntary hospitals and observed that 'Not only do neighbouring hospitals compete against each other in their appeals but they make no attempt to reach any common agreement as to their functions' (cited in Forsyth, 1966: 85). It recommended the establishment of a Hospitals' Commission to administer a central government grant to be spent on the co-ordination of voluntary hospitals. The Sankey Report (British Hospitals Association, 1937) drew attention to the lack of progress in achieving the aims of the Cave Committee and called for the establishment of regional machinery to co-ordinate hospital provision.

The 'personal social services'

Local government managed to acquire a significant role in the provision of education and health care between the wars. The notion of the voluntary sector as an 'extension' of state services was gaining ground with it being increasingly represented as appropriate for experimental or highly individualised work rather than as a supplier of mainstream services (Lewis, 1999: 60). Local Councils of Social Service and 'Guilds of Help' – prepared to work in partnership with local government and accept grants – developed in many areas. However, local authority Public Assistance Committees, hampered by their poor law antecedents, found it difficult to develop services and the voluntary sector continued to play an important role in the supply of a variety of residential and 'community' services.

AREA SELECTIVITY

Slum clearance in the nineteenth century was 'area selective' – its objective being to eliminate zones of 'social pathology'. Area selectivity returned to the political agenda in the 1930s but with improvement added to the nineteenth century fixation on demolition. Under the Greenwood Act, passed in 1930 by a minority Labour Government, 'improvement' areas where 'the houses are not all so far gone as to justify wholesale clearance of the area', could be declared. It was believed that 'if the worst are dealt with and the area opened out and air and sunshine let in, it could be made reasonably healthy'. (Greenwood, 1930: 6). In April 1933, the Minister of Health issued a circular requiring local authorities to concentrate on slum clearance rather than building for 'general' needs.

The issue of unfit dwellings was considered by the Moyne Committee set up in 1933. The desire to remove local authorities, not only from the provision of 'general needs' housing but also from meeting needs arising from slum clearance, was reflected in the Committee's recommendation that 'public utility' societies should be involved in the reconditioning of older homes and providing new dwellings in urban areas. However, the Labour Party was beginning to gain electoral support by highlighting the housing issue, and evidence presented to the Moyne Committee identified overcrowding as a serious problem. The Conservatives therefore adopted a strategy, aimed at confining the inhabitants of unfit and overcrowded dwellings to their 'areas of origin', of restricting the state to removing 'pathological' conditions while leaving private enterprise to build the vast majority of new dwellings in the suburbs (Yelling, 1992). This was reflected in the 1935 Housing Act, which granted subsidies 'directed straight to the problem of re-housing the worst-paid workers on the most expensive sites' (Clarke, 1937: 255). The Minister of Health outlined the aim of the legislation as the re-housing of overcrowded families at or near the site of the original home by building upwards in flats. Working class families living in slums were to be excluded from the developing suburbia.

LABOUR MOBILITY AND WORK CREATION

In an attempt to reduce unemployment, the Government introduced schemes to assist workers to move to regions where employment opportunities were being generated by new industries based on the production of electrical goods and motor cars. An Industrial Transference Board was established in 1928 to set up centres where unemployed workers from 'depressed areas' could be trained for work in the more prosperous regions and to distribute grants to create work in depressed areas. About 140,000 people were taken off the unemployment register by work creation schemes but, in 1932–3, the Government ended grants for public works using the argument that this type of expenditure 'depleted the resources of the country which are needed for industrial restoration' (cited in Stevenson and Cook, 1977: 63). Nonetheless, the Special Areas (Development and Improvement) Acts of 1934–5, enabled assistance to be given to local authorities and voluntary agencies to start improvement schemes for water supply, sewerage, hospital building and factory location. In 1936 a Special Areas Reconstruction Association was created to encourage the development of small businesses and trading estates. These measures were targeted on the areas with the highest unemployment; South Wales, Cumberland, Durham, Northumberland and West Scotland.

THE FAMILY

Reviewing two major investigations into family life, conducted in the 1930s, Aldridge concluded: 'the entire message is ... framed around the bringing of new standards of health and convenience to the conventional duality of men/employment and women/children/home' (Aldridge, 1996: 29). Helen Bosanquet's idealised notion of the family was even more secure in the late 1930s than at the turn of the century. In 1935 the first-marriage rate for men was higher than it had been in 1901 and, although divorce was on the increase, only an average of 4784 petitions per year were filed in the period 1931 to 1935. The illegitimacy rate, at 5.2 per 1000 live births, was lower than the rate at the end of the nineteenth century (Coleman, 1988). Opportunities for women to obtain paid employment had increased but only 10 per cent of women continued to work after marriage (Moroney, 1976: 19). The dominant idea was 'a woman's place is in the home' especially in times of high male unemployment and a growing concern about the quality of Britain's children. The 'cult of domesticity' (Pugh, 1992) dominated social policy. Despite the reluctance to give cash assistance to mothers, services providing advice and assistance were expanded in order to develop the 'mothercraft' believed to be absent in many working class homes. Beddoe (1989: 38–9) notes: 'In London in the mid 1930's girls spent two afternoons a week undergoing cookery instruction for forty-four weeks a year in the last two years of their school life' and in 'South Glamorgan, senior girls spent one afternoon a week in the local infant welfare clinic'. However, attempts to establish a domestic curriculum for girls in grammar schools were successfully resisted (McKibbin, 1998: 219).

SOCIAL EXCLUSION

'Malingers'

Despite the high levels of recorded unemployment between the wars the search for the 'scrounger' persisted. When monitoring the impact of the centres set up to transfer labour from north to south the Ministry of Labour noted some of the men entering the centres had become 'soft' and required 'hardening' before transfer (Colledge, 1989: 6). In 1929 the minority Labour Government set up residential labour camps, offering a three-month 'training' course in hard labour (King, 1999: 156) and centres were established to train young women in domestic service including one, financed jointly by the British and Australian governments, to prepare young women for service in Australia (Webb and Webb, 1929: 693). Married women in work were also identified as potential 'malingers'. In the 1920s it was noticed that the sickness rate of married women was three times that of unmarried women (Gilbert, 1970: 286) and this difference was interpreted as a sign that married women had less commitment to paid work. In 1932 the sickness benefit rate for married women was reduced and the regulations governing eligibility were tightened: married women in work were to be denied sickness benefit if still capable of carrying out their household duties (Whiteside, 1999: 30).

'Tramps'

The number of 'people without a settled way of living' increased during the depression; in 1929 the Webbs estimated the 'host on the road' at 50,000 to 60,000 people (Webb and Webb, 1929: 948). Despite evidence that a high proportion of these men were looking for work, the deterrent principles applied in the workhouse casual wards persisted as can be seen in the modest request made by one tramp for reform. He claimed every 'casual' ought to be supplied with 'a straw mattress and a pillow, a bath and a clean night-shirt and the opportunity to wash his shirt and socks' (A Casual's Report on Vagrancy Reform, cited in Webb and Webb, 1929: 953–62). Many itinerant workers shunned the workhouse in favour of lodgings houses. Here, so George Orwell reported, 'Twopenny Hangovers' could be purchased where 'you spent the night sitting on a bench leaning over a rope which was unceremoniously dropped in the morning by an assistant' (cited in Humphries and Gordon, 1994: 185).

'Good' and 'bad' tenants

Little consideration was given to the criteria to be used in allocating the new dwellings built under the 1919 Housing Act. Price acted as a rationing device because, despite the central subsidies to reduce rents, the poorest households could not afford to live in the 'homes fit for heroes'. Even the better-off struggled to pay. As Olecnowicz (1997: 7) has observed:

Becontree tenants represented an economic elite among the working class. Most paid a higher proportion of their weekly income in rent than previously and had to find the money for travel to jobs in inner London. They resorted to strategies that had served them in the old areas: the pawnshop, hire purchase, reducing expenditure on food, or taking in lodgers ... If these strategies failed, they either received notices to quit for non-payment of rent or more often decided to return to the inner-city districts ... a continual process of self-selection and adaptation occurred on Becontree: only those who could cope remained.

The high local authority rents, nationally about 20 per cent above the controlled rents of the private landlord sector and double this in some areas (Bowlby, 1945: 114), were supplemented as a rationing device by local authority checks on the 'suitability' of applicants. It was not until the 1935 Housing Act that councils were obliged 'to give reasonable preference to persons who are occupying insanitary or overcrowded houses, have large families, or are living under unsatisfactory housing conditions'. Until the slum clearance drives of the 1930s local authorities allocated their homes according to normative notions of the 'good' tenant – usually being a male breadwinner capable of earning sufficient to pay the rent, motivated to tend the garden and with a spouse who had skills in house-wifery (Giles, 1995: 73–8).

Inferior stock

In the period between the wars the Eugenics Society continued to investigate the links between receipt of public assistance and inherited intelligence. It sponsored research projects, including Lidbetter's examination of the 'pedigrees' of those receiving relief from the Boards of Guardians in East London during the 1920s (Lidbetter, 1933b). Summarising the findings of this research the President of the Eugenics Society said:

> That natural inheritance does play an important part in human destiny is indicated in Mr. Lidbetter's pedigrees by the continued reappearance of certain defects known to be little affected by environment ... The best in civilisation is the best biologically. What is therefore necessary today is attention to the problems of reproduction and its control. (Lidbetter, 1933b: foreword by Darwin)

The influence of eugenics continued until the outbreak of the war. Cattell's *The Fight for Our National Intelligence* 'congratulated the Nazis on being the first government to adopt sterilization of the unfit as a means of racial improvement' (Carey, 1992: 13).

Means testing

The negative working-class experience of means testing in the inter-war period has been cited by some commentators as a major reason for the introduction of more 'universal' forms of social provision after the Second World War. Ably assisted by the books of Wal Hannington (1937, 1940), the leader of the National Unemployed Workers' Movement, the hatred of the means test penetrated deep into the collective consciousness of working class communities. This antagonism developed from the specific nature of the tests applied rather than from the intrinsic qualities of means testing.

The means tests used by local Public Assistance Committees varied from area to area. Often the scales were not published because publication would create 'a presumption that any person with an income below that indicated by the scale is destitute and has some form of claim to relief' (Annual Report of Ministry of Health, 1927). The Relief Regulation Order, 1930, declared the able bodied could qualify for assistance outside an institution only if at least half of the relief was given in kind and the recipient was 'set to work' (Macleod and Powell, 1952: 12). Most of the able bodied applying for relief from the public assistance committee had no entitlement to unemployment insurance benefits either because they had exhausted their rights to 'extra benefits' or because they were not included in the scheme. Although coverage was extended in the 1920s, agricultural workers, domestic servants and all those without a 'contract of service' such as homeworkers were not allowed to join the insurance scheme (Webb and Webb, 1929: 676). Even though the regulations demanding in-kind and work tests were often ignored, the discretionary elements in the maintenance scales were the source of fear and resentment. However, it was the activities of the Unemployment Assistance Board that made the means test the *bête-noire* of the working class. The national benefit rates introduced by the Unemployment Assistance Board in January 1935 involved benefit cuts of up to 35 per cent in those areas where the most 'generous' local public assistance committees had administered the means test. Thus, the new 'means test' authority was immediately associated with harshness and unfairness. These cuts were quickly modified in response to popular protest (Hutt, 1972: 262–5) but the image of the Unemployment Assistance Board was tarnished. The form of means test – the 'household' test – also provoked antagonism. If a member of a household applied for financial help then the income of all the other people living in the dwelling was included in the assessment. This meant that a long-term unemployed man – the 'head of the household' – could find himself dependant on the income of a son, daughter, brother or sister who was in work. It was not surprising that many sons and daughters moved in with friends and relatives before the 'means-test man' arrived for the home visit, regarded as essential to the efficiency of the means test.

The test embraced all items of income including friendly society and trade union benefits leading many of the 'thrifty' working class to ponder whether their 'self help' had been worthwhile. The 'wage stop' was an additional source of resentment. Individuals were not allowed to receive 'a sum which is equal to or greater than the amount which would obviously be available by way of earnings' (Unemployment Assistance Board, 1935, cited in Walker, 1983: 12).

Means testing was also applied to housing subsidies. The 1930 Housing Act allowed local authorities to concentrate subsidies on the poorest council tenants by relating rent to income. Some local authorities introduced 'differential' rents in schemes arising from slum clearance (Bowlby, 1945: 128) but very few councils adopted authority-wide 'differential rent' schemes. When such schemes were proposed they met with fierce resistance from better-off tenants who realised that lower rents for their poorer neighbours meant higher rents for themselves (Schifferes, 1976: 55). Free school meals were means tested. Only 2 per cent of children received free school meals in 1939 (Mason, 1998: 7) and sometimes they were provided in special 'feeding centres'. Means testing was also applied to school fees. Fees had to be paid for secondary education and, after 1932, 'special' places, carrying full or partial exemption from fees, could only be offered subject to a test of means. The specifics of the test of income were left to the discretion of each local education authority but the Board of Education declared that it was unwilling to approve a fee of less than £9.45 a year [£350] and indicated that an income less than £3–£4 per week [£110–£148] should qualify a family with one child for free education. However, there is no evidence that this means test offended or deterred those who qualified, indeed being a 'scholarship' boy or girl was a badge of honour.

In health care, destitution and deterrence as principles of hospital admission were modified as the 'external' benefits of isolation hospitals and asylums were appreciated and improvements were made to Poor Law infirmaries. People who were not 'paupers' were admitted to public hospitals and efforts were made to recover the cost of treatment through charges made according to locally determined means tests. Voluntary hospitals directed people with more than £4 per week to private wards (Macleod and Powell, 1952: 17) and appointed almoners to recover the cost of treatment from people admitted to public wards.

SOCIAL JUSTICE

Territorial justice

Between the wars rates remained the main source of revenue for social welfare services. The uneven burden of unemployment was, in part, responsible for central government absorbing a higher share of the costs of unemployment but the general imbalance between local needs and the ability of local authorities to meet them attracted only limited attention. Central government grants increased from 22 per cent of local expenditure in 1914 to 38 per cent in 1936/7 (Newton, 1980: 98), but this increase was to mainly compensate for rate concessions granted to industry and agriculture in 1929 (Cronin, 1991: 95). Between 1921 and 1940 local authority spending on education increased by 44 per cent, but education grants from central government increased by only 14 per cent (Stevenson, 1984: 313). The main 'block' grant, introduced in 1929, had links to 'local needs' but the formula was crude and other grants often covered only a percentage of expenditure incurred. The impact of this complex system of distribution is difficult to assess but there is little doubt that the poorest areas were severely handicapped in their service provision. Using data for 1938 Hicks (1954) reached the conclusion that the high rates charged by 'low spending' authorities were due to their attempt to maintain standards in the face of large needs. Helen Wilkinson, MP for Jarrow, noted in her book *The Town That Was Murdered* that the low rateable values in the town meant:

Every attempt to improve the condition of the people, all that valuable local desire to organise things better communally, which is the most hopeful thing in Britain's local life, is damped and crushed by this terrible problem of the rates. (Wilkinson, 1939: 250)

Market forces modified by philanthropy and municipal pride determined the geographical distribution of health care resources in the 1930s. At the end of the Second World War there were 10.2 beds per 1000 population in London compared to 4.9 in South Wales. Intra-regional variations were even more diverse.

... while all of Yorkshire had an overall 6.6 beds for a thousand of population there were immense differences between Dewesbury with 10.3 beds and Halifax with 10.8 on one hand and the North Riding with only 3.1 and York with 4.9 on the other. (Eckstein, 1958: 57)

The availability of voluntary hospital beds reflected the supply of specialists to deliver treatment and the local supply of specialists was influenced by the availability of private patients. The 1945 Ministry of Health Hospital Survey noted that 'the chief determining factor is not whether there is enough work to keep a specialist busy, but whether there is enough private practice to make it worth his while to settle in the place concerned' (Carling and McIntosh, 1945: 19). Thus, in many areas, specialist treatment was difficult to obtain. For example, in the Sheffield and East Midlands area:

> Thoracic surgery has developed very little. In Sheffield two surgeons, and in Derby one, have done some as a sideline to general surgery, but the most active work is done in Nottinghamshire by a Newcastle surgeon and in Leicester by a London surgeon who visit at intervals of several weeks. (Parsons, et al. 1945: 9)

Municipal hospital provision reflected local political factors and, according to Powell, '... voluntary provision tended to favour the less needy areas (the inverse care law)' whereas 'municipal provision tended to favour the needy areas (territorial justice)' (Powell, 1997b: 35). Market forces also influenced the distribution of general practitioners. By 1938, although over 90 per cent of GPs received some remuneration from 'panel patients', they needed a supply of private work to supplement their income and many preferred to work in pleasant areas.

The distribution of income and wealth

There is a dearth of information on the distribution of income and wealth between the wars and the available statistics reflect the dominant concern of political economy at the time – the respective shares of the GDP obtained by labour and capital. In the late 1930s wealth remained highly concentrated with the top 1 per cent owning 55 per cent and the top 10 per cent owning 88 per cent of total wealth (Atkinson, 1972: 21; Laybourn, 1990: 137).

The impact of the inter-war recession was spatially concentrated with the South experiencing considerable economic growth based on the new car and electrical goods industries, the expanding service sector and the boom in house construction for home ownership. Between 1913 and 1938 national real income per head increased by a third. The share going to labour (wages and salaries) expanded from 47 per cent in 1910–14 to 59 per cent in 1935–9 (Aldcroft, 1970: 386) indicating that, despite setbacks such as the defeat of the General Strike, labour made gains at the expense of 'capital'. Real wages increased by 17.2 per cent between 1913 and 1930 and by a further 7.7 per cent between 1930 and 1939 (Aldcroft, 1970: 364). Nonetheless, in 1938, the 87.2 per cent of income receivers who formed the 'working class' – earning less than £250 [£8750] per annum – received only 55.5 per cent of total income. In contrast the top 5 per cent received 29 per cent before tax and 24 per cent after tax (Seers, 1951: 34; Lydall, 1959).

Expenditure on social welfare increased threefold in real terms between the wars and, by 1938, absorbed 11.3 per cent of GDP (Peacock and Wiseman, 1961: 184–91). Barna (1945), using information for 1937, reached the conclusion that about 5 per cent of national income was redistributed from 'rich' to 'poor' reducing the incomes of the upper and middle class by 10–18 per cent and increasing the incomes of the working class by 8–14 per cent. Income tax was progressive because most working class incomes fell below the tax threshold, but Macmillan noted that of the £504 million devoted to social service expenditure in 1935 only £234 million came from the National Exchequer (Macmillan, cited in Pope et al., 1986). Indirect taxes and national insurance contributions were regressive. Aldcroft comments:

> ... no less than two thirds of all indirect taxes were paid by those earning less than £100 per annum. Thus a married man with three children all under 16 earning £100 a year paid 14 per cent of his income in tax (all indirect) in 1937–8 as against only 5.4 per cent in 1913–14. Altogether persons with incomes below £250 a year paid £14 million in direct taxes, £407 million in indirect taxes and £57 million in social insurance contributions. (Aldcroft, 1970: 372).

CONCLUSION

The theoretical formulations of collectivism developed at the turn of the century remained fundamentally unchanged in the inter-war period. Ellison (1994) has identified three visions of how social justice might be achieved. 'Technocratic socialism', often using Marxist language, looked to physical planning and nationalisation to resolve the contradictions of capitalism. 'Keynesian socialism' calculated that demand management supported by the redistribution of wealth, better access to social welfare and general 'social improvement' would produce greater equality of opportunity. 'Qualitative socialists' such as G.D.H. Cole and R.H. Tawney 'believed in their different ways that socialism had to be rooted in a democratic and communal conception of socialism' (Ellison, 1994: 21). Cole's erratic and idiosyncratic combination of economic planning and industrial democracy had limited appeal but Tawney's development of 'new' liberal ideas into 'ethical socialism' (Dennis and Halsey, 1988) had lasting influence. His most influential book, *Equality*, first published in 1931, was a restatement of the ideas of Hobhouse, but with a stronger emphasis on the role of public services as a means to promote equality of status. Tawney was anxious to stress that equality of status in access to services does not mean the pursuit of equality of outcome.

So to criticise inequality and to desire equality is not, as is sometimes suggested, to cherish the romantic illusion that men are equal in character and intelligence. It is to hold that, while their natural endowments differ profoundly, it is the mark of a civilised society to aim at eliminating such inequalities as have their source, not in individual differences, but in its own organization, and that individual differences, which are a source of social energy, are more likely to ripen and find expression if social inequalities are, as far as practicable, diminished. (Tawney 1938: 39–40)

He believed that the 'social income which is provided from the surplus remaining after the necessary costs of production and expansion have been met' should be available to all on equal terms (1938: 141) but the 'social surplus' must not be used primarily to make cash incomes more equal. Public services, especially high quality education, should have precedence so that people can become conscious of their common humanity through a shared communal life.

It is not the division of the nation's income into eleven million fragments, to be distributed, without further ado, like cake at a school treat, among its eleven million families. It is, on the contrary, the pooling of its surplus resources by means of taxation, and the use of the funds thus obtained to make accessible to all, irrespective of their income, occupation, or social position, the conditions of civilisation which, in the absence of such measures, can be enjoyed only by the rich. (Tawney, 1975 [1931]: 122)

Thus, for Tawney, equality meant social justice in a moral community in which no 'social groups are deprived of the necessities of civilisation which others enjoy' (1975 [1931]: 117).

5

The Welfare State
and Social Justice

If we speak of economic reconstruction, we think less of maximum production (though this too will be required) than of equitable distribution.

Times Editorial, July 1 1940

The first use of the term 'welfare state' is credited to William Temple who, when Archbishop of York, published *Citizen and Churchman* in which he contrasted the 'power' states of the dictators with the 'welfare' states emerging in democracies. Clement Attlee adopted the phrase as a campaign slogan in the 1950 General Election and, by the early 1950s, it was in widespread use. It entered the *Oxford English Dictionary* in 1955 aptly described as 'a polity so organised that every member of the community is assured of his due maintenance and the most advantageous conditions possible for all'.

THE BEVERIDGE REPORT

In 1941 Sir William Beveridge was invited to chair a committee of civil servants to undertake a 'survey of the existing national schemes of social insurance and allied services, including workmen's compensation, and make recommendations' (Beveridge, 1942: v). From these innocuous terms of reference Beveridge produced a report described as 'the most significant political event of the war' (Fielding, 1998: 43) and acclaimed as the 'Magna Carta of the welfare state' (Harris, 1999: 21). As a context for his specific recommendations on social security, Beveridge made three assumptions: the state would promote full employment, provide children's allowances and deliver a comprehensive national health service. Taken together these assumptions were more radical than the proposals contained in his main report.

Children's allowances

'State maintenance' for children was discussed at a Trades Union Council conference in 1905 when the majority of the delegates rejected cash payments for children but supported school meals provided by the state as a necessary consequence of compulsory education (Hall et al., 1975: 159). Sydney Webb backed family allowances as an 'endowment of motherhood' to enable the population to be 'recruited from the self-controlled and foreseeing members of each class, rather than those who are feckless and improvident' (Webb, 1907a: 19). Eleanor Rathbone harboured more radical thoughts. For her, family allowances were the way to reconcile equal pay for women with the entrenched claim that male earnings should be sufficient to support a family. If child support could be separated from the issue of wages then equal pay might be achieved (Alberti, 1996: 140). In *The Disinherited Family* Rathbone argued against a family 'living wage', paid to the wage-earner for his labour, because it 'assumes acceptance of a supposition ... that all men are heads of families and that all families are of the same size ...' (Rathbone, 1986 [1924]: 122). Using contemporary poverty research she demonstrated how a minimum wage would

> be totally inadequate ... at least so long as we proceed on the assumption that no advantage can be given to the family of three, six or eight persons that is not equally extended to the single man and even (if 'equal pay for equal work' be conceded) to the single woman. (Rathbone, 1986 [1924]: 155)

Moreover, citing evidence that 'out of the total Drink bill, £263 million represents the expenditure on beer – the working-man's drink' (Rathbone, 1986 [1924]: 167), she claimed a 'family wage', if paid to the father, would not be spent on children.

In the 1920s trade unions remained lukewarm on family allowances suspecting state support for children might drive a wedge between single and married men thereby undermining the pressure for wage increases. Their apprehension was justified – Treasury officials were interested in the idea of family allowances as a mechanism to reduce wage demands (Macnicol, 1978: 194). Beveridge supported allowances for children with Rathbone's argument that a national minimum for families of every size could not be secured by the wage system alone. He also claimed the gap between income during work and unemployment should be as large as possible, an objective that could only be achieved, if subsistence was to be guaranteed, by giving allowances for children in times of earning and non-earning alike. In addition, children's allowances would help to restore the birth rate, a desirable objective because 'with its present rate of reproduction the British race cannot continue' (Beveridge, 1942: 154). Later, in *The*

Pillars of Security and Other War-Time Essays (1943), Beveridge supported non-means tested allowances because, by neutralising the economic advantages of the small family characteristic of the middle class, they would reduce 'dysgenic' pressures (Wolfe and Klausen, 1997: 238). Initially, Beveridge planned to pay family allowances for all children but modified this proposal in response to Treasury concern about the cost of his scheme. His final recommendation was not to pay an allowance to the first child, which he justified with the argument that parents and the state should share the cost of raising children.

Comprehensive health and rehabilitation services

Beveridge's second assumption was the establishment of a 'comprehensive national health service'. This made it unnecessary for him to consider medical treatment benefits as part of the social security system. The main reason given for integrating the cost of treatment into a comprehensive health service was the requirement to link prevention, treatment and rehabilitation to promote national efficiency. 'Rehabilitation', 'is a new field of remedial activity with great possibilities, but requiring expenditure of a different order of magnitude from that involved in the medical treatment of the nation' (Beveridge, 1942: 158–9). He believed a preventative, rehabilitative National Health Service would mean that, after 20 years, there would be no real increase in the cost of health care (Peden, 2000: 347).

The maintenance of employment

Beveridge emphasised how social insurance could work effectively only within a context of the elimination of the 'waste' of idleness. He argued:

> income security which is all that can be given by social insurance is so inadequate a provision for human happiness that to put it forward by itself as a sole or principal measure of reconstruction hardly seems worth doing. It should be accompanied by an announced determination to use the powers of the State to whatever extent may prove necessary to ensure for all, not indeed absolute continuity of work, but a reasonable chance of productive employment. (Beveridge 1942: 163)

Principles of social security

Contributions in return for benefit   Beveridge believed 'the popularity of compulsory insurance, the growth of voluntary insurance and the strength of popular objection to any kind of means test demonstrated that benefit in return for contributions, rather than free allowances from the State, is what the people of Britain desire'. Means tests penalised 'what people have come to regard as the duty and pleasure of thrift, of putting pennies away for a rainy day' (Beveridge, 1942: 11). Accordingly as many people as possible were to be included in the 'comprehensive' insurance scheme making them 'deserving' of benefit by virtue of a contributory record.

Subsistence   The benefit to be paid in return for contributions was 'intended in itself to be sufficient without further resources to provide the minimum income needed for subsistence in all normal cases' (Beveridge, 1942: 122). Food, clothing, fuel, light, household sundries, and rent plus 'a margin for inefficiency in spending' were taken into account in determining the minimum income necessary for 'subsistence' but Beveridge constantly modified the detail of his estimates 'to rationalise the rough benefit levels already decided upon by the coalition government' (Parker, 1998: 5). The 'subsistence' principle set both a floor and a ceiling to the involvement of the state. 'To give by compulsory insurance more than is needed for subsistence is an unnecessary interference with individual responsibilities … individual social security should be a combination of three distinct methods … social insurance for basic needs; national assistance for special cases; voluntary insurance for additions to the basic provision' (Beveridge, 1942: 121).

Pooling of risks   Risk pooling was at the heart of Beveridge's concept of social insurance. *Social* insurance was a 'new type of human institution … The term implies the pooling of risks except so far as separation of risks serves a social purpose' (Beveridge, 1942: 13). Pooling of risks meant middle class exclusions from contributions, a feature of social insurance between the wars, had to be abolished and the risk rating applied by some approved societies had to end (Hewitt, 2000: 51). Nonetheless, although the insurance scheme was designed to be universal in coverage, it was also adapted to the requirements of different groups who would be obliged to contribute variable amounts in return for different benefit packages. Beveridge divided the population into six classes. Only 'employees' would contribute towards the full benefits package: the other five classes would receive benefits according to different levels of contribution. Housewives would be insured by their husband's contributions, which would meet the 'marriage needs of a woman', namely:

1   Marriage, met by marriage grant.
2   Maternity, met by maternity grant in all cases, and, in the case of a married woman in gainful occupation also by maternity benefit for a period before and after confinement.
3   Interruption or cessation of husband's earnings by his unemployment, disability or retirement, met by share at benefit or pension with husband.

4   Widowhood, met by provision varying according to circumstances including temporary widow's benefit for readjustment, guardian benefit while caring for children and training benefit if and when there are no children in need of care.

5   Separation ... met by adaptation of widowhood provisions including separation benefit, guardian benefit and training benefit but not to be paid when the woman was the 'guilty party' in the separation.

6   Incapacity for household duties met by provision of paid help in illness as part of treatment. (Beveridge, 1942: 133)

These recommendations for married women reflected Beveridge's views on the role of women in the family and society.

> In any measure of social policy in which regard is had to Facts, the great majority of married women must be regarded as occupied on work which is vital though unpaid, without which their husbands could not do their paid work and without which the nation could not continue. In accord with Facts the Plan for Social Security treats married women as a special insurance class of occupied persons and treats man and wife as a team ... During marriage most women will not be gainfully employed. (Beveridge, 1942: 49–50)

So, on marriage, a woman became a new person for insurance purposes. Her contributions before marriage would be redeemed by the marriage grant. Thereafter, as a housewife with 'vital if unpaid work' to perform, she would be entitled to a special package of insurance benefits acquired through her partner.

The special case of 'old age'   Provision for the needs of elderly people was clouded by the projected increase in the proportion of elderly people – 12 per cent in 1941 increasing to 20.8 per cent in 1971. Prompted by the Treasury (Means and Smith, 1998: 114), Beveridge argued 'every shilling added to the pension is extremely costly', so pensions should be awarded only to those who had retired from work. The retirement condition would also act as an incentive for older people to give up work and so release jobs for younger people. The full 'subsistence' pension would not be paid until contributions had been made for 20 years because the 'insurance' principle 'required that people pay for their pensions' (Beveridge, 1942: 99).

Flat rate contributions and flat rate benefits   Beveridge made a clear distinction between taxation and insurance. 'Taxation', he argued, implies regard to the means but 'insurance contributions for the same benefits, whether or not it varies with the risk, should not vary with the means of the person who pays it'. (Beveridge, 1942: 107). The 'flat rate' (same for all) contribution was the logical outcome of the notion of subsistence benefits. If it was the duty of the state to 'abolish want' by meeting basic needs then, given that insurance was the basis of the plan, it followed that everyone should pay the same contribution in return for the same 'subsistence' level protection from want. Lloyd George's 'tripartite' system of contributions to the National Insurance Fund from employer, employee and state was adopted with each share calculated by determining the actuarial cost of the scheme over an average lifetime and then dividing by three.

Compensatory payments   Existing legislation placed a legal liability on an employer to compensate any employee for loss of earning capacity due to 'personal injury by accident or industrial disease arising out of and in the course of his employment' whether or not this incapacity was due to the employer's negligence. Beveridge listed nine disadvantages of this legislation including the failure of some employers to insure against claims and the tendency for the lump sum compensation to be 'injudiciously expended' (Beveridge, 1942: 36). Accordingly, Beveridge recommended incapacity for work due to industrial injuries or disease should become part of his national insurance scheme and benefits should be based on two-thirds of past earnings up to a maximum of £3 [£160]. This departure from the flat rate subsistence principle was justified with the argument that 'many industries vital to the community are especially dangerous and that 'a man disabled during the course of his employment has been disabled while working under orders' (Beveridge, 1942: 39).

The role of national assistance

A step was taken towards making means-tested assistance more acceptable to the working class when, in 1940, responsibility for assistance to elderly people and widows was transferred from local government to the Unemployment Assistance Board – renamed the 'Assistance Board'. Aid to elderly people was called 'supplementary pension' and the Determination of Needs Act abolished the household means test, which had meant that other people living in a dwelling were obliged to contribute to the maintenance of an elderly person. These reforms led to a dramatic increase in the number of assistance recipients. In 1939, 250,000 pensioners were receiving outdoor relief but by the end of 1940 the Assistance Board was paying over a million supplementary pensions (Lafitte, 1945: 18). Somewhat against the spirit of this reform, Beveridge announced 'assistance must be felt to be something less desirable than insurance; otherwise the insured persons get nothing for their contributions' (Beveridge, 1942: 41). He put the matter more bluntly in a paper tabled during the preparation of his report. 'An assistance scheme, which makes those assisted unamenable to economic rewards or punishments while treating them as free citizens is inconsistent with the principles of a free society' (cited in Glennerster, 1995: 29). Under Beveridge's influence the term 'supplementary pension' fell out of use; 'pension' was a term to be attributed only to payments arising from insurance contributions. Initially, Beveridge thought of national assistance as covering only 'Cripples and deformed, deaf and dumb, mentally deficient, and vagrants and moral weaklings' (Beveridge, 1942, cited in Evans and Glennerster 1993: 23). However, as the preparation of his report progressed, other groups fell into the national assistance net by virtue of their exclusion from insurance on cost grounds.

THE IMPLEMENTATION OF THE BEVERIDGE REPORT

Churchill thought Beveridge was 'an awful windbag and a dreamer' promoting 'false hopes and visions of Eldorado' (Cockett, 1995: 62). A secret committee was set up to prepare a brief on the report for the leaders of the Conservative Party. It claimed the subsistence element of the proposals was too expensive and would 'encourage malingering and laziness' (Clarke, 1998: 242) and the scheme's 'universality' was denounced as excessively redistributive (Cockett, 1995: 61). The Conservative leadership did not attack Beveridge's scheme in public but Churchill gave only lukewarm support to its principles and the report was 'booted into post-war touch' (Hennessy 1992: 76). This lack of enthusiasm from the Conservatives probably re-enforced Labour's claim that the Tories 'running true to form, would be likely to cut social provisions on the pleas that the nation could not meet the cost' (Labour Party, 1945: 12).

Family allowances

Despite a strong lobby inside the Treasury for allowances to be paid in 'kind' rather than in cash (Land et al., 1992: 38) the Family Allowances Act 1945 introduced child allowances. The issue of payment to the father or the mother was hotly contested with the White Paper *Social Insurance* (1944) suggesting it should be legally paid to the father but it was 'natural and appropriate' for him to appoint his wife to draw the money (Pederson, 1993: 345). The Cabinet eventually decided to leave the matter to a free vote in Parliament. Mothers won but the cost of the scheme was reduced by paying what Barbara Castle called the 'paltry sum' of 25 pence [£5], not the 40 pence [£8] recommended by Beveridge, to the second and each subsequent child. This failure to provide for the full subsistence needs of children was justified with the argument 'nothing should be done to remove from parents the responsibility of maintaining their children' (Ministry of Reconstruction, 1944: para 50) and that any deficiency would be made up by services in kind such as school milk and meals. The 1944 Education Act laid a duty on LEAs to provide milk and a meal and, in 1945, a charge was made for the meal with remissions for children on low incomes.

National insurance

The Labour Government implemented most of Beveridge's recommendations, but with some noteworthy omissions. Domestic help benefits were discarded and the end of marriage grant was abandoned because the social security department may have found it difficult to determine guilt in a separation case and hence become involved in 'subsidising sin' (Department of Health and Social Security, 1974: 145). Unemployment benefit, which Beveridge recommended should be paid for the duration of unemployment, subject to attendance at a training centre, was restricted to 30 weeks, but with the possibility of extension when a persuasive case was made to a local tribunal (Barnett, 1986: 125). Beveridge thought benefits should be paid personally by visitors from a friendly society both to prevent fraud and offer personal assistance (Gladstone, 1979: 15). However, friendly societies were not involved in the running of the new scheme despite a campaign for inclusion based on the claim that they were the working man's 'guide, philosopher and friend' (Newman, 1945: 4).

Pension payments, which Beveridge believed should reach 'subsistence' level on a phased basis, were paid at the same level as other benefits and 400,000 old people, mainly from the middle class, who were exempt from contributions under the 1925 scheme, received the new pension (Lynes, 1963: 1). The retirement age was set at 65 for men and 60 for women ostensibly in response to the National Spinsters Association's argument that women lost their jobs earlier than men and that the lower pension age would benefit the married woman who could retire at the same time as her husband – women marrying men who were, on average, five years older (Thane, 1998: 200). However, despite this charming rationale of different qualifying ages, the decision was probably the outcome of the desire to shed female labour to ensure full employment for males after the war. Eligibility for the pension was conditional on retirement and earned income brought a pound-for-pound reduction in pension after a small disregard (Brown, 1992: 29). At 70 (65 for women) this thinly veiled means test was not applied; the pension became 'universal' and paid at a higher rate in recognition of extra contributions.

The failure to set the general rate of benefit at 'subsistence' level was the most important departure from Beveridge's principles. In the 1930s Rowntree maintained 'working people are just as human as those with more money – they cannot live just on a "fodder basis"' (Rowntree, 1937: 126) and so he included a sum for personal expenditure in his poverty line. However, Beveridge excluded this personal expenditure from his definition of subsistence and the Labour Government failed to allow for the full impact of inflation in updating the calculations made by Beveridge at 1938 prices (Field, 1981: 89; Deacon, 1982). According to Kincaid (1975: 60) 'a Beveridge minimum would have required benefits at £1.70 [£32.30]a week for a single person and nearly £3 [£57] a week for a married couple'. Instead, benefits were paid in 1948 at £1.30 [£24.70] for a single person and £2.10 [£40] for a married couple. Thus, in terms of actual purchasing power, the 1948 adult benefit rate gave only three-quarters of the standard of living regarded by Beveridge as 'an irreducible minimum'. Insurance benefits for the sick and unemployed were lower in real terms than the payments made before the war (Abel-Smith, 1953: 3). Some authors have claimed the failure to set benefits at subsistence level was not deliberate – the Government simply miscalculated inflation (Heb, 1981: 306; Atkinson, 1995). However, the impact of inflation on Beveridge's calculations was known. In 1942, Hubert Henderson, a Treasury official, commented that Beveridge's allowance for subsistence

> may be fully sufficient to supply the minimum needs of an adult living in a cheap cottage with a vegetable garden in a country district. It is almost certainly insufficient for the majority of the people in large towns if every possibility of aid from other sources is disregarded. Moreover, the cost of living has already risen by more than 25 per cent above pre-war; and we shall be fortunate if the post-war level is not at least one-third, rather than one-quarter, above pre-war. (Henderson, 1942: 77)

As Brown (1990: 290) has noted the Coalition Government 'had disliked the idea of subsistence rates and indicated its likely rejection of them'. The White Paper *Social Insurance* (Cmd 6550, 1944) maintained that the level of social security payments must not undermine personal responsibility and must take into account the 'maximum contribution which the great body of contributors can properly be asked to bear'. The Labour Government, concerned about the impact of flat rate national insurance contributions on the lowest paid, acquiesced in the setting of insurance benefits at an 'austere' level. (Tomlinson, 1998: 69)

National assistance

The National Assistance Act 1948 set up a National Assistance Board, which assumed responsibility for assisting persons 'without resources to meet their requirements'. The main role of the Board would be 'to care for those people whose lives are so afflicted that they do not come inside the insurance field at all' (Griffiths, 1947). The national scale assistance was set at £2 [£40] weekly for a single person plus rent – well above national insurance rates.

JOBS FOR ALL

Blaug (1990: 25) claims that 'within the space of about a decade, 1936–46, the vast majority of economists throughout the western world were converted to the Keynesian way of thinking'. The notion that public spending was the key to avoiding high levels of unemployment had been in circulation throughout the 1930s. However Keynes' *The General Theory of Employment, Interest and Money* (1936) gave precision to the idea of the multiplier impact of spending on public works by his introduction of the concept of the 'consumption function'. Keynes' theorising and the example of Roosevelt's New Deal in the USA began to animate confidence in the notion that the state could regulate the economy to reduce the incidence of unemployment. The White Paper on *Employment Policy*, published in 1944 by the Coalition Government, contained a bipartisan commitment to a 'high and stable level of employment' and Labour's 1945 manifesto promised to achieve this objective by a combination of demand management, the control of investment and redistribution of income to prevent underconsumption. In fact aggregate demand was high between 1945 and 1951 so the explicit application of Keynesian theory was not required (Tomlinson, 1997: 168).

THE NATIONAL HEALTH SERVICE

In the 1930s the Labour Party was committed to the establishment of a comprehensive health service, free at the point of consumption, with services provided by staff on full-time salaries, working, at 'primary care' level, in publicly funded health centres. The new service would be administered by a multi-purpose system of regional government (Webster, 1988: 24). The story of how elements of this blueprint were incorporated into plans produced by the Coalition Government and then eroded in the course of establishing the National Health Service has been told many times (Eckstein, 1958; Willcocks, 1967; Webster, 1988; Jacobs, 1993). The compromises embodied in the National Health Service Act and the outcome of the subsequent brouhaha with the British Medical Association produced a National Health Service with the following features.

- The Minister of Health was given responsibility 'to provide the establishment in England and Wales of a comprehensive health service, designed to secure the prevention, diagnosis and treatment of illness and for that purpose to provide or secure the effective provision of services' (National Health Service Act, 1946: 1).
- Aneurin Bevan claimed 'A free health service is pure Socialism and as such is opposed to the hedonism of capitalist society' (Bevan, 1952: 81). All forms of health care were free at the point of consumption and financed mainly by general taxation but with a contribution from

the National Insurance Fund. Free health care had two justifications. It was unfair that illness, not any fault of the individual, should bring lack of treatment or financial hardship and free treatment would increase national efficiency by preventing ill health and by promoting rehabilitation to ensure an early return to work. Bevan believed that 'It is cardinal to a proper health organisation that a person ought not to be financially deterred from seeking medical advice at the earliest possible stage' (Bevan, Second Reading of the National Health Service Bill, 1946). He said that charges for health care were a deterrent to early treatment and, when the backlog of the 'silent suffering of the 1930s' had been overcome, then the cost of health care to the nation would diminish as people received earlier and hence cheaper treatment. Despite this robust justification of free care, in 1949 the Government announced it would introduce prescription charges. Bevan managed to prevent the immediate implementation of these charges but he resigned from the Government in 1951 when charges were imposed on dentures and spectacles (Campbell, 1987: 242–4).

- On Bevan's instructions the voluntary and municipal hospitals were nationalised (Webster, 1998: 14). Bevan's justification of the nationalisation of hospitals was:

  > … it is repugnant to a civilised community for hospitals to have to rely upon private charity. I believe we ought to have left hospital flag days behind … Because the local authorities are too small … I decided that local authorities could not be effective hospital administrators. I decided that the only thing to do was to create an entirely new hospital service, to take over the voluntary hospitals, and to take over the local government hospitals and to organise them as a single hospital service. (Bevan: Parliamentary Debates (Commons), 422, 30 April 1946, pp. 46–50)

- Drawing on the successful regional structure of the Emergency Medical Service established at the start of the Second World War (Forsyth, 1966: 82) Regional Hospital Boards were established to plan the service. Hospital Management Committees and Boards of Governors in teaching hospitals were responsible for the management of the service at 'local' level. Bevan wanted to 'universalise the best' (Green and Thorogood, 1998: 58) and it was thought that state ownership of hospitals would enable capital and revenue expenditure to be planned to ensure equality of access to services. Planning was also thought to be necessary to improve administrative efficiency in the delivery of health care and to provide the comprehensive health centres that were to be a mechanism for uniting the fragmented administrative structure at the point of delivery to the patient.

- Services provided by family doctors, dentists, pharmacists and opticians were loosely supervised by Executive Councils whose membership included substantial representation from the professions.

- Local authorities retained control over public health measures, the care of mothers and young children, the provision of midwifery, health visiting, home nursing, ambulance services and the super-vision of mentally ill and mentally handicapped people in the com-munity. In addition they were made responsible for building health centres from which a comprehensive primary care service was to be developed.
- Private practice continued, indeed consultants were allowed to treat private patients in National Health Service hospitals.

EDUCATION

A settlement of the religious issue was critical to an improvement in educational standards. The voluntary sector could not afford to restruc-ture its provision into primary and secondary schools as advocated by the Hadow Report, let alone introduce specialisation into secondary edu-cation. Indeed it had been cost factors that led to resistance from the voluntary sector to the raising of the school leaving age in the 1930s (McKibbin, 1998: 213). Rab Butler, having spent a great deal of time in negotiations with the leaders of the Churches (Butler, 1971: 95) produced the final settlement embodied in the 1944 Education Act. Church schools would have a choice to become either 'controlled' or 'aided'. 'Controlled' schools would provide religious education according to an agreed syllabus and would be controlled by local education authorities who would pay the costs, appoint the teachers and a majority of the governors. 'Aided' schools would have their costs met by the local education authority but would have to provide 50 per cent of the building costs (with the assistance of government grants). In return for their financial contribution the sponsors of aided schools could appoint teachers, the majority of governors and could direct religious education. The 1944 Education Act abolished tuition fees in all maintained schools and made provision for the school leaving age to be raised to 16. Local education authorities were charged with ensuring there were sufficient primary and secondary schools available for their area to give all pupils opportunities for educa-tion according 'to their different ages, abilities and aptitudes'. Moreover, education authorities had to 'have regard to the need for securing' provi-sion for nursery schools, special educational treatment and boarding education and were required to make provision for recreation, social and physical training, medical inspection and treatment of schoolchildren as well as provide milk, meals and other refreshments to infants. Since 1927 a number of independent, non-boarding, grammar schools had received direct grants from the Ministry of Education on the condition that a proportion of their pupils (usually 25 per cent) should be admitted from public elementary schools either free of charge or on reduced fees. This arrangement was continued under regulations issued in 1945 that also allowed local authorities to nominate pupils for 'reserved places' in the direct grant schools.

THE PERSONAL SOCIAL SERVICES

Parker (1970: 105) has defined the personal social services as those 'lying outside the general fields of health and education, which are adjusted in some special way to the particular social needs of individuals, families or groups and which require personal contact between provider and recipient'. The term 'personal social services' did not exist in 1945. Responsibility for such services was dispersed between different statutory and voluntary organisations.

Services for children

In the 1930s services for children 'deprived of a normal home life' were supplied by different departments according to the reason the child required special attention. At central level, the Home Office and the Ministries of Health and Education were involved and, at local level, public assistance, education and health committees all held responsibilities. Correspondence in *The Times* attracted attention to the poor conditions of children in care and the Curtis Committee was set up to investigate the situation. It documented the administrative disarray and was highly critical of the general standards of care noting 'the smaller children's almost pathological clamour for attention and overt affection, and the older children's slowness, backwardness, lack of response, habits of destructiveness and lack of concentration' (Boss, 1971: 13–14). The Curtis Committee recommended the establishment of a specific children's committee in each local authority responsible for a Children's Department headed by a Children's Officer. These recommendations were incorporated in the 1948 Children Act. The Children's Committee was required to ensure that each child in public care was treated 'so as to further his best interests and to afford him opportunity for the proper development of his character and interests'; a provision that led to the creation of the profession of child care officer (Donnison, 1962).

During the war 7.5 million women were in paid employment. Many of these women workers had been conscripted into 'war work' and, when the war was over, only 25 per cent of women expressed a desire to continue in paid work (Fielding, 1998: 39). Most women had no wish to continue the 'double shift' of paid employment plus running a home. The Ministry of Health declared that 'in the interest of the child no less than the benefit of the mother, the proper place for the child under two is at home with his mother' (Ministry of Health, 1947: 2). Day nursery places, which had received substantial Treasury subsidies during the war, especially in areas where there was a shortage of female labour, were reduced. Local authorities were informed that day nurseries had been set up 'for wartime purposes' and would 'gradually cease to function' (Bridgen and Lowe, 1998: 255).

Adult services

The National Assistance Act 1948 completed the process of making financial assistance the responsibility of central government by transferring to the Assistance Board, henceforth to be known as the National Assistance Board, the remaining responsibilities of local authorities in respect to cash assistance to the sick, the disabled, the blind, old people who did not qualify for a pension, separated wives, unmarried mothers and others. Local welfare authorities, the successors of the public assistance committees, shorn of their powers to provide financial assistance, were left with the responsibility to provide services in kind. The National Assistance Act placed a duty on local authorities to provide residential accommodation

> for persons who by reason of age, infirmity or any other circumstances are in need of care and attention which is not otherwise available to them, temporary accommodation for persons who are in urgent need thereof, being need arising in circumstances which could not reasonably have been foreseen. (National Assistance Act 1948, Part 111, Section 21.1)

Permissive powers were available to make arrangements for 'promoting the welfare' of people who were 'deaf, dumb, blind or substantially handicapped' but on the presumption that such arrangements would be made through voluntary organisations, encouraged by grants from local government. Local authorities were allowed to give grants to voluntary organisations to provide meals on wheels but had no power to provide this service directly. The 1946 National Health Service Act permitted local authorities to employ home helps and gave 'very general powers for the care and aftercare of persons suffering from illness and for preventive measures relating to health' (Tinker, 1981: 99). These powers were usually exercised through health committees.

PHYSICAL PLANNING

The report of the *Royal Commission on the Geographical Distribution of the Industrial Population* (Barlow Report, 1940) concluded that the growth of population in the prosperous areas of the Midlands and the South was generating 'conurbations' that were damaging to health, congested by traffic and vulnerable to mass bombing. The suggested remedy was central control of the location of industry to disperse the population. The desirability of land use planning was endorsed by the report of the *Committee on Land Utilisation in Rural Areas* (Scott Committee, 1942). Good agricultural land, it asserted, was a priceless national asset to be protected from development. The report of the *Expert Committee on Compensation and Betterment* (Uthwatt Committee 1942) considered the issue of development gain, absent from the government agenda since the abandonment of Lloyd George's development tax in 1921. Undeveloped rural land should be nationalised with compensation based on values at a specified date. Local government should carry out all development in existing built-up areas, compensating landowners according to current land values. In addition all property owners should pay a regular betterment levy of 75 per cent of the increased value of a site between valuations.

The 1945 Distribution of Industry Act required an industrial development certificate for all new industrial plant and allowed central government to offer incentives for industry to set up in development areas. The 1947 Town and Country Planning Act imposed taxes of between 40 per cent and 100 per cent on the 'betterment' value of development land and established a Central Land Board with powers to purchase land compulsorily. It also placed a duty on local authorities to prepare development plans for their areas and allowed them to control most of the development and acquire land by compulsion. The New Towns Act of 1946 made provision for the establishment of new towns as a method of relieving congestion in the major cities and providing workers with homes in a fully planned environment.

HOUSING

Public opinion polls carried out in 1945 demonstrated that the public believed housing to be the most urgent issue (Francis, 1997: 115). On the stringent definition of overcrowding contained in the 1935 Housing Act – more than two people per room with all rooms counted as available for occupation – about 4 per cent of working class dwellings were overcrowded (Stevenson, 1976: 176) and local authorities, with little effort, had identified about 250,000 slums. The war intensified the problem; 458,000 houses were destroyed and over 3 million were damaged.

Aneurin Bevan believed the boom in home ownership in the 1930s had solved the housing problems of the middle class. He was strongly in favour of local authority development for rent at least until the housing crisis was solved (Francis, 1997: 119) because local authorities were 'plannable instruments' and could allocate homes based on need. He allowed building for home ownership only when the prospective owner could demonstrate 'housing need'. Bevan insisted that the new local authority homes should be of high quality with, for example, a water closet, both upstairs and downstairs, in each family dwelling. The Housing (Financial and Miscellaneous Provisions) Act tripled the central government subsidies available in the late 1930s and the 'prefabs' programme was ended on the argument they were 'rabbit hutches' with long-term maintenance problems. Bevan's vision of local authority housing as replicating the social mix of the Welsh village was signified in the 1949 Housing Act. This removed the requirement, present in all previous Housing Acts, that public housing should be supplied only to 'the working classes' (Ambrose, 1994: 87). He encouraged local authorities to reserve plots for 'the higher income groups at higher rents' (Bevan quoted in Francis, 1997: 125) to be used when the housing crisis had been overcome.

THE WELFARE STATE: DISTRIBUTIVE PRINCIPLES

The term 'welfare state' soon became the subject of academic discourse and political rhetoric as an entity with a particular moral significance. The term incorporated 'representations' of relationships between social classes, individuals and the state and came to have symbolic importance as a description of the changed nature of British society. It embodied the shape of a new society in which the state would have a major role in determining the distribution of wealth, income and life chances.

Equality of educational opportunity

In the 1940s the dominant notion of equality of educational opportunity was based on the psychological studies of intelligence published in the 1930s. In 1938 the Spens Report stated:

> Intellectual development during childhood appears to progress as if it were governed by a single central factor, usually known as 'general intelligence', which may be broadly described as innate all-round intellectual ability ... it is accordingly evident that different children from the age of 11, if justice is to be done to their varying capacities, require types of education varying in certain important respects. (Board of Education, 1938: 357–8)

The Norwood Report (Board of Education, 1943) supported Spens's conclusions by identifying three types of pupil. First, 'the pupil who is interested in learning for its own sake, who can grasp an argument or follow a piece of connected reasoning'. Second, the pupil 'whose interests and abilities lie markedly in the field of applied science or applied art'. Third, the pupil who 'deals more easily with concrete things than with ideas' with 'much ability ... in the realm of facts' (Board of Education 1943: 124). Three types of school were recommended to suit these three classes of children. Norwood also endorsed a curriculum divided according to gender declaring 'knowledge of such subjects [Needlework, Cookery and Laundrywork] is a necessary equipment for all girls as potential makers of homes' (Board of Education, 1938: 127–8).

The 1944 Education Act did not forbid 'multilateral' (comprehensive) schools but, in the implementation of the Act, the idea of equality of educational opportunity was interpreted as meaning the removal of financial barriers to different types of secondary education to allow selection according to ability and aptitude as recommended in the Spens and Norwood reports. The promise of 'parity of esteem' to be granted to the grammar, secondary modern and technical schools and the notion that grammar schools, free of fees, provided a 'ladder of opportunity' for working class children meant that the pressure for comprehensive schooling from within the Labour party was contained. Attlee and his education ministers supported the tripartite system and 'sanctioned ministerial circulars which discouraged the multilateral school as anything but exceptional' (Rubinstein, 1984: 18).

Citizenship rights, equality of status and social integration

Tom Marshall was the first academic to analyse the significance of the welfare state. In *Citizenship and Social Class* (1963 [1950]) he identified three types of rights: civil, political and social. Marshall argued that the social rights embodied in the welfare state marked the final stage in the organic evolution of citizenship. Social rights were expressions of equality of status.

> The extension of the social services is not primarily a means of equalising incomes. In some cases it may, in others it may not ... What matters is that there is a general enrichment of the concrete substance of civilised life, a general reduction of risk and insecurity, an equalisation between the more and the less fortunate at all levels – between the healthy and the sick, the employed and the unemployed, the old and the active, the bachelor and the father of a large family. Equalisation is not so much between classes as between individuals within a population which is now treated for this purpose as though it were one class. Equality of status is more important than equality of income. (Marshall, 1963 [1950]: 107)

'In their modern form [social rights] imply an invasion of contract by status, the subordination of market price to social justice, the replacement of the free bargain by the declaration of rights' (Marshall, 1963 [1950]: 115). Marshall's ideas reflected R.H. Tawney's vision of a society in which all men should be able to live a life of dignity and culture with certain goods and services 'planned as far as is possible to emphasise and strengthen not the class differences which divide but the common humanity which unites them' (Tawney, 1975 [1931]: 49).

Richard Titmuss also developed the notion of the welfare state as an integrative mechanism. Titmuss 'was not the architect of the Modern British welfare state, but he soon made himself its ideologue, although as much as its critic as its advocate' (Reisman, 1977: 1). He believed the institutions of the welfare state, created in the period 1944 to 1948, reflected the upsurge in community spirit generated in The Second World War.

the mood of the people changed, and in sympathetic response, values changed as well. If dangers were to be shared, then resources should also be shared ... dramatic events on the home front served only to reinforce the war-warmed impulse of people for a more generous society. (Titmuss, 1950: 508)

Thus, for Titmuss, welfare institutions provided the foundation for a new form of society based on 'man's desire to serve the community' (Titmuss, 1941, cited in Oakley, 1996: 152) but they required development if their full potential as integrating mechanisms for society was to be attained. Titmuss developed his rationale of state welfare over 25 years and in *Social Policy: An Introduction* (1974) he outlined three models of social policy.

MODEL A The Residual Welfare Model of Social Policy

This formulation is based on the premise that there are two 'natural' (or socially given) channels through which an individual's needs are properly met: the private market and the family. Only when these break down should social welfare institutions come into play and then only temporarily...

MODEL B The Industrial Achievement-Performance Model of Social Policy

This incorporates a significant role for social welfare institutions as adjuncts of the economy. It holds that social needs should be met on the basis of merit, work performance and productivity...

MODEL C The Institutional Redistributive Model of Social Policy

This model sees social welfare as a major integrated institution in society, providing universalist services outside the market on the principle of need... (Titmuss, 1974: 31–2)

Titmuss' mission was to justify Model C – the model he believed was embodied, at least in an embryonic form, in the welfare state. He made a distinction between 'economic' and 'social' policy equating the 'economic' with the mechanisms of the market. Economic policy was based on the exchange of equivalents or on 'quid pro quo'. It was founded on egoism and hence produced divisions in society. In contrast 'social' policy – when based on the institutional redistributive model – was a reflection of the gift or unilateral transfer.

> The grant or the gift or unilateral transfer – whether it takes the form of cash, time, energy, satisfaction, blood or even life itself is the distinguishing mark of the social ... just as exchange or bilateral transfer is a mark of the economic. (Titmuss, 1968: 22)

Social policy helped to integrate society by allowing opportunities for people to demonstrate altruism. Its focus was on 'integrative systems; on processes, transactions and institutions which promote an individual's sense of identity, participation and community and allow him more freedom of choice for the expression of altruism and which, simultaneously, discourage a sense of individual alienation' (Titmuss, 1970: 223–4). Titmuss believed 'the National Health Service in Britain has made a greater contribution to integration and ethnic tolerance than brigades of lawyers and platoons of social workers' (1968: 9). It promoted blood donorship because it 'institutionalised' altruism; people could give blood in the knowledge that it would be used to help those in greatest need and not sold as a commodity.

> Voluntary blood donor systems ... represent one practical and concrete demonstration of fellowship relationships institutionally based in Britain in the National Health Service and the National Blood Transfusion Service. It is one example of how such relationships between free and equal individuals may be facilitated and encouraged by certain instruments of social policy. (Titmuss, 1970: 273)

Preventative and rehabilitative measures, delivered by society as a whole, were a third positive outcome of the institutional redistributive model of social policy. Titmuss regarded many state welfare services as 'not essentially benefits or increments to welfare at all' but 'partial compensations for disservices, for social costs and for social insecurities which are the product of a rapidly changing industrial society' (1968: 133). 'Private' systems of compensation through the legal system were inadequate due to the unequal power relationships between perpetuators and victims. State compensatory systems were more efficient, not least because of their ability to foster institutions whose very operations would compensate for diswelfare. In contrast, social welfare systems, established on the 'residual' model, produced undesirable consequences.

- Market-based systems of compensation (claiming damages from the perpetrator) founder because it is difficult to identify a causal agent (Titmuss, 1974: 82).
- Welfare institutions based on market principles often compound the inequalities of the economic system. Occupational pensions, for example, are frequently based on final salary, which discriminates against manual workers whose earnings are likely to be highest when they are young and fit.
- Private enterprise social service institutions operate by excluding 'bad risks'. Thus, private occupational schemes exclude the chronically sick, the disabled, the elderly, the mentally handicapped, new entrants and most categories of women – especially unmarried mothers – and private medical institutions exclude 'the bad risks' of the over-80s, the indigent and so-called charitable cases (Titmuss: 1974: 42–3). These 'bad risks' are left to the residual state welfare system and, in the context of powerful private welfare markets, services for the poor 'tend to become poor standard systems' (Titmuss, 1968: 143). Recipients of such services are likely to be stigmatised as 'self-confessed failures' (Titmuss, 1974: 45) with the means tests being the primary mechanism in the promotion of stigma. The 'fundamental objective of means tests is to keep people out; not to let them in' and recipients of such services 'must, therefore, be treated as applicants or supplicants; not beneficiaries or consumers' (Titmuss, 1968: 134).

THE 'WELFARE' STATE: RHETORIC AND REALITY

Did the form of welfare established between 1944 and 1948 embody, albeit in embryo, the characteristics described by Marshall and Titmuss? Marshall's notion of citizenship certainly captured the mood of the time. The day after the publication of the Beveridge Report, the headline in the *Daily Mirror* proclaimed the new social security system would cover 'from a duke to a dustman' and Attlee claimed social insurance was 'designed not for one class but for all' (Attlee, 1946, cited in Gregg, 1967: 44). Nonetheless, qualifications need to be made to Marshall's notion of state welfare as the embodiment of 'citizenship' rights and to Titmuss' idea of state welfare as the actualisation of altruism and hence the route to social integration.

The 'inclusiveness' of citizenship

Feminists have highlighted the 'gendered' nature of the citizenship rights established between 1944 and 1948 (Wilson, 1977; Lister, 1997: 168–94). The welfare state was constructed around 'two-track' citizenship with male citizenship defined in relation to paid work in the 'productive' economy and female citizenship in relation to the domain of unpaid work in the home and the valued role of 'motherhood'. Female citizenship was reflected in the payment of family allowance to the mother and the absence of a requirement on single parents to register for work when claiming national assistance. Other female 'welfare rights' came through the husband as the 'male breadwinner' in the anticipation that a married woman would have an income (a share in her husband's earnings) and would not require her own insurance. In contrast most male 'welfare rights' came directly to the man as the 'insured person'. Thus, as Pederson (1993: 10) has pointed out, the welfare state was 'deeply structured along gender lines, distributing rights-based entitlements to men both for themselves and for their wives and children and providing lesser, means-tested assistance to women only in the absence of men'.

   In order to cement the full inclusion of the working class, the 'residuum' – to use the term common at the turn of the nineteenth century – continued to be excluded from full citizenship. The cash benefits available from the National Assistance Board were to be 'less eligible', in status if not in amount, than insurance benefits. In effect Beveridge had created a three tier social security system linked to degrees of worth defined via work – high benefits for those involved in industrial accidents, non-means tested benefits for those with connections to the labour force and less eligible means tested benefits for the remainder. Allocation of a local authority house also signified the privileged status of the 'respectable' working class (Murie, 1997) – an offer was made only after detailed investigations of worthiness. Moreover, the welfare powers granted to local authorities under the 1948 National Assistance Act allowed extensive local discretion in the treatment of homeless families. The requirement to prevent 'queue jumping' in a severe housing shortage, as well as Poor Law attitudes carried over into welfare departments, led to forms of provision reflecting the premise that prolonged homelessness was caused by the homeless themselves. The standard of temporary accommodation was low, married men were often separated from their wives and some authorities set up classes in household management for homeless mothers. The 'homeless condition' was linked to the 'problem family'. The report *Our Towns* identified 'problem families' as part of the 'submerged tenth, always on the edge of pauperism and crime, riddled with mental and physical neglect, a menace to the community, of which the gravity is out of all proportion to their numbers' (cited in Macnicol, 1999: 71). *Problem Families*, published by members of the Pacifist Service Units identified the 'feckless mother' as the primary cause of unclean and badly nourished children (Starkey, 2000). A study of a thousand families in Newcastle upon Tyne estimated that 2 per cent of the families studied were 'problem famlies' with parents 'whose capacity for creating a home and family life is limited and who sometimes break down under the strain' (Spence et al., 1954: 246). Such families were considered 'pathological' and in need of treatment from 'clinical scientists' to restore them to the mainstream. This approach reflected 'the emergence of a more cosmetically-acceptable "reform eugenics" that stressed positive eugenics rather than more controversial negative eugenic policies (such as sterilisation)' (Macnicol, 1999: 730). 'Idle' male workers formed a third dimension of the 'residuum'. The National Assistance Board retained the power, granted to the Unemployment Assistance Board in 1934, to withdraw support as a check on voluntary unemployment and the 'wage stop' – restricting benefit to less than received in the applicant's 'normal occupation' – was retained. Reception and rehabilitation centres were set up for men 'without a settled way of living'.

The nature of citizenship

The rights embodied in the notion of citizenship were not enforceable through the legal system. Campbell (1983: 147–8) has called such rights 'socialist' rights – not 'centred on courts of law' but 'directives and enablements' signifying 'the proper ends and capacities of organised society rather than the ultimate recourse of aggrieved individuals'. As Habermas (1994: 31) has explained, 'Social Rights signify from a functionalist viewpoint the installation of a welfare bureaucracy'. The consumption of social welfare depended mainly on obligations placed on political, professional and administrative elites to provide services at an unspecified standard rather than rights to an optimum standard, vested in individuals and enforceable through the courts. These 'social rights', by enabling professionals and bureaucrats to define the requirements of 'the people', contained an ingrained paternalism.

Similar doubts surround Richard Titmuss' formulation of the nature of the welfare state as an expression of altruism. Titmuss never made a clear distinction between the reality of state welfare and his formulation of an ideal welfare system. 'It is now (*or should be*) an objective of social policy to build the identity of a person around some community with which he is associated' (Titmuss, 1974: 38, emphasis added). The reality of state welfare, as established in the late 1940s, certainly did not conform to Titmuss's 'ideal type' nor did its genesis reflect the altruism he identified as the fountainhead of the welfare state. Titmuss totally digested the notion of the organic evolution of society associated with the 'new' Liberalism and assumed 'the British welfare state, historically speaking, bubbled up from the collective consciousness' (Reisman 1977: 33). Had he attempted to formulate a systematic explanation of the development of state welfare he may have realised that class interests and class conflict provided the context for its development (Faulks, 1998: 4).

State welfare, social justice and national efficiency

Clause Four of Labour's 1918 constitution embodied the notion that the capitalist mode of production was the fundamental cause of social injustice because it denied workers 'the full fruits of their industry'. Although, by 1939, supplementary ways to tame capitalism had been devised (Ellison, 1994), Labour's 1945 manifesto was true to its constitution. 'The Labour Party is a Socialist Party, and proud of it', it declared, 'there are basic industries that are over-ripe for public ownership and management in the direct service of the nation' (Labour Party, 1945: 5).

The 'new' Liberal idea – reflected also in Fabian Socialism – of 'undeserved' gains being legitimately available for redistribution formed a second dimension of Labour's approach to social justice. The confiscation of the capitalist's 'undeserved profit' in those domains not yet 'ripe for public ownership' was linked to securing the resources necessary for a 'living wage' and the offer of equal access to 'optimal' health, education and housing (Jay, 1946: 197). However, universal welfare, financed by the taxation of 'surplus wealth', received less emphasis than nationalisation in Labour's 1945 manifesto. Tomlinson's claim that, between 1945 and 1951, Labour's disposition to social services was 'conditioned by ... fear of insecurity ... rather than one of equality' (Tomlinson, 1997: 266) rings true. Perhaps this explains why the Labour leadership readily accepted the flat rate insurance principle with its redistribution of income over the lifetime of the working man (Glennerster, 1995: 13). Without the fear of insecurity male workers could press for higher wages in industries under public ownership and those yet to be nationalised. As Richard Crossman noted in 1952, 'the planned Welfare State is really the adaptation of capitalism to the demands of modern trade unionism' (cited in Bedarida, 1990: 198). The social insurance elements of the welfare state, based on the Fabian/'new' Liberal notion of a national minimum to meet basic needs, provided a degree of social security. However, for the male working class and its union leaders, the 'fair' wage, to be secured primarily by nationalisation, remained the path to social justice (Dell, 2000: 25).

Robust elements of the Fabian quest for national efficiency permeated the welfare state programme of the Labour Party. In two influential books, *The Audit of War* (1986) and *The Lost Victory* (1995) Correlli Barnett asserts that politicians, influenced by upper-class 'visionary dreamers', set out to construct a 'New Jerusalem'. The result was the neglect of investment in 'productive' industries and the ultimate creation of a dependency culture. However, whereas Barnett tells part of the story, he ignores the emphasis on 'human capital' evident in the construction of state welfare. The detailed notes on Beveridge's plan, discovered in Hitler's bunker, include the comment that the plan was 'proof that our enemies are taking over national-socialistic ideas' (Timmins 1995: 25). As Hayek identified in *The Road To Serfdom* (1944), there were strong elements of national socialism in the form of the post-war British Welfare State, not least in the belief that investment in people would produce a strong nation state. Five examples demonstrate the point. First, Beveridge's national minimum was directly related to Rowntree's 1901 notion of physical efficiency – labour would be maintained at a level sufficient to ensure its productivity. Second, education was to be organised so that children would be efficiently allocated to the type of schools that would maximise their future economic potential. Third, social provision would be preventative, hence the Beveridge and Bevan 'fallacy' that state health care would save resources. Fourth, the efficient and 'natural' division of labour in the family between women as carers and men as providers would enhance productivity and ensure that an orderly workforce would be available. Finally, state provision of housing was justified because it could be directed to the most efficient locations in terms of industrial productivity. This relationship between state welfare and national efficiency helps to explain the limitations of Marshall's notion of 'social rights' as an element in social justice. Marshall's conception of social rights was conditional on making a reciprocal contribution to the efficiency of the nation and thereby the claims of those unable to contribute were restricted (Marshall, 1981: 91). National efficiency was also an important element in Titmuss's conception of altruism. Altruism was the will for the 'common good', which Titmuss interpreted to mean the 'British' good – a civilisation that had 'slowly evolved a higher way of life' (Titmuss, cited in Jacobs, 1985: 10). Titmuss regarded the decline in the British birth rate during the 1930s as a symptom of egoism:

> For a century we have preached the value of morals and practised the immorality of acquisitiveness ... Modern war is a temporary index of a morally unhealthy society – a declining replacement rate is a permanent expression of the same thing. The former results from man's physical control over the internal combustion engine, the latter from control over fertility. In both cases he is destructive of life; he kills the living and destroys the desire to reproduce ...
> (Titmuss, 1941, cited in Oakley, 1996: 152)

The distribution of income and wealth

The share of the top 5 per cent in total personal wealth diminished in the period 1938 to 1948 (Atkinson, 2000) and earnings became more equal during and after the war. In 1935/6 unskilled manual workers (men and women) received 20 per cent of the earnings of higher professionals but by 1955/6 this had increased to 28 per cent (Atkinson, 1975: 74). The Attlee Government retained the steeply progressive income tax established during the war and increased surtax and death duties. Thus income distribution after direct taxation became more equal between 1938 and 1949 with the Gini coefficient (a measure of overall inequality) falling from 43 to 35, mainly as a result of a decline in the disposable income of the richest 10 per cent (Johnson, 1999: 21). However, contrary to Labour's policy in the 1930s, indirect taxes were increased to reduce consumption of imported goods (Francis, 1997: 179, 181). There are no available estimates of the impact of indirect taxation on the redistribution of income, and the impact of the incidence of state social security, health care, personal health service, education and housing spending is also uncharted.

6

Redistributive State Welfare?

It is commonplace to portray the welfare state as it existed between 1944 and 1976 as a single entity. Dubbed the 'classic welfare state' (Lowe, 1999; Digby, 1989; Digby and Stewart, 1996; Gladstone, 1999) it has been represented as the outcome of a range of 'post war settlements', gradually 'developing into a systematic structure' (Clarke and Langan, 1993: 30) and enduring until the 'unsettlements' of the late 1970s (Hughes and Lewis, 1998). However, by 1976, the welfare state had changed sufficiently to cast doubt on the notion that it belonged to the same genus as the welfare state of the late 1940s.

STOP/GO: CONSERVATIVE SOCIAL POLICY 1951 TO 1964

Rowntree's third poverty study concluded 'whereas the proportion of the working-class population living in poverty has been reduced since 1936 from 31.1 per cent to 2.77 per cent ... it would have been reduced to 22.18 per cent if welfare legislation had remained unaltered' (Rowntree and Lavers, 1951: 40). Despite this endorsement of state welfare the Conservative's 1951 manifesto stressed the undesirable consequences of high public expenditure. 'No community living in a world of competing nations' can possibly afford such frantic extravagances', it said, but then displayed Tory ambivalence about welfare by making only vague promises 'to prune waste and extravagance in every department'. The only specific proposal was a cut in food subsidies 'to ensure public money is spent on those who need help and not, as at present, upon all classes indiscriminately'.

In power, the Conservatives did not attempt to change the nature of the welfare state directly by legislation. Instead, they froze its 'universal' dimension, chipped away at its structure and relied on economic growth to nurture private provision (Cronin, 1991: 215). As promised in their *Industrial Charter* (1947), the 'directing role' of the state in the economy was retained to ensure the maintenance of employment and the state continued to supply social services. However, as Rab Butler explained in *The Art of the Possible* (1971), Conservative objectives also included:

> ... the improvement of incentives through reduced taxation, the encouragement of a high level of personal savings, the steady and orderly reduction of physical controls, the overhauling of the top-heavy administrative machine and the shrinking of the Civil Service ... (Butler, 1971: 149)

Electoral considerations influenced the wariness of the Conservative retreat from Labour's 'New Jerusalem'. The Conservatives had won 231,000 fewer votes than Labour in the 1951 General Election and recognised the popularity of the welfare state (Jeffreys, 1987: 12).

Between 1951 and 1954 the value of insurance benefits declined in real terms (George, 1968: 211) and, taking into account benefit levels between elections, only just kept pace with inflation up to 1957 (Dilnot et al., 1984: 20). Means-tested national assistance payments more than exceeded price rises but lost value relative to average earnings (Atkinson, 1969: 20). Expenditure on health care, especially capital expenditure, was severely restrained with an average annual growth of 0.5 per cent (Webster, 1996: 6). By 1954/55 the proportion of GDP absorbed by the NHS had declined from 4.2 to 3.5 per cent and revenue sources such as payments and National Insurance contributions increased from 8.7 per cent of health care spending in 1949 to 18.5 per cent in 1958/9 (Webster, 1996: 6). Education fared better than social security and health care but the rise in educational provision was insufficient to accommodate the additional children born in 1945/6 as they progressed through the system. The proportion of children in classes of over 40 in primary schools increased from 30 per cent in 1952 to 37.6 per cent in 1955. This dearth of capital and revenue resources prevented reorganisation of schools on 'multi-lateral' lines by those local authorities inclined towards this system. The provision in the 1944 Education Act for school leavers to have one full day's further education in county colleges was ignored.

At first, housing was the exception to the general spending freeze. At the 1950 Conservative Party Conference, the delegates passed a resolution calling for a target of 300,00 houses per year to be built. By reducing the size of council houses and increasing subsidies, this target was reached in 1953 with over two-thirds of the new dwellings in the local authority sector (Malpass, 1990: 48). Conservative attention then turned to the promotion of home ownership and the revival of the private landlord sector. In the mid-1950s local authority building was restrained by making big cuts in the subsidies supporting building for 'general needs'. Available central resources were concentrated on requirements arising from slum clearance and the 'special' housing needs of elderly people. Home ownership was stimulated by abandoning the 'betterment levy' on developed land, relaxing the licensing of building materials and the introduction of mandatory improvement grants for the installation of basic amenities. The Rent Act 1957 was an attempt to revive the private landlord sector. Rents of dwellings above a rateable value of £30 were decontrolled and 'creeping decontrol' was allowed when a dwelling of lower rateable value became vacant.

In the late 1950s, under the growing influence of the 'middle way' espoused by Harold Macmillan (George and Wilding, 1994: 46–73), state welfare began to expand. The watershed came in 1957 when the Treasury lost a battle with the spending ministries over a proposed freeze on public sector investment, a charge for the 'hotel' costs of hospital treatment and the abolition of family allowances for the second child (Jarvis, 1998: 33). Between 1958 and 1963 the average annual real growth rate in public expenditure was 7.7 per cent on education, 4.8 per cent on health care, 5.6 per cent on social security and 4.6 per cent on housing. Education – regarded by the Conservatives as a mechanism for creating an 'Opportunity State' to rival Labour's Welfare State – was at the centre of this new commitment to improving the quality of public services. 'One Nation' Conservatism, directed at absorbing the trade unions into the ethos of welfare capitalism, was also reflected in Macmillan's embrace of economic planning and his search for a prices and incomes policy. He established a National Economic Development Council and a National Incomes Commission and promoted a more proactive regional policy. In addition there was a modest move towards earnings-related pensions and an attempt to promote a 'third arm' for housing in the form of non-profit rent and co-ownership housing associations. The Conservatives even revived earlier policies such as the payment of 'general needs' subsidies to encourage local authority building. By 1963 there were distinct signs of dampness in Conservative social policy. Within the National Assistance Board internal discussions were in progress about the adequacy of the scale rates and the impact of the wage stop (Veit-Wilson, 1999). Reforms such as the promotion of community care and the expansion of higher education were introduced and the Housing Minister, Sir Keith Joseph, set a housing target of 350,000 dwellings per year.

DISTRIBUTIVE PRINCIPLES CIRCA 1963

Full employment

The Conservative Party's 1947 *Industrial Charter* promised policies to generate full employment in return for co-operation from the unions (Charnley, 1996: 136). Throughout the Conservative term of office unemployment was never more than 2.6 per cent and, for most of the period, was less than 2 per cent with a low point of 1.2 per cent in 1955. The maintenance of full employment met with little opposition. Its impact on 'economic efficiency' caused some concern in the Cabinet in the mid-1950s but no politician was prepared to speak out in public against the objective. Full employment meant unemployment benefit attracted scant political attention and those with a good contributory record were allowed to claim 'added' days when their entitlement to benefit had expired.

Occupational and 'fiscal' welfare

By 1963 almost 50 per cent of the total working population, mostly men, had joined an occupational pension scheme (Dilnot et al. 1994: 17). The meagre level of the state pension encouraged the growth of 'occupational welfare' but its expansion was also fostered by 'fiscal welfare' – the granting of tax allowances for 'social' purposes. In the 1950s tax breaks formed part of a premeditated attempt to reduce tax and encourage 'personal' provision of welfare. By 1964, allowances were available for retirement provision, life assurance, marriage, children, wife's earned income, housekeepers and mortgage interest with a combined value, in terms of revenue foregone by the Exchequer, of £2753 million per year (Walsh, 1972: 217). Tax relief on mortgage interest was the most important element of fiscal welfare. Until 1963 owner occupiers paid Schedule A tax on the imputed income assumed to be paid to themselves as rent thereby putting them in a similar position to private landlords who paid tax on their rental income. In return for the payment of Schedule A tax, owners of dwellings were allowed to deduct their mortgage interest payments from their income tax. When Schedule A tax was abolished for resident owners, tax relief on mortgage interest continued thereby creating a substantial subsidy for owner occupiers.

Selective benefits

Beveridge's objective was to guarantee a national minimum through insurance benefits. Whereas his original scheme did not achieve this he anticipated fewer people would apply for national assistance as his insurance scheme matured. In fact, weekly national assistance payments increased from 1 million in 1951 to 1.45 million in 1962 with 70 per cent of all assistance payments made to supplement insurance benefits, mainly the pension. The Phillips Committee, appointed in 1953 to examine the financial consequences of Labour's welfare legislation, captured the dominant tone of the Conservative approach to social security. It endorsed the role of means tests, insisting that 'there is nothing to suggest that the present arrangements for national assistance are not fully capable of playing their part in securing a minimum standard of living for all old people' (Phillips Committee, 1953: 83). The permanence of national assistance in the Conservative Party's vision of social security was revealed in 1959 when the White Paper *Improvements in National Assistance* announced that the recipients of national assistance would be given 'a share in increasing national prosperity' (Ministry of Pensions and National Insurance, 1959: 3), a promise not extended to claimants of insurance benefits. Beveridge's principle of flat rate benefits in return for flat rate contributions provided a rationale for not increasing insurance benefits. If benefits were increased then contributions must also increase and, because the same contribution was paid by every worker, including the lowest paid, the government had a choice between keeping benefit recipients poor or making the 'working poor' poorer. Indeed, one senior Treasury official suggested the dominant principle for setting benefits should be what could be afforded from the contributions of the lowest paid workers (Bridgen and Lowe, 1998: 103).

The scheme for graduated pensions revealed a different application of the principle of 'selectivity'. Beveridge based his recommendations for retirement pensions on contributions related actuarially to future pension costs but 'by the end of the 1950s pensions were financed purely on a pay-as-you-go basis' (Secretary of State for Social Services, 1985: 1). The White Paper *Provision for Old Age* declared the 'burden in respect of pensions for which inadequate contributions have been paid' meant that 'National Insurance is thus confronted with a very large uncovered liability in future years for which no adequate income is provided by the scheme as it stands' (Ministry of Pensions and National Insurance, 1958: 3). To solve this problem a new graduated contribution was proposed for use in financing *existing* flat rate pensions entitlements. In return, contributors would be entitled to a very modest graduated pension, which would not be inflation-proofed. The scheme was 'selective' in that members of occupational pension schemes could 'contract out' of entitlement to the additional state pension provided their occupational pension was equivalent to that offered by the state. Hence, people with insecure and poorly paid jobs – those unlikely to be included in an occupational pension scheme – were 'selected' for inclusion in a scheme offering a very poor return for the contributions paid. They were caught between Treasury demands to keep the National Insurance Fund out of deficit and Conservative ministers who wanted to shield their supporters from the full impact of an earnings related scheme (Bridgen and Lowe, 1998: 110–12).

The withdrawal of food subsidies also illustrates the application of selectivity. As these subsidies were curtailed, family allowances were increased but, when all food subsidies ended, family allowances were frozen. By 1964, state assistance to children represented an addition to earnings (before tax) of only 9.5 per cent for a manual worker on average earnings with five children (Holman et al., 1970: 6). A fourth form of selectivity was manifest in the Conservative approach to council house rents. In 1956 the Minister for Housing declared that 'the justification for housing subsidies is need and ... need alone' (cited in Young and Rao, 1997: 67). Changes were made in the subsidy system aimed at concentrating central government assistance on people with low incomes thereby forcing the better off to consider home ownership. Rents increased faster than prices and, by 1963–4, 39 per cent of authorities operated a rent rebate scheme compared to 8.2 per cent in 1949 (Malpass, 1990: 96, 98).

Territorial justice

Health care In 1968 Bleddyn Davies coined the term 'territorial justice' to refer to 'an area distribution of provision of services such that each area's standard is proportional to the total needs for the service of its population' (Davies, 1968: 39). Some attention was given to 'territorial justice' when the NHS was established. A Medical Practices Committee was set up to control the distribution of GPs. This Committee divided England and Wales into 1400 administrative areas and classified them into groups. Grants were paid to GPs prepared to set up in 'designated' areas (with an average list size of more than 2500) and doctors could be prevented from working in restricted areas (with a list size of less than 1700). This system worked well in the 1950s when 'the distribution of general practice was transformed as vacancies in the less attractive areas were gradually filled' (Haynes, 1985: 69). However, in the late 1950s, its efficiency as a redistributive mechanism declined due to a shortage of GPs and the failure to adjust the absolute definitions of 'restricted' and 'intermediate' areas as the average list increased. In 1953 a similar system was established for the hospital sector. All requests for new consultant posts had to be submitted to an advisory Committee on Consultant Establishments whose role it was to ration requests in order to assist underprovided regions. This made little impact on the distribution of specialists as 'relatively unpopular areas probably already had posts unfilled for want of applicants' (British Medical Association, 1969: 205). Dentists were not subject to any controls and by 1963 the range of dentists available per 10,000 population varied from 6 in Chester to 0.9 in Norfolk. (British Medical Association, 1969: 206)

Local government The Local Government Act 1948 abolished the 'block' grant replacing it with the 'Exchequer Equalisation Grants' payable to local authorities with rateable values below the national average thereby helping to rectify the injustice identified in the 1930s by Helen Wilkinson. Ten years later most of the remaining percentage grants were replaced by an additional 'block' grant and distributed according to a new formula designed to relate local income to local need. It failed to achieve this objective because the need indicators adopted – population, number of old people, school population, density of population, road mileage – did not fully reflect the socio-economic variables generating different levels of need. Using indicators of needs and standards Davies (1968) discovered large variations in levels of provision unrelated to the incidence of needs.

Area selectivity

In the 1930s the Conservatives devised a housing strategy to ensure the urban poor stayed in the city centre thereby leaving developing suburbia free for occupation by the more affluent (Yelling, 1992). This 'exclusion' strategy was revived in the mid-1950s. By concentrating subsidies on slum clearance and increasing financial assistance in accordance with the number of storeys in a block, the Government encouraged local authorities to deal with slums without 'overspill' into rural locations. The negative planning powers available to county councils and the tight green belts drawn around urban areas comple-mented the positive promotion of 'stay put' for inner city dwellers. Manchester, for example, was prevented from developing a new town for its 'overspill' population by objections from Cheshire. The Government supported Cheshire's objections claiming Manchester's overspill problem could be reduced by building at higher densities in the city boundaries (Hall et al., 1973: 588–92).

'Less eligibility'

The relative decline in the value of insurance benefits helped to ensure that workers would be better off in employment. However, the more generous increases in national assistance and the relative decline in the value of family allowances presented a potential work disincentive for unemployed people eligible to claim national assistance. This problem was solved by the retention of the 'wage stop' that survived, almost unchanged, from the days of the Unemployment Assistance Board. The 'wage stop' prevented an unemployed person from receiving national assistance payments greater than 85 per cent of his or her earnings in 'normal' employment. 'Less eligibility' also continued in the treatment of council tenants and homeless people. A report of the Central Housing Advisory Committee discovered many local authorities dealing with people unable or unwilling to pay their rent by moving them to poorer qual-ity housing (Central Housing Advisory Committee, 1955: 17). Mounting pressure on temporary accommodation in the late 1950s resulted in the continued application of deterrent principles to homeless people. Greve (1971: 126), records that 'Croydon, for example, had at that time very strin-gent admission rules: no husbands were admitted; no "blameworthy" cases (homelessness due to quarrels, rent arrears, etc.) were admitted unless with children under five; stay was strictly limited to six months'.

Institutional and community care

In the late 1950s 'community care' was gaining support but the phrase meant different things in different contexts to different people. The dominant interpretation referred to the closing down of the large institutions and their replacement with smaller residential care homes. On this interpretation of 'community care' some headway was made in the 1950s and early 1960s but, if community care is taken to mean state help for people cared for in their own homes, then little progress was made. Townsend and Wedderburn in *The Aged in the Welfare State* (1965) revealed the deficiencies of the health and welfare services in meeting need. 15 per cent of elderly people needed home helps but 4 per cent received the service, 7 per cent needed meals on wheels but 1 per cent received a meal. The supply of services varied considerably in different parts of the country. Rotherham, for example, employed 1.3 home helps per 1000 population whereas Tynemouth employed 0.06 per thousand population (Webster, 1996: 11).

Jones et al. (1983: 102) trace the origins of the modern community care movement for people with a mental disorder to the Royal Commission on Mental Illness and Mental Deficiency, 1954–57. It recommended the expansion of local authority services such as residential care and occupational/training centres but the development of other local authority services had to wait until the early 1960s when local authorities were asked to submit plans for the development of community care. The National Assistance Act 1948 gave local authorities the power to develop domiciliary services for people with physical, visual and sensory impairments but the only mandatory element was the development of services for blind people. The provision of services for other groups did not become mandatory until 1960, which meant that the home help service was the main local authority community care service for people with a physical disability (Means and Smith, 1998: 25).

Taxation

During the 1950s income tax was charged at different rates on each slice of income and a special surtax was levied on people with very high incomes. The Conservatives gradually lowered all the rates of tax but a large part of the lost income was recouped by the failure to raise personal tax allowances in line with inflation. This 'fiscal drag' meant the starting point for the payment of income tax by a single person declined from 39.4 per cent of average earnings in 1949/50 to 24.7 per cent in 1962/3 (Field et al., 1977: 32). Between 1948 and 1964 the proportion taken by tax and national insurance of the income of a man with average earnings and two young children increased from 3 per cent to 9 per cent (Jackson et al., 1972: 66). Nicholson's study of income distribution between 1949 and 1963 found that the distribution of income in Britain was becoming more equal until about 1957 when the movement towards equality ended (Nicholson, 1964). In an earlier study Nicholson had attempted to measure the redistribution of income in 1953, 1957 and 1959 using information from the Ministry of Labour's Family Expenditure Survey. The tables presented combined families with different characteristics (e.g. pensioners and younger single people were placed in the same grouping) but it is possible to make some useful comparisons. In 1957, before taxation and the value of benefits in cash and kind had been taken into account, the 10 per cent of families containing two adults and two children with the lowest incomes had an income of 25 per cent of the highest decile. After redistribution the lowest decile held 38.7 per cent of the resources of the highest decile (Nicholson, 1964).

LABOUR 1964 TO 1970: THE EXPANSION OF STATE WELFARE

The 'rediscovery' of poverty

The new Labour Government was presented with three reports detailing the nature and extent of poverty in Britain. *The Poor and the Poorest* (1965) criticised the 'subsistence' standard used in Rowntree's studies. It claimed 'Poverty is a relative concept. Saying who is in poverty is to make a relative statement – rather like saying who is short or heavy' (Abel-Smith and Townsend, 1965: 63). Abel-Smith and Townsend adopted two 'relative' poverty lines – below national assistance (the poorest) and national assistance plus 40 per cent (the poor). They found the percentage of the population living on an income less than 40 per cent above the national assistance scale had increased from 7.8 per cent in 1954 to 14.2 per cent in 1960 with 3.8 per cent of the population having an income below the basic national assistance level. These findings were confirmed by two Government reports. *Financial and Other Circumstances of Retirement Pensioners* (Ministry of Social Security, 1966b) showed that 14 per cent of retirement pensioners could have received National Assistance but they had not applied for it. The reasons given by pensioners for not claiming assistance were lack of knowledge, they were 'managing all right' or they disliked applying to the National Assistance Board because of pride and aversion to charity (Atkinson, 1969: 58). *Circumstances of Families*, (Ministry of Social Security, 1966a) revealed that about 125,000 families containing nearly 500,000 children had incomes below the supplementary benefit and many of the 'breadwinners' in these families were in full-time work.

Abel-Smith and Townsend redefined rather than rediscovered poverty and from the mid-1960s, an income below the national assistance scale became the 'official' poverty line, despite its limitations as a measure of poverty. What standard of living was represented by the national assistance scales? Is it not illogical that an increase in national assistance scales should produce an increase in poverty? Given these limitations it is fruitful to speculate on the reasons why such a measure became widely accepted as the poverty line. It had a rationale in that it represented the national minimum approved by Parliament but its adoption also defined a potential work incentive problem. As the Supplementary Benefits Commission noted 'The wage stop is not, therefore, a cause of family poverty: it is a harsh reflection of the fact that there are many men in work living on incomes below the Supplementary Benefit standard' (Ministry of Social Security, 1967: 2).

Labour's response to the problem of family poverty and work incentives was to increase family allowances and to 'claw-back' some of the cost from those paying income tax by reducing child tax allowances. Richard Crossman described the measure as 'one of the most ingenious pieces of legislation passed under this Government which means tested the better off rather than the poor' (Crossman, 1969: 17). However, the strategy was unpopular because, by 1969, many low-income families found that the reduction in tax allowances had pulled them back into the income tax net. 'Claw-back' became a mechanism 'that simply meant that money received by mothers was withdrawn from the father's pay packet' (Secretary of State for Social Services, 1985: 44).

Labour's 1964 manifesto promised to help elderly people by increasing existing insurance benefits, thereafter linking them to average earnings, to introduce an Incomes Guarantee under which 'those whose incomes fall below the new minimum will receive as of right, and without resource to National Assistance, an income supplement' and to set up a 'new wage-related insurance scheme' (Labour Party, 1964 cited in Craig, 1975: 265). In power, Labour did not establish a statutory link between benefits and earnings but it did increase benefits at a rate above the rise in earnings. The Incomes Guarantee for pensioners was dropped and replaced by an attempt to change the image of national assistance by renaming it 'supplementary benefit'. 'Applicants' were renamed claimants and emphasis was placed on the 'supplementary pension' paid as a right rather than as a handout from the state. A bill making provision for earnings-related pensions was introduced in 1969 but lapsed when Parliament was dissolved in 1970.

Benefits for those not in employment and under pension age were improved as part of a social security package aimed at assisting industrial restructuring. A redundancy payments scheme was introduced in 1965, which provided compensation of one weeks' pay for each year's service under the age of 41 and one and a half weeks' pay for each year's service over that age, subject to a maximum. In 1966 earnings-related sickness, industrial injury, widows and unemployment benefits, paid in return for additional earnings-related contributions, were introduced. These benefits, lasting up to 28 weeks, were justified with the argument:

> the scale of commitments which people undertake depends upon what they earn ... thus his [a family man's] social insurance benefit needs to be a high proportion of his weekly earnings ... need cannot be met by flat rate benefits alone. (Ministry of Pensions and National Insurance, 1966, cited in Micklewright, 1989: 529).

However, earnings-related contributions eroded Beveridge's flat rate contributory principle and supplied a source of finance for higher basic benefits. Earnings-related payments and higher basic benefits meant the gap between income in and out of work narrowed from 55 per cent in 1964 to 25 per cent in 1968 (Stewart, 1972: 95). Later, anxiety about work incentives led to the introduction of a 'wage stop' on *insurance* benefits set at 85 per cent of the earnings on which benefit was calculated.

Health care

Two related issues, the role of charges and resources, dominated the health-care debate. Labour's 1964 manifesto stated 'the most serious attack on the Health Service made by Conservative Ministers has been the increased burden of prescription charges'. It promised to abolish these charges declaring its aim as 'to restore as rapidly as possible a completely free Health Service' (Labour Party, 1964, cited in Craig, 1975: 261). Commitments were also made to increase capital spending on hospitals and to increase the number of doctors and nurses. The election pledge to abolish prescription charges was quickly fulfilled but charges were reintroduced in 1968 (with exemptions covering 40 per cent of the population) as part of an economic package to shift resources from home consumption to exports. Nonetheless, under Labour, healthcare spending increased from 3.86 per cent of GNP in 1964 to 4.9 per cent in 1969 (Townsend and Bosanquet, 1972).

Education

In its opposition years, there was a marked shift in Labour's policy on education. In 1955, the party favoured 'encouraging comprehensive secondary schooling' only, but, in 1964, the manifesto stated 'Labour will get rid of the segregation of children into separate schools caused by 11-plus selection: secondary education will be reorganised on comprehensive lines' (Labour Party, 1964 cited in Craig, 1975: 263). This stronger support for comprehensive education was the result of mounting research evidence on the talent wasted by the tripartite system (Crowther Report, 1959; Central Advisory Council for Education, 1963; Douglas, 1964) plus Labour's growing preference for social welfare, rather than public ownership, as the engine of social justice. In 1965, the government requested local authorities to prepare plans for comprehensive education and a circular, issued in 1966, announced that the government intended to refuse loan sanctions for building programmes based on grammar and secondary modern schools.

In 1962, Tony Crosland reformulated the concept of equality of educational opportunity. He made a distinction between 'weak' and 'strong' versions of the concept. The 'weak' version assumed 'access to elite education is based not on birth or wealth, but solely on intelligence as measured by IQ tests, and hence that all children of the same measured intelligence at the appropriate age have completely equal access' (Crosland, 1962: 12). In contrast, the strong version claimed that 'granted the differences in heredity and infantile experience, every child should have the same opportunity for *acquiring* measured intelligence, so far as this can be controlled by social action' (Crosland, 1962: 173, emphasis added). This meant a return to the 'environmental eugenics', popular at the turn of the century. The state should do everything in its power to remove the social and economic conditions influencing educational attainment and the measure of success would be the extent to which social differences in attainment were reduced. Halsey expressed the idea succinctly, asserting that equality of outcome is achieved:

> ... if the proportion of people from different social, economic and ethnic categories at all levels and in all types of education are [sic] more or less the same as the proportion of these people in the population at large. In other words the goals should not be the liberal one of equality of access but equality of outcome for the median member of each identifiable non-educationally defined group, i.e. the *average* woman, negro or proletarian or rural dweller should have the same level of educational attainment as the average male, white, suburbanite. (1972: 8)

Crosland's notion of equality of educational opportunity was reflected in the Plowden Report on primary schooling published in 1967. Plowden focused on children in deprived areas stating that 'the homes and neighbourhoods from which many of [the] children come provide little support and stimulus for learning' (Central Advisory Council for Education, 1966:

para. 151). Plowden argued that 'the principle that special need calls for special help should be given a new cutting edge'. Positive discrimination in favour of schools located in deprived areas was necessary:

> going well beyond an attempt to equalise resources ... The first step must be to raise the schools with low standards to the national average; the second, quite deliberately to make them better ... The schools must supply a compensating environment. (Central Advisory Council for Education, 1966: para. 151)

Labour allocated extra resources to deprived areas through its Educational Priority Areas Programme. These resources were used for school building, additional payments to teachers and to support and 'increase the involvement of parents in the children's education to increase the "sense of responsibility" of their communities' (Halsey, 1972: 57). The 'area' approach to deprivation, with its emphasis on 'people change', was also manifest in the establishment of the Urban Programme in 1968 and the Community Development Programme set up in 1967.

Housing

By 1964 Labour had turned away from the 1945–51 policy of promoting a local authority monopoly of housing in favour of a balanced approach to local authority tenants and homeowners. Labour's growing taste for home ownership was reflected in its declaration that the expansion of the public sector was a response to 'exceptional needs' whereas 'the expansion of buildings for owner occupancy ... is normal' (Ministry of Housing and Local Government, 1965). Owner occupation was stimulated by the introduction of an 'option mortgage' scheme allowing a person with a low income, who did not benefit from tax relief on mortgage interest, to receive a low interest loan. Nonetheless, Labour gradually began to restore the equilibrium between public and private sector building that had tipped towards owner occupation in the late 1950s and early 1960s. The gap between the two sectors narrowed from 96,000 in 1964 to 23,000 in 1969. A substantial part of Labour's new build programme was targeted on the needs arising from clearance and a range of pressures, especially the shortage of bricks, meant the use of industrialised building techniques and the erection of high-rise blocks of flats (Dunleavy, 1981). New mechanisms were set up to regulate rents giving tenants and landlords the opportunity to ask Rent Assessment Committees to determine a 'fair' rent for a property. The 1969 Housing Act promoted a switch from clearance to improvement by reviving the notion of improvement areas first introduced in 1930. Local authorities were allowed to declare General

Improvement Areas in which they would have enhanced powers of compulsory purchase, the power to pay higher grants and make environmental improvements. Ministers promoted this change in emphasis as a positive measure stressing the ways that clearance had disrupted established communities. However, the policy was also a response to the financial crisis of 1967 – rehabilitation was cheaper than demolition and new build.

The personal social services

In the mid-1960s, what are now called 'the personal social services' remained the Cinderella of the welfare state. Responsibility for such services was divided between three principal local authority departments – Welfare, Health and Children's – with other departments such as Education and Housing having a 'welfare' arm. Local authorities had a duty to provide residential care but care of adults 'in the community' remained mainly permissive on the assumption that the voluntary sector should play a major role in service provision. The Ministry of Health adopted a laissez faire attitude to local provision content; to 'advise and exhort' but 'not to seek to direct' (Grifffiths, 1966: 489, 518). The Seebohm Committee (1968: 29–32) summarised the problems of the personal social services as inadequate in the amount, range and quality of provision accentuated by poor co-ordination and difficult access. Seebohm diagnosed the causes of these failings as lack of resources, inadequate knowledge and divided responsibility, and recommended the creation of a single Social Services Department in each authority. A unified department would 'provide better services for those in need because it will ensure a more co-ordinated and comprehensive approach to the problems of individuals and families and the community in which they live' (Seebohm Committee, 1968: 44). The Chronically Sick and Disabled Persons Act 1970 stimulated the attempt to detect and meet 'need'. It strengthened the duties of local authorities to meet needs and made them responsible for estimating the number of people requiring services as a foundation for service planning. The growing emphasis on 'need' as the guiding principle of social allocations was also reflected in the Children and Young Persons Act 1969, which made provision for the age of criminal responsibility to be raised, in stages, to 14 and for 'intermediate treatment' facilities to be developed to meet the needs of children 'in trouble'.

Taxation

Spending on state welfare grew substantially between 1964 and 1970 and tax increases were necessary to finance this expenditure. The standard rate of income tax increased from 38.75 per cent to 41.25 per cent but the major addition to the income tax yield came, yet again, from the failure to increase tax allowances in line with inflation. Extra resources were also raised from the introduction of capital gains tax, increases in corporation tax, a new selective employment tax and higher taxes on consumer spending on tobacco, alcohol and the purchase and running of cars.

STOP/GO: CONSERVATIVE SOCIAL POLICY 1970 TO 1974

In opposition the Conservative Party entered a 'dry' period (Willetts, 1992). Radical proposals for curtailing state welfare were afloat in Conservative circles but fear that such reforms would be unpopular led to their exclusion from official policy statements. The 1970 Conservative Party manifesto emphasised reducing income tax but was short on the detail of how this might be achieved. 'Reductions will be possible because we will cut out unnecessary Government spending and because we will encourage savings. And as our national income rises we will get a larger revenue with lower tax rates' (Conservative Party, 1970: 12).

Social security

In the countdown to the 1970 General Election the Conservatives committed themselves to increasing family allowances and clawing back some of the cost by further reductions in child tax allowances (Field, 1971: 30). However, the unpopularity of Labour's earlier transfer of income from the 'pay packet to the purse' persuaded the Conservatives not to proceed with their scheme. The value of family allowances declined in real terms during Edward Heath's term of office but Family Income Supplement, aimed at families on a low income where the head of the household was in work, was introduced. Prescribed levels of income were set according to the number of children in the family (unlike family allowances, the first child was included) and the benefit was 50 per cent of the difference between this prescribed level and the income of the family. Criticism from the Labour Party focused on the disincentives to longer hours of work contained in the scheme, its low 'take-up' rate of 48 per cent (Deacon and Bradshaw, 1983: 81) and its payment to the male as head of the household.

Strategy for Pensions (Secretary of State of the Department of Health and Social Security, 1971) returned to the late 1950's theme of the 'demographic timebomb'. It noted that the growing number of pensioners could not be supported by the existing 'pay as you go' system with its basic reliance on flat rate contributions. 'In the Government's view an equitable and enduring solution can only be found in a system of earnings-related contributions for basically flat-rate benefits' (1971: 1–2). Accordingly, the Government proposed contributions to the state pensions scheme should become earnings related up to a fixed ceiling. Provision for an income in retirement above the basic pension would be made through state-regulated occupational pensions underpinned by a fully funded State Reserve Scheme run on the lines of an occupational scheme by an independent Board of Management. This plan became law as the 1973 Social Security Act, but was not implemented. Nonetheless, some of the Conservative social security reforms had a lasting impact. The Government announced it would develop the social security system 'along selective lines'. This statement marked the formal abandonment of the Beveridge principle of equal benefits across all contingencies except for the requirements arising from industrial injury. In the 1970s the social security system was marked by increasing diversity in the form and level of the benefits available. A distinction was made between short-term illness and long-term disability by the introduction of a new invalidity benefit, paid after 28 weeks of illness and at a more generous rate than sickness benefit. Moreover, Unemployment Benefit was separated from other categories of benefit entitlement. As Lynes commented at the time:

> What is new is the decision to treat the unemployed, even while still entitled to unemployment benefit, less generously than the sick. For the first twenty-eight weeks sickness and unemployment benefits are identical. After that the unemployed revert to the basic flat-rate benefit. There is nothing comparable to invalidity benefit for the long-term unemployed. (Lynes, 1974: 77)

The separation of need associated with unemployment from other needs was also injected into the supplementary benefits scheme. The long-term rate of supplementary benefit, introduced in 1973, was not made available to unemployed people (Supplementary Benefits Commission, 1974: 14).

Health care and the personal social services

Real expenditure on health care increased by over 20 per cent between 1970 and 1974 (Merrison, 1979: 433), but spending relative to rising need and demand remained a major political issue. The phrase 'We will consider the financing of the health service with a view to finding ways of devoting more resources to the nation's health without increasing the burden on the taxpayer' had been included in the draft Conservative Party manifesto. This was an oblique reference to a plan, based on the

British Medical Association's report *Health Service Financing* (1969), to provide 80 per cent of health care through the National Health Service and to force 20 per cent of the cost onto private health insurance, subsidised by the state (Heath, 1998: 452). This plan was abandoned before the General Election and the Conservatives directed their attention towards securing greater efficiency by administrative reorganisation to promote 'rational planning'. A new formula to relate expenditure to need was introduced to be phased in over ten years. However, this formula gave a 50 per cent weighting to supply factors such as the number of occupied beds and the number of cases treated (Webster, 1996: 609) and would not have equalised access to hospital care because no allowance was made for health care needs in different areas. (Culyer, 1976: 121).

The Seebohm Committee (1968), whose recommendations formed the rationale for the reorganisation of the personal social services under the Social Services Act, 1970, maintained that a single Social Services Department would attract more resources. Indeed, the new Social Services Departments were successful in attracting extra finance. Real growth averaged 10 per cent per year (Davies, 1998: 216) but additional demands were imposed on the new departments by an ageing population and of the run-down large hospitals for people with a mental disorder.

Education

The Conservative's 1970 manifesto declared 'Many of the most imaginative new schemes abolishing the eleven-plus have been introduced by Conservative councils', but imposing a system on 'rigid lines is contrary to local democracy'. In accordance with the spirit of the manifesto Mrs Thatcher withdrew Labour's Circular 10/65, which had requested plans from local authorities for comprehensive reorganisation. Nevertheless, plans continued to be submitted, often from Conservative-controlled authorities: 3600 proposals were considered of which only 9 per cent were rejected (Thatcher, 1995: 171). In 1972 a White Paper *Education: A Framework for Expansion* was published. Educational expenditure in the schools sector was planned to increase by 3 per cent per annum up to 1981–2 and it was anticipated that the relative decline in the predicted number of children entering primary schools and a reduction in the rate of higher education expansion would free additional resources to develop nursery education.

Housing

Selectivity was applied to housing policy in two ways. The White Paper *Fair Deal For Housing* proposed a national rent rebate scheme to carry through 'the Government's central policy of subsidising people not bricks and mortar' (Secretary of State for the Environment, 1971: 11). The Housing Finance Act 1972 made provision for local authority rents to be determined by the 'fair' rent procedures already applied to private landlordism. Since 'fair' rents meant higher rents for local authority tenants their impact was cushioned by a national system of rent rebates. 'Fair' rents would also generate a substantial surplus in many local authority housing revenue accounts. The Act included provisions to ensure a proportion of this surplus was to be paid to the Treasury. The Act also introduced a national rent allowance scheme for tenants of private landlords. The second dimension of selectivity in housing was heralded in the White Paper *Better Homes: The Next Priorities* (Department of the Environment, 1973). This contained proposals to allow local authorities to declare Housing Action Areas and thereby target the resources available for improvement on the most needy areas. The Conservatives lost office before the White Paper could be implemented.

Despite the move to greater selectivity in social policy between 1970 and 1974 state expenditure on social welfare increased. This can be explained as the outcome of the displacement of social policy objectives by political reality. During its 'dry' period in the late 1960s the Conservative party formulated a robust policy of greater selectivity in social service provision. The Chancellor expressed this in October 1970: 'We intend to adopt a more selective approach to social services … instead of the present indiscriminate subsidies, help will be given where it is most needed' (Barber, 1970, cited in Timmins, 1995: 281). Selectivity as a policy objective was retained throughout the period 1970 to 1974 but was overlaid by a U-turn on economic policy. As unemployment reached almost one million the policy of letting 'lame-duck' industries go under was reversed. More money was injected into the economy via social welfare to gain union support for an incomes policy and to promote employment (Dutton, 1991: 68). The quadrupling of oil prices in 1973 also led to additional spending in order to maintain domestic demand. The aim of the 1972 and 1973 budgets was to raise the growth of GDP to an annual rate of over 5 per cent by allowing for a 50 per cent increase in the Public Sector Borrowing Requirement.

LABOUR 1974 TO 1976: LET'S HAVE A PARTY

Labour's February 1974 manifesto claimed 'Clearly, a fresh approach to the British crisis is required, and Labour insists that it must begin with an entirely new recognition of the claims of social justice' (Labour Party, 1974a, cited in Craig, 1975: 402). It promised big increases in social welfare spending financed by 'an annual Wealth Tax on the rich; … a new tax on major transfers of personal wealth; a heavy tax on speculation in property – including a new tax on property companies and the elimination of tax dodging across the whole field' (Labour Party, 1974a cited in Craig, 1975: 402). The October manifesto repeated the theme declaring 'We believe that men and women will respond to difficult challenges if there is a sense of underlying fairness in society. Labour believes, for instance, that taxation must be used to achieve a major redistribution of both wealth and income' (Labour Party, 1974b cited in Craig, 1975: 427).

In its first two years the Labour Government introduced a number of egalitarian social security measures. Child tax allowances, which benefited the families with the highest incomes, were replaced by a new, untaxed Child Benefit payable to the mother in respect to all children. The introduction of Family Income Supplement in 1971 had reduced the impact of the wage stop and it was anticipated that the introduction of Child Benefit would further reduce the number of families whose income, when claiming supplementary benefit, was greater than their potential income in work. In 1976, when the wage stop was abolished, there were only 6000 families affected by the wage stop compared to the 35,600 in 1970.

Barbara Castle's 1975 Social Security Act made National Insurance Contributions (NICs) earnings-related up to a ceiling and the Social Security Pensions Act 1975 introduced a state earnings-related pensions scheme (SERPS). SERPS would pay a pension related to the earnings history of the recipient over his or her 20 best years of earning. The pension would be based on contributions paid on earnings between the lower earnings limit, broadly equal to the basic pension, and an upper earnings limit of 7.5 times the state pension. Every year of contributions would secure a pension of 1.25 per cent of the earnings on which contributions had been paid. The Act also put widows' and invalidity pensions on an earnings-related basis and enabled women to obtain the same benefit rate as men with equivalent earnings. The right of married women to opt to pay a lower rate of contribution but receive no pension was abolished although women already paying the special lower rate could continue making a reduced payment. The 1975 Social Security Benefits Act provided a non-contributory invalidity pension for non-insured disabled men and women under retirement age. These measures, together with the decision to increase the basic state pension by 25 per cent and then keep it in line with earnings or prices, whichever was the higher, had an egalitarian impact. However, the improvements in social security and the initial failure to link personal tax allowances to price rises produced troublesome results. The tax threshold for a married couple with two children under 11 was lower than the supplementary benefit threshold (Barr, 1980: 240) and the gap between the real take-home pay of workers with the lowest earnings and those claiming benefits narrowed. As Barr (1980: 231) commented '... real benefits rose relative to earnings. It is this fact that has strengthened assertions that a man can be better off receiving benefits than he would be if earning'.

Barbara Castle's egalitarian impulse also focused on health care. She tackled the issue of 'pay' beds by phasing them out of the National Health

Service and introduced a new mechanism for distributing funds to Regional Health Authorities. The RAWP formula, as it was known, attempted to phase in a system of resource allocation based on objective measures of the relative need of each region for expenditure on health care (Department of Health and Social Security, 1976). In *Priorities for Health and Personal Social Services* (1976), growth in health services was directed towards the requirements of elderly people and people with a learning disability. *Better Services for the Mentally Ill* (Department of Health and Social Security, 1975) reviewed the progress made in establishing community care services. In her foreword, Barbara Castle claimed the improvements of the late 1960s and early 1970s were 'not getting to the core of the problem'. She developed a two-pronged response to the problem. Guidelines were set for community provision – 60 local authority day places per 100,000 population for example – in the hope of prompting local authorities and health authorities to increase spending on the 'Cinderella services' and a new mechanism was introduced to transfer resources from health authorities to local government.

Labour's February 1974 election manifesto promised to expand education by 'finally ending the 11+'. A short Act was passed giving the Education Secretary the power to require local authorities to submit plans for a comprehensive system of secondary education. By 1978, 80 per cent of children attended comprehensive schools and more schemes were in the pipeline. The system of direct grants paid by central government to independent schools was abolished with the affected schools given the choice of complete independence or absorption into the local government comprehensive system. Most chose independent status.

On gaining office Labour immediately imposed a freeze on council house rents and then restored the right of local authorities to set their own rents. Rent control was applied to furnished properties and the Government stated that its objective was the gradual replacement of private landlords through a process of 'municipalisation'. Subsidies to local authorities increased four-fold in response to rising land prices and interest rates.

In the mid-1970s central government grants to local authorities were distributed through the Rate Support Grant mechanism based on two principal elements – 'needs' and 'resources'. The 'needs' element was designed to take into account the social and economic circumstances that generated divergent levels of need. This element was calculated by isolating the variables that accounted for different expenditure levels and then weighting them according to their incidence in a particular area and the contribution made by each variable to explaining national divergence in expenditure. The 'resources' element was intended to compensate those authorities with low rateable values (Loughlin, 1986: 23–9). The effect of this mechanism was to shift resources to the urban areas with the greatest needs, mainly under Labour control and away from the rural counties

(Rhodes and Bailey, 1979). Government grants to local authorities increased rapidly in the mid-1970s; by 1976 central grants provided 66.5 per cent of local government spending.

DISTRIBUTIVE PRINCIPLES: CIRCA 1976

Social harmony

In the 1940s, welfare provision was linked to economic growth and social justice by the notion of 'human capital'. The state should invest in people and, because the working class needed the most investment, this strategy would promote social justice. As the economy expanded, this connection between social welfare investment and economic growth, indicated in Richard Titmuss's third model of social policy – the Industrial Achievement-Performance Model (Titmuss, 1974: 31–2) – was sidelined. Although elements of welfare provision were sometimes justified by their positive economic impact (Donnison, 1965) Titmuss' preferred model of welfare – the Institutional Redistributive Model – held centre-stage in academic and political discourses on welfare. As the 'human capital' approach receded, the role of state spending on 'universal' welfare services as a route to social justice and hence industrial harmony became dominant. Part of Heath's policy 'U-turn' in 1972 consisted of extra welfare spending and, by the mid-1970s, the idea of the 'social' wage delivered by the 'corporate state' was an important component of the social contract forged between the Labour Government and the Trade Unions. Barbara Castle expressed the mood of the minority Labour Government in 1974 when she said:

> We had fought the election on our Social Contract with the unions as the best hope of winning their co-operation in restraining excessive wage demands … In obedience to union pressure we declared that we would repeal the Industrial Relations Act in its entirety, increase pensions and other benefits, keep the price of key foods down by subsidies, legislate on equal status for women, press ahead with comprehensive secondary education … (Castle, 1994: 454–5)

Full employment

The ideal of 'full employment', to be achieved by demand management, remained intact in the early 1970s. As unemployment increased towards one million the Conservative party changed its economic policy and, on attaining office, Labour's first budget injected new demand into the economy and unemployment started to fall.

Need

By 1976 'need' had become the dominant principle for the distribution of 'decommodified' state services but, when compared to the late 1940s, its meaning and application had changed. In the late 1940s individual need was linked to the 'national' requirement for a healthy, efficient, educated workforce – a link that helped separate 'needs' from 'wants' and with the capacity to cap potential claims to scarce resources. By 1976, under the influence of professional forms of organisation, the growth of consumerism and the appeasement of the trade unions, individual need had been uncoupled from 'national' need.

The characteristics of a profession include the mastery of an intellectual technique, unavailable to the 'laity', that performs a service for society (Hall, 1979: 38). Professions also represent themselves as 'client-orientated'; because the professional has the authority to state what is good or bad for the 'client', then individual 'client' welfare – not the 'common good' – is the paramount professional ethic. When the state assumed financial and administrative responsibility for the 'welfare' of its citizens, it left decisions on individual need in the control of established professions and those occupations aspiring to professional status (Foster and Wilding, 2000: 144). These 'organisational professions' (Young and Laffin, 1990: 9) not only claimed expertise in interpreting individual need according to professional norms they also claimed authority in determining 'aggregate' need – 'aggregate' need being the sum total of individual need as interpreted by the professionals. In doing so, according to 'public choice' theorists, they expanded their spheres of influence and their incomes (Niskanen, 1973). Enoch Powell expressed the frustrations of some of the spending and Treasury ministers when he said:

> The unnerving discovery every Minister of Health makes at or near the outset of his term of office is that the only subject he is ever destined to discuss with the medical profession is money ... The vulgar assumption is that there is a definable amount of medical care 'needed', and that if that 'need' was met, no more would be demanded. This is absurd. (Powell, 1975 [1966]: 14, 23, 26)

Social security contained no 'organisational professionals' and so the role of 'apolitical' interpreters of 'need' was assumed by social scientists. In 1965 Townsend and Abel-Smith, as an adjunct to their interpretation of poverty as a relative concept, had used National Assistance plus 40 per cent to identify the 'poor'. Although Townsend had not formulated a coherent alternative to this 'below state minimum approach', in 1973 he stated 'Poverty can be defined objectively and applied consistently only in terms of relative deprivation'. (Townsend, 1973: 15)

Who would dare to lay down a scale of necessities for the 1970s for a young woman consisting of: one pair of boots, two aprons, one second-hand dress, one skirt made from an old dress, a third of the cost of a new hat, a third of the cost of a shawl and a jacket, two pairs of stockings, a few unspecified underclothes, one pair of stays and a pair of old boots worn as slippers (1973: 15, the clothing standard set by Rowntree in 1901).

This theme of relative poverty was developed in *Poverty in the United Kingdom* (1979) where Townsend attempted to achieve his goal of a relative but objective poverty line by devising a number of deprivation indicators. He argued that if the sum of these deprivations was used as a 'deprivation score' and this score was related to income, a 'poverty line' may emerge 'at which withdrawal [from participation in society] escalates disproportionately to falling resources' (Townsend, 1979: 57). Townsend claimed to have discovered such an objective, 'scientific' poverty line and identified 26 per cent of the population as living below this 'objective', 'relative deprivation' standard.

Desert

In the 1940s and 1950s, despite the prominence given to citizenship status in the consumption of welfare services, considerable emphasis was placed on 'desert' criteria in the operation of the welfare state. During the 1960s and early 1970s this 'desert' dimension began to recede as a more relaxed approach to 'traditional' morality developed and professional expertise in need determination became dominant. Two examples will demonstrate subordination of desert to need.

Single parent families   In 1974, the report of the Finer Committee on one parent families recommended that all lone parent families, 'regardless of the cause of their status should be entitled to a new social security benefit which we call guaranteed maintenance allowance ...' (Department of Health and Social Security, 1974a: 501). This was a radical proposal because the allowance was set at a rate above existing benefit levels and gave *all* single parents the security of a guaranteed basic income with the state being responsible for claiming maintenance from liable relatives. The Labour Government did not introduce such a guaranteed maintenance allowance but the Child Benefit Act 1975 made provision for additional child benefit to be paid to all single parents and increased the supplementary benefits available to children in lone parent households.

Housing allocations   The report of the Central Housing Advisory Committee (Central Housing Advisory Committee, 1969) declared:

Our wider conception of 'housing need', however, embraces more than economic circumstances. There are also social circumstances which, though often complicated by inadequate income, demand attention in their own right – the fatherless family, the family with a mentally ill mother, and that highly diverse group which are termed 'problem families'. It is not easy for a council to justify to its electorate the rehousing of families in arrears of rent, unmarried mothers or, indeed, any group which does not conform to the accepted canons of good behaviour. Yet these are often the very people (and electors) whose social needs demand attention by local authorities. (Central Housing Advisory Committee, 1969: 22)

Although the Government did not legislate to change the broad rules under which local authority housing was allocated the Central Housing Advisory Report had an impact on the practices of local government. Moreover in 1977 the Housing (Homeless Persons) Act was passed, which placed an obligation on local housing authorities to provide accommodation for homeless people. In response to claims the original bill was 'a charter for the rent dodger, scrounger and home leaver' (Mr Rees Davies, MP for Thanet West, cited in Thompson, 1988: 8), 'intentionally' and 'local connection' clauses were introduced. Nonetheless, by making exclusions more transparent and subject to a statutory process, the Act amounted to the provision of basic entitlements to housing for homeless people.

Social justice

As Glennerster (1995: 122–51) has indicated and Phillips (1999) has explained, 'simple' equality of real income appeared to be the lodestar of social democrats in the early 1970s. The term 'equality', unqualified by notions of fair acquisition, came to be used more frequently as a proxy for social justice.

In the 1940s, the welfare state was geared to the promotion of social justice through equality of status and greater equality of educational opportunity. However, the Labour movement attached the generation of social justice – in the sense of a more equal distribution of income and wealth – to the economic policies of nationalisation, the regulation of 'industry', demand management for full employment and the push for higher wages. In the 1950s common ownership of the means of production, as the route to social justice, started to recede in the minds of the Labour leadership (Macfarlane, 1998: 259). The welfare state, financed by progressive taxation, assumed greater importance as the mechanism for reducing inequalities in outcome. Moreover, new inequalities, indirectly related to the economic order, were beginning to be identified, adding to the claims made on the state and compounding the problem of 'government overload' (King, 1975).

Gender and 'race'

Until the mid-1970s, the issue of gender inequality was a muted theme in the analysis of social policy. As Wilson observed:

> The British Welfare State has been copiously discussed since its beginnings. What has never been discussed is its impact on women. Yet women are central to its purposes, and it has always cast its safety net around the housewife and mother in her home. (Wilson 1977: 170)

In the 1930s discussions about the role of women had concentrated on the inadequate recognition of 'motherhood' in the system of social welfare. The payment of family allowances to the female partner was one outcome of this 'endowment for motherhood' campaign and Eleanor Rathbone would have rejoiced at the Equal Pay Act 1970, which stated that 'like' work should receive 'like' pay. The theme of due recognition of motherhood remained influential in the early 1970s as was revealed when 'welfare feminists' successfully resisted an attempt by the Heath Government to convert family allowances into tax credits, paid to the male 'breadwinner'. Nonetheless, there was a growing appreciation that 'Beveridge principles' were unjust to women. Married women, outside the paid labour force, were not insured in their own right, women received lower sickness and unemployment benefits than men and the infamous 'half test' meant that, if a woman had not paid contributions for at least half of the years between her marriage and retirement, then she received no pension in her own right. Barbara Castle's SERPS scheme rectified some of these injustices but a more fundamental critique of state social welfare had started to unfold. Some feminists began to claim that 'Social Welfare policies amount to no less than the state organization of domestic life' (Wilson, 1977: 9). This identification of the cause of the subordination of women in the institution of the family was to produce a variety of remedies, ranging from more provision of state services to free women from their domestic role, to the payment of wages for housework.

In the 1960s the analysis of 'racial' inequality focused on what has come to be called 'direct' discrimination. Legislation designed to reduce discrimination was linked to immigration control and to policies to promote the integration of immigrants. The Race Relations Act 1965 made it unlawful to discriminate in public places. However, rather than making racial discrimination a criminal offence, a Race Relations Board was established to supervise a conciliation process involving local committees. In 1966 an Urban Programme was announced bringing together various priority area projects and the funds granted under section 11 of the 1966

Local Government Act to areas with a high proportion of immigrants. The Race Relations Act 1968 extended the 1965 legislation to cover housing, employment and commercial and public services. This extension of the scope of anti-discriminatory legislation prompted the requirement to create a positive role for government to temper the atmosphere generated by tighter immigration controls, but discrimination research also played a part. *Political and Economic Planning* sent applicants, matched on all criteria other than colour, in search of jobs and housing. In a series of applications for accommodation a West Indian was discriminated against by private landlords on 45 out of 60 occasions, on 20 out of 30 occasions by estate agents and in 14 out of 18 occasions by accommodation bureaux (Deakin, 1969: 168).

In the 1970s the developing interest in equality of outcome was reflected in the identification of 'institutional' discrimination. The idea of institutional racism rests on the assumption that if the outcomes of established policies and procedures is unequal then there must be some entrenched racism, perhaps unintended, operating through the power structure of the agency. Although the 1971 Immigration Act – with its 'patrial' and 'non-patrial' distinction – embodied institutional racism the state directed its attention to some of the 'internal' manifestations of 'secondary' discrimination. The Race Relations Act 1976 made it unlawful to apply a condition to employment, housing, etc. 'such that the proportion of persons of the victim's racial group who can comply with it is considerably smaller than the proportion of persons not of that group who can comply' (Race Relations Act, 1976, Ch. 74: 1) but these provisions did not apply to government regulatory activities such as immigration control, the administration of the prison service and the law enforcement activities of the police. The Act gave the Commission for Racial Equality, a replacement for the Race Relations Board, the power to organise a formal investigation into any organisation in which discrimination was suspected and to issue a non-discrimination notice if discrimination was confirmed. However, the notion that the opportunities of ethnic minorities could be promoted by positive discrimination received a chilly response. An idea born in the USA, positive discrimination suggested that it is necessary to give extra rights to 'racialised' groups both to compensate for past discrimination and to enhance 'social utility' by, for example, 'enriching decision making by the presence of employees from different backgrounds' (McCrudden, 1990: 144). The most radical form of such preferential treatment in the USA was the designation of quotas of jobs or places in higher education reserved for people from ethnic minorities. The 1976 Race Relations Act specifically outlawed quotas but allowed 'positive action' – a weaker form of positive discrimination – in the form of outreach activities, training initiatives, etc. (Edwards, 1995).

THE DISTRIBUTION OF INCOME AND WEALTH

The share of the top 5 per cent in total personal wealth fell in the early 1970s from 60 per cent in 1968 to 48 per cent in 1976. Overall income inequality also declined and, perhaps as a result of the Equal Pay Act 1970, the earnings of women relative to male median earnings increased. Spending on social welfare expanded significantly between 1973–4 and 1976–7: in *real* terms by 23 per cent on health care; 46 per cent on housing subsidies; 32 per cent on personal social services; 16 per cent on social security and 9 per cent on education. Labour's 1974 February manifesto had promised to 'bring about a fundamental and irreversible shift in the balance of power and wealth in favour of working people and their families' (Labour Party, 1974a: 20). Indeed, the Labour Government raised the higher rates of income tax – the top rate to 83 per cent – but, in the absence of the introduction of the promised wealth tax, the revenue obtained from the 'rich' was insufficient to fund the expansion of welfare (Dell, 2000). The Chancellor's paper on public expenditure (1976: 1) noted how, in recent years, the tax burden had 'greatly increased'. 'In 1975–76 a married man on average earnings is paying about a quarter of his earnings in income tax, compared with a tenth in 1960–61. At two-thirds average earnings, he is paying about a fifth compared with less than a twentieth'. Not only was the standard rate of income tax increased to 33 per cent but the thresholds at which tax became payable had been reduced mainly as a consequence of 'fiscal drag' – the impact of inflation on the value of tax allowances. In 1976–7 a man with two children started to pay income tax at a level of income 23 per cent lower than the tax threshold in 1965–6 (Field, 1977: 4). Nonetheless, the overall impact of taxation and social benefits on the distribution of income was significant. In 1977 the Gini coefficient had reached a low post-war point of 22 (Johnson, 1999: 21). In the same year the poverty rate, measured as the proportion of the population below half the average national income equivalised for family size, was 6 per cent – a reduction of 5 per cent since 1972 (Burgess and Propper 1999: 261).

7

State to Market: Market to State

LEAN YEARS

By 1976, the modest economic growth promoted by Labour's expansionist strategy had declined sharply. The balance of payments was in deficit, unemployment almost doubled and inflation, fuelled by another OPEC oil price hike, was 24 per cent. 'Stagflation' had hit Britain. The recession of the early 1970s had been countered by pure Keynesian techniques but the seeming failure of Keynesian economics to supply a lasting solution provided a window of opportunity for alternative economic and social approaches to attract attention.

In early 1976, a Treasury paper announced that 60 per cent of the GDP was devoted to public expenditure (Chancellor of the Exchequer, 1976: 1). It claimed:

> When world demand picks up, more resources – capital as well as manpower – will be needed for exports and investment … Unless we are prepared to see rising taxation reduce take home pay, these resources can be made available only if we keep public expenditure at roughly the same level for several years. Changing the structural distribution of resources in this way is the only means of restoring and maintaining full employment. (Chancellor of the Exchequer, 1976: 1)

The Treasury imposed cash limits on all departments but, by Autumn 1976, the value of the pound was falling fast. The Government applied for a loan from the International Monetary Fund to prevent a further run on sterling and promised additional cuts in public spending in return for the loan. The Prime Minister explained the new reality in a speech delivered in September 1976:

> The post-war world we were told would go on forever, where full employment could be guaranteed by a stroke of the Chancellor's pen … We used to think that you could just spend your way out of recession … I tell you in all candour that this

option no longer exists and in so far as it ever did exist, it only worked ... by injecting a bigger dose of inflation into the economy, followed by a higher level of unemployment. (cited in Callaghan, 1987: 426–7)

Callaghan's speech reflected influential views in circulation at the time. Bacon and Eltis (1976), for example, claimed Britain's economic problem was 'too few producers'. The 'marketed' sector was 'productive' because it created a surplus for reinvestment whereas the 'non-marketed' sector, mainly state services, supplied no such surplus and was therefore 'non-productive'. Moreover, the 'marketed' sector satisfied the wants of both the 'productive' and 'non-productive'. Accordingly, Britain's economic problem was too many 'unproductive' people and a 'productive' sector stoking inflation by demanding higher wages to compensate for the taxation they paid to support the 'unproductive'.

1976 to 1979 were svelte years for public expenditure. It fell from 45.6 per cent of GDP in 1975–6 – the figures in the 1976 Treasury paper were exaggerated – to 39.8 per cent in 1978–9. Spending on education declined from 6.4 per cent to 5.3 per cent of GDP, on the National Health Service from 4.9 per cent to 4.5 per cent, on personal social services from 1 per cent to 0.8 per cent and capital spending on housing was cut by 25 per cent (Hills, 1991). As this spending break was applied, the distributive principles dominant in 1976 were reformulated to conform to the Treasury's demand to prioritise 'expenditure designed to maintain or improve our industrial capacity' (Chancellor of the Exchequer, 1976: 2).

Having rejected the injection of more demand into the economy to reduce unemployment, the Government tried to alleviate worklessness by special measures such as the Job Creation programme, the Work Experience programme and the Youth Opportunities programme. The 'social' ministries, the Home Office and the Department of Education and Science, with their 'people changing' emphasis, were superseded by the Department of the Environment as the driving force in delivering small area selectivity. The Inner Urban Areas Act 1978 established a number of partnerships between central and local government to try to lever private capital into urban economic revival, and public expenditure on housing renewal in inner city areas was reduced (Monck and Lomas, 1980). Benn and Chitty (1996: 12) claim that 'during the last years of Labour's term of office the cause of comprehensive education slipped progressively from view' as educational debate was directed to content rather than form. In a speech at Ruskin College in 1976 Callaghan accepted that there was a concern among employers about the basic standards of educational achievement. In an attempt to steer education away from 'child centred learning' towards greater emphasis on the future economic role of children he called for a 'great debate' on education. At the same time civil servants began work on the preparation of a national curriculum. The conclusions of a Government review of housing policy also reflected the new climate of public expenditure restraint. A 'more selective and discerning approach to housing policy' adapted to 'present realities' was recommended (Secretary of State for the Environment and Secretary of State for Wales, 1977: 7). Local Housing Investment Strategies were the mechanism for delivering this new approach. Each local authority would have to present central government with an account of the local housing situation and proposals for action to justify a request for additional funds.

THE WELFARE STATE IN CRISIS?

In the late 1970s the Left began to produce its own versions of the 'too few producers' thesis thereby converting a crisis of 'collectivism' into a crisis of 'welfare capitalism' (Mishra, 1984). The dual state theory, for example, made distinctions between the 'accumulation', 'control' and 'legitimation' functions of the state. Certain state activities such as state investment in worker productivity directly helped the development of capitalism while other activities retarded its progress. 'Social expenses' (spending on the maintenance of social control) and 'social consumption' (keeping the workers happy through service provision) were necessary for social harmony under capitalism but a long-term drain on capitalist accumulation (Offe, 1984). Expansion of social expenses and social consumption costs had produced a crisis for capitalism (Wolfe, 1977).

In the mid-1980s, the centre-left supplied few convincing explanations of the economic and social difficulties of the late 1970s. However, William Robson's *Welfare State and Welfare Society* provided the basis for a later 'social democratic' analysis of the 'crisis' in state welfare. He argued that a welfare state provides services whereas a welfare society 'is what people do, feel and think about matters which bear on the general welfare' (Robson, 1976: 7). Later, David Marquand developed this theme by claiming:

> 'Keynesian social democracy' – the 'governing philosophy' of the post-war period – had broken down. It had done so because economic change had exposed its fundamental weakness: that it was a philosophy of public intervention, without a notion of the public realm or public good. Because of this, it could not provide the moral basis for the hard choices that had to be made when the economic climate turned cold; as a result, the public sector became a battleground for predatory private interests instead of the instrument of a coherent public purpose. (Marquand, 1997: 26)

He augmented his thesis with the assertion that the mechanisms on which the centre-left relied to achieve its objectives – economic planning and 'top down' redistribution by the state – lacked moral justification. The result was:

> Revisionist social democracy depended on communitarian ties, but it could not speak the language of community. All too often, it became a technocratic philosophy rather than a political one: a philosophy of social engineering rather than of argument, negotiation and persuasion ... its view of government ... was 'mechanical' not 'moral', emphasising outward changes of structure and law rather than inner changes of value and belief. (Marquand, 1990: 3)

THE CONSERVATIVE RESPONSE

In 1975, Sir Keith Joseph initiated a change in Conservative Party thinking that was to have a lasting impact. Claiming 'we are now more socialist in many ways than any other developed country outside the Communist bloc' (quoted in Young, 1991: 85), he embraced 'monetarist' economic policy. Monetarist theory insisted spending on public services 'crowded out' the private, surplus-generating economic sector by its impact on interest rates and that 'printing money' had allowed governments to postpone difficult decisions (Heald, 1983: 47). If the state simply controlled the supply of money in the economy in a predictable way, then automatic adjustments would take place in the balance of supply and demand. Eventually inflation would be driven out of the system as each worker realised an increase in wages would lead to an increase in unemployment and that he/she might be the one without a job. But, Joseph insisted, 'the unflinching control of money supply though essential is not enough' (Joseph, 1977, cited in Clarke et al., 1987: 135–6). Reform of social policy was also necessary. *In Equality* (1979) he claimed political demands for income redistribution stemmed from the base motive of envy and the aim of 'equality of results' was at odds with equality of opportunity.

> [Equality of results] implies that the tendency which exists in a society of equal opportunities for some people to make better use of them than others should be corrected by the preferential intervention of the State, so that, although some run faster than others, all shall finish in the same place. Discrimination between different kinds of citizen, absence of which is the essence of equality of opportunity, is the central feature of equality of results. (Joseph and Sumption, 1979: 31)

He mocked the idea that greater equality would produce a more harmonious society. The effect of egalitarianism 'is simply to shift the competition to another field. Instead of competing for the favour of the consumers of the fruits of their labour, men will instead compete for the favour of the State' (1979: 38–9). Joseph also claimed the relief of relative poverty, 'from which egalitarianism has derived much of its emotional force' (1979: 21), is counterproductive. Government should alleviate absolute poverty 'if it [a family] cannot afford to eat' (1979: 27). Moreover 'to the extent that confiscatory rates of tax discourage the creation of wealth the poor are actually worse off than they would be in a society of sharp contrast' (1979: 27).

Although the favoured candidate of the Right to challenge Heath for the leadership of the Conservative Party, Joseph's star fell following some unfortunate remarks on the threat to the 'human stock' of children 'born to mothers least fitted to bring children into the world and bring them up' (Joseph, 1974 cited in Denham and Garnett, 2001: 267–8). However, Margaret Thatcher, elected leader of the Conservative Party in 1975, shared Joseph's convictions. She firmly believed Hayek's *The Constitution of Liberty* provided a blueprint for reform (Ranelagh, 1991: ix) and she 'listened to Friedrich von Hayek like a schoolgirl her face glowing with attention (William Rees-Mogg, cited in Campbell, 2000: 372). Nonetheless, as 'an incremental pragmatist with convictions' (Cockett, 1995: 266), Thatcher was well aware that political constraints required a gradual approach to reform. The Conservative's 1979 manifesto was cautious in its attack on state welfare. The Conservatives, it said, wanted to work with 'the grain of human nature, helping people to help themselves and others' (1979: 3). Controlling inflation and cutting income tax were placed at the centre of the manifesto's objectives but it made few specific proposals for cutting expenditure.

STATE TO MARKET, MARKET TO STATE

Conservative social policy between 1979 and 1997 can be divided into four phases. In the first phase, lasting from 1979 to 1987, social policy was driven by a desire to cut taxation and promote self-reliance but preoccupation with the economy and trade union reform meant these aspirations lacked systematic application (Ridley, 1991: 83). Phase two, marked by the introduction of market principles into publicly financed social services, lasted from the 1987 General Election to the downfall of Margaret Thatcher. The short interlude from John Major becoming Prime Minister to the 1992 General Election appeared to indicate a change of direction towards 'One Nation Conservatism' but economic difficulties led to a fourth policy phase. This was marked by further spending restraints, the development of a 'managerial' approach to public service and, under the influence of neo-Conservatism, the promotion of 'underclass' explanations of social disadvantage.

1979–1987: CUTTING PUBLIC EXPENDITURE?

Housing

The 'right to buy' was the most fundamental welfare reform in the first phase of Conservative social policy. The Housing Act 1980 made the purchase of a local authority dwelling the individual right of a tenant resident in a council house for three years. Discounts on the market price of up to 50 per cent, later raised to 60 per cent for houses and 70 per cent for flats, were offered. Higher local authority rents, achieved by the withdrawal of government subsidies, also acted as an incentive to buy. The capital receipts generated by council house sales were used to boost improvement grants and thereby help to prevent any future requirement to build council homes due to the slum clearance. Renovation grants to private owners increased from 80,000 in 1979 to 319,000 in 1983 only to decline to 158,000 in 1987 as 'right to buy' receipts were directed elsewhere.

Social security

The announcement that pension increases would be linked only to prices meant substantial savings on projected state expenditure and, with economic growth, pension expansion could be channelled into the private sector (Pierson, 1994: 59). Additional reductions in the cost of social security were achieved by abolishing earnings-related supplements to unemployment and sickness benefits, taxing basic benefits and immediate cuts in the real value of short-term insurance benefits.

The Green Paper *Reform of Social Security: Programme for Change* (Secretary of State for Social Services, 1985a) announced three objectives to guide further reform of social security. The system should be capable of meeting 'genuine need', it should be consistent with the Government's economic policy – social security being held responsible for the present tax burden and for undermining work incentives – and it should be easier to understand and administer. Although the abolition of SERPS and its replacement by a second pension from the private sector, supported by state fiscal incentives, was the 'flagship' recommendation of the Green Paper, the White Paper *Reform of Social Security: Programme for Action* (Secretary of State for Social Services, 1985c) abandoned the plan to abolish SERPS. The Chancellor objected to the cost of the tax exemptions arising from the compulsory second pension and Margaret Thatcher believed there would be no political support for abolishing SERPS without an adequate private pension supported by tax concessions (Lawson, 1992: 590). So SERPS survived, albeit in a truncated form. Entitlement was to be based on lifetime earnings rather than best 20 years and calculated on 1 per cent of relevant earnings per annum rather than 1.25 per cent. Spouses would inherit only half rather than all of the deceased's SERPS.

The White Paper's proposals on other benefits were more in line with the recommendations of the Green Paper. Maternity Allowance was to be paid through the employer rather than the state, Supplementary Benefit was to be renamed Income Support and the existing householder/non – householder distinction in benefit entitlement was to be replaced by age-related allowances that would reduce payments to people under 25. Grants for extraordinary circumstances were to be abolished in favour of discretionary loans from a 'Social Fund'. Family Income Supplement was to be renamed Family Credit and paid through the wage packet – a proposal later rejected by the House of Lords (Levin, 1997: 148). Entitlement to Family Credit was aligned with Income Support and the withdrawal rate was set at 70 per cent rather than the 50 per cent applied to Family Income Supplement. Parents in work lost entitlement to free school meals. Eligibility for Housing Benefit was aligned with Income Support and a much sharper cut-out rate – 65 per cent compared to 40 per cent – was applied. These proposals were implemented in the 1986 Social Security Act.

Education

The 'Black' papers on education (Cox and Boyston, 1975; Cox and Dyson, 1977), with their arguments against comprehensive and 'progressive' education, had attracted support from the Conservative Party but the first eight years of Conservative power produced meagre reform. The Government revoked the requirement on local government to submit plans for comprehensive education and made it compulsory to publish information on school performance. An 'assisted places' scheme was introduced to enable less well off parents to claim part or all of the fees from a special government fund if their children attended designated private schools. Parental choice of state secondary schools was enhanced by abolishing school catchment areas and setting more generous 'standard numbers' for admission to schools.

As Secretary of State for Education Sir Keith Joseph attempted to devise a system of educational vouchers to enable parents to send their child to a school of their choice with resources automatically flowing into 'successful' schools. However, in 1983, he announced to the Conservative Party conference that 'the voucher, at least for the foreseeable future, is dead' (quoted in Chitty, 1992: 28) – assassinated, according to Seldon (1986: 37–42), by determined opposition from the civil servants in the Department of Education. Spending on education declined from 5.3 per cent of GDP in 1978/9 to 5.1 per cent in 1986/7 but the smaller number of pupils entering the system enabled class sizes to be reduced. In 1981 21.8 per cent of primary school children were taught in classes with 31 or more pupils. This had declined to 19 per cent in 1986. In secondary schools the comparable figure showed a reduction from 8.2 per cent to 6.1 per cent (Hills, 1991: 55).

Health care

The Conservatives abolished the Health Services Board, established by
Labour to restrain the growth of private health care and ended the phasing out of pay beds in the NHS. Minor tax concessions for low earners to
stimulate the growth of private health insurance were introduced and
there were big increases in prescription charges. Area Health Authorities
were phased out, general managers were appointed by District Health
Authorities and a system of competitive tendering for support services to
health care was set up. As Ranade (1997: 57) has commented 'for a radical
government committed to "rolling back the state", these changes, though
controversial, were not large'. Spending on health care, measured in
volume terms, taking into account changes in input prices such as wages,
grew at average annual rate of only 0.9 per cent (Hills, 1991: 96).

Personal social services

Margaret Thatcher's 'instinct' on the personal social services was to place
greater responsibility for care on informal networks, especially the family.
The 1979 Conservative Party manifesto stated 'In the Community, we
must do more to help people to help themselves and the family to look
after their own'. This attitude was reflected in early policy pronounce-
ments of the new Government. *Care in Action* (1981a) stressed the potential role of the voluntary sector and *Growing Older* declared that 'the
primary sources of support and care for elderly people are informal and
voluntary ... Care in the community must increasingly mean care by the
community' (DHSS, 1981b: para. 1.9).

The Government appears to have believed that, if the state withdrew
from provision, then informal welfare would develop spontaneously to
fill the vacuum. This approach was manifest in the abandonment of
central guidelines for levels of local authority provision, the devaluing of
'planning' to meet 'future' needs and year-by-year reductions in central
support for personal social service expenditure (Hills, 1991: 212, 224). In
the case of elderly people the gap to be filled by informal support was
likely to be large as the number of people aged over 75 was projected to
increase by 722,000 between 1981 and 2001 (Rossiter and Wicks, 1982: 9).
In the event the shortfall in care was met, not by 'informal' welfare, but
by the rapid expansion of private sector residential care. In 1980 people
with a low income living in private and voluntary residential and nursing
homes had their eligibility to claim their care fees from the social
security system clearly established (Fimister, 1995: 11). Despite the
capping of the residential care costs payable by the state the changes in
the social security rules coincided with a rapid expansion of beds in
the 'independent' residential and nursing home sector. Nursing home

provision grew by 400 per cent and residential homes increased by
334 per cent between 1980 and 1991 (Wistow et al., 1994). Supplementary
benefit/income support spending to assist people in these homes
increased from £10 million in 1979 to over £1000 million in 1989 (DoH,
1989: para. 8.5). Other 'special needs' groups experienced a similar
growth in private residential care – places for people with a learning
difficulty increased sevenfold between 1978 and 1990 and private home
places for people with a mental illness increased from 593 new places in
1977 to 2660 new places in 1990.

Local government

> Next to trade unions, Thatcherism's greatest bugbear has been 'local
> government'.
>
> (Letwin, 1992: 159)

In 1979, despite the subordinate constitutional position of local government, local autonomy was still at least a semi-sacred cow of Britain's
unwritten constitution. Local government was regarded as different
from other agencies involved in service provision because local councillors were elected by universal suffrage and local government derived
part of its finance from a locally imposed tax – the rate. However,
Margaret Thatcher believed local government was the principal culprit
in promoting spending above the level that the nation could afford. The
Local Government Planning and Land Act 1980 reduced central support to those local authorities with high needs and high resources –
mainly the large cities under Labour control. Many local authorities
responded to these cuts by increasing the rates and there followed a
series of attempts by central government to curtail local expenditure.
One such device was to 'fine' specific local authorities for 'overspend-
ing' by grant penalties thus breaching a long-standing convention that
'local authorities could spend what they thought to be necessary, provided only that they raised local taxes to cover expenditure over and
above their grants' (Newton and Karran, 1985: 117). Some local authorities met these fines with a combination of increased borrowing and yet
higher rates. This central/local conflict produced a substantial reduction in central government support (down in real terms by 30 per cent
between 1978/9 and 1986/7) but greater use of service charges and a
big increase in the rates (Douglas and Lord, 1986: 24–5). The Rates Act
1984 closed one route to higher spending by awarding the Government
the power to cap the rate set by local councillors. Nonetheless, the
option of higher borrowing and 'creative accounting' to finance extra
spending remained.

Taxation

The Conservative Manifesto declared 'We shall cut income tax at all levels'. Given this promise the decision, made in 1979, to increase VAT from 12.5 per cent on luxury items and 8 per cent on other goods and services to a standard 15 per cent, was a masterstroke. This VAT increase, together with privatisation proceeds, the expanding revenues from North Sea Oil and an increase in the level of NICs allowed cuts in other forms of taxation despite the rapidly mounting social security bill for unemployment. Between 1979 and 1983 the basic rate of Income Tax was cut from 33 per cent to 27 per cent, the highest rate was reduced from 98 per cent to 60 per cent and personal tax allowances were increased in real terms. The top rate of Inheritance Tax was reduced by 10 per cent and the main rate of Corporation Tax by 17 per cent.

1987–1990: BRINGING THE MARKET TO THE STATE

Thatcher declared that the 1987 Conservative Party Manifesto 'went to the heart of my convictions' (Thatcher, 1995: 572). In her third term she would:

> give ordinary people the kind of choice and quality in public services that the rich already enjoyed ... Conservative policies must liberate and empower those whom socialism traps and then contemptuously ignores. (Thatcher, 1995: 572)

Some academics have attempted to give intellectual coherence to the reforms introduced in health, education, 'social housing' and the personal social services during the late 1980s by employing the concept of a 'quasi-market'. According to Bartlett and Le Grand (1993: 10) quasi-markets are 'markets' 'because they replace monopolistic state providers with competitive independent ones' but they are 'quasi' because 'they differ from conventional markets in a number of key ways'.

> ... all the organisations are not necessarily out to maximise their profits: nor are they necessarily privately owned ... consumer purchasing power is not expressed in money terms in a quasi-market. Instead, either it takes the form of an 'earmarked' budget or voucher confined to the purchase of a specific service allocated to users, or it is centralised in a single state purchasing agency. Also it is important to note that, in most cases, it is not the direct user who exercises the choices concerning purchasing decisions, instead those choices are often delegated to a third party, such as a social services department or care-manager in community care, and a GP or a health authority in health care. (Bartlett and Le Grand, 1993: 10)

The notion of a 'quasi-market' captures, in part, a basic rationale underlying the Conservatives' 1987–1990 reforms but there was a range of sub-texts contained in the specifics of each reform.

Education

Kenneth Baker, the Secretary of State for Education declared his aim was 'to achieve the results of a voucher scheme, namely real choice for parents and schools that responded to that choice by improving themselves' (Baker, 1993: 212). Indeed, Baker's Education Reform Act 1988 was an attempt to mimic the voucher idea while avoiding the pitfalls identified by civil servants opposed to vouchers (Seldon, 1986: 37–42). School budgets for staff, premises and services became the responsibility of individual schools and this delegated budget was based on a formula reflecting the number of pupils in a school. The admission of pupils to a particular school was to be determined by a standard number, not to be lower than the number of pupils admitted in 1979, thereby introducing competition between schools for pupils where there was surplus local capacity. Local management gave schools substantial autonomy from local government but greater independence could be acquired by opting out of the local educational system to become a grant-maintained school. To obtain grant-maintained status a majority of parents would have to vote for the change following a resolution by the Governors or a petition from at least 20 per cent of the parents of children in the school.

The idea of a National Curriculum had been floating within the Department of Education for many years (Glennerster, 1995: 198) but the proposed move to a more market-orientated approach meant the curriculum vacuum had to be filled. Markets can generate 'value pluralism' and the Government was concerned that 'traditional values' were already being undermined in certain schools. Margaret Thatcher asserted:

> Children who need to be able to count and multiply are learning anti-racist mathematics – whatever that may be. Children who need to be able to express themselves in clear English are being taught political slogans. Children who need to be taught respect for traditional moral values are being taught that they have an inalienable right to be gay. (Thatcher, 1987)

The 1988 Education Act placed a duty on the Secretary of State for Education to establish a National Curriculum for all state schools and set out 'attainment targets' by which the performance of children at the ages of 7, 11, 14 and 16 would be measured. The 1988 Local Government Act prohibited the promotion of homosexuality in schools.

Housing

Reflecting on housing policy in 1987, Michael Heseltine noted the £20 billion backlog in local authority house repairs. Heseltine's solution was to sell the remaining council homes to housing trusts, housing associations or other 'approved' landlords to enable private finance to supply the resources necessary to meet the repairs backlog (Heseltine, 1987: 208). These ideas were incorporated in the White Paper *Housing: The Government's Proposals* (Department of the Environment, 1987) and given legislative backing in the 1988 Housing Act and the 1989 Local Government and Housing Act. Under this legislation local authorities would become 'enablers' of housing provision, helping other agencies to provide and manage dwellings. Three mechanisms to supplement the right to buy – higher rents, 'Tenant's Choice' and Housing Action Trusts – would divest local government of its housing stock. Incorporating the cost of Housing Benefit into each local government housing revenue account would push up rents. This would ensure that most housing revenue accounts would be in deficit thereby giving central government the power to control rents by variations in housing benefit subsidy. Tenant's Choice allowed independent landlords to acquire local authority housing if tenants voted in favour of the transfer. Housing Action Trusts were to be set up by the Government to acquire local authority land and property, refurbish the dwellings and sell them on to a range of 'alternative' landlords. It was envisaged that housing associations – called 'independent' landlords in the 1987 White Paper – would be major participants in the transfer of the local authority stock. The rents charged by private landlords were decontrolled and housing associations were expected to rely more on private finance and to shift their rents closer to market rents. Nicholas Ridley, the Secretary of State for the Environment at the time, explained the rationale of this move to market rents.

> I was determined to weaken the almost incestuous relationship between some councils and their tenants. Absurdly low rents, and a monopoly position in providing rented housing, allowed some councils to make their tenants entirely dependent on them ... I saw the solution as being to provide housing benefit on a sufficiently generous scale to enable all tenants to be in a position to pay their rents, and at the same time to bring rents up towards market levels. This would put all three classes of landlord ... into the same competitive position, giving tenants a choice. (Ridley, 1991: 86–8)

Health care

In education and housing power in the 'quasi-market' was to reside with the state-supported consumer. Parental choice would determine the

finances of schools and schools unable to satisfy the wants of parents
would go out of business. The fortunes of 'social housing' providers
would depend, in part, on the tenant's choice of landlord with Housing
Benefit acting as a sort of 'portable voucher' by helping to pay the rent of
low income households. The quasi-markets introduced into health care
and the personal social services were different in that they relied on
'quasi-consumers' to do the purchasing.

Mrs Thatcher was not fond of the NHS. She had considered reform
before the 1983 and 1987 elections but, aware of the popularity of the
service, backed away from including any proposals in her manifestos.
Then, in January 1988, she suddenly announced a review of the NHS by
a small cabinet committee. The committee considered several options,
including floating the middle class into private health insurance through
tax concessions, but eventually the chosen reforms were based on the
'internal' market idea first put forward by Professor Alian Enthoven
(1988). The White Paper *Working For Patients* (Department of Health, 1989)
declared that the future task of District Health Authorities would be to
survey the range of options available to secure the best health care in an
area and then achieve 'value for money' by making appropriate arrangements with suppliers. These suppliers could be 'arms length' public
provider units, independent NHS Trusts holding nominal capital assets or
the private sector. GPs working in practices of over 11,000 patients could
elect to hold their own budgets and purchase a limited range of services –
up to a cost of £5000 for any patient – from the independent suppliers. The
only trace of the idea of tax concessions to move part of the cost of health
care to private insurance was to allow people over 65 to offset the cost of
private insurance against their tax liability. The purchaser/provider proposals of the White Paper were given legislative authority in the National
Health Service and Community Care Act 1990.

Personal social services

In response to two critical reports on community care (Audit Commission
1985 and 1986) Sir Roy Griffiths was appointed 'to review the way in
which public funds are used to support community care policy and to
advise … on options which would improve the use of these funds as a contribution to more effective community care' (Griffiths, 1988: 1). His report
was damning. 'In few areas can the gap between political rhetoric and
policy on the one hand, or between policy and reality in the field have
been so great' (Griffiths, 1988: iv). There was a lack of co-ordination
between the various agencies involved in supplying community care and
the system of paying for residential care by 'open-ended' income support
payments – when care in the community was cash limited – created 'perverse' incentives. Griffiths' remedy was that 'one authority should be

responsible for assessing needs and organising suitable care' and that local government was 'best placed to assess local needs, set local priorities and monitor performance' (Griffiths, 1988: vii). In future, each local authority should draw up a plan demonstrating how it would co-operate with other agencies, including the private and voluntary sector. In implementing this plan local authorities should act as 'enablers' rather than 'providers' using funds from an earmarked community care budget. People with the necessary resources should pay the full cost of their services. Griffiths' main recommendations were given legislative authority in the National Health Service and Community Care Act 1990. Income support funds for the payment of nursing home and residential home fees were transferred to local authorities that became purchasers of a range of services on behalf of social service 'customers'.

Local government

The Community Charge – a uniform levy on all the electors in an area with a reduced rate for the poor – was aimed at reducing the political impediments to lower local government expenditure that had bedevilled the Government in the 1980s. The 1987 Conservative Party manifesto stated that community charge 'should encourage people to take a greater interest in the policies of their local council and in getting value for money' (Conservative Party, 1987). Nicholas Ridley, the Minister responsible for the community charge legislation, put the matter more directly:

> The second defect [of the rates] was the effect of rates rebates for the less well-off ... By the 1980s these rebates had had the effect on average of leaving less than half the population paying full rates. But that average concealed the fact that in some areas in the cities as few as 18 per cent or 20 per cent of the residents paid full rates. This had enabled high-spending Labour councils, like Liverpool, Lambeth and Newcastle, to levy a very high rate, knowing that most of their supporters would not have to pay, although they benefited from the spending. (Ridley, 1991: 121–2)

The Community Charge was introduced in Scotland in 1989 and in England and Wales in 1990. Changes in taxation and social security produce winners and losers. In the past Mrs Thatcher had been careful to ensure that the losers were gradually phased out of entitlement usually by ensuring that any reductions applied only to new claimants. The phased introduction of the community charge – quickly to become known by the Labour Party tag of 'poll tax' – presented greater problems in that everyone faced a demand for local taxation on an annual basis. Schemes were devised to provide safety nets for the very poor and to phase in the new tax but the impact of these measures was to nullify the overall argument in favour of the poll tax. When the first bills were sent out a substantial number of people were losers not least because some local authorities, aware this unpopular tax was associated with the Conservatives, increased their expenditure. Unfortunately for Mrs Thatcher, the Ribble Valley constituency, normally a solid Conservative seat, contained a large number of losers. The Conservatives lost the Ribble Valley by-election in 1990 on a swing of 24.8 per cent to the Liberal Democrats. Leading Conservatives believed that the poll tax was 'hated' and 'it was clear that so long as Margaret Thatcher remained, so would the poll tax' (Lawson, 1992: 1001). The move to unseat the Prime Minister gained momentum.

The poll tax attracted all the media attention but the Local Government and Housing Act 1989 was of more lasting importance in the subordination of local government. The controls established in the 1980s had given central government some control of revenue expenditure but the lack of robust curbs on capital expenditure enabled 'creative accounting' to be used as a way of avoiding revenue cuts (Stanton, 1996: 11). The Local Government and Housing Act provided a rigorous definition of capital expenditure, brought all forms of capital expenditure into a single system and provided central government with a mechanism for setting a limit to the capital spending of individual local authorities. Thus an important source of local government autonomy was blocked and central government gained tight control of local government finance.

Taxation and social security

The 1988 Budget cut the higher rate of income tax and inheritance tax to 40 per cent and reduced the standard rate of income tax to 25 per cent. Personal allowances were raised and, in an attempt to boost the status of marriage, the married man's allowance was increased. Professor Arthur Laffer's theory that high rates of tax reduced tax revenue by their impact on incentives and tax avoidance provided part of the rationale of these tax cuts for the affluent. Some of the lost revenue was recouped by restricting tax relief on mortgage interest to mortgages of £30,000 per property rather than per person, by reducing the tax advantages of 'perks' such as company cars and by aligning rates of capital gains tax with those of income tax.

Single parents

Between 1981 and 1990 the number of lone parents increased by 400,000 and the cost of their state benefits increased from £1750 million to

£3600 million (Maclean, 1998: 227). Influenced by Charles Murray's allegations that the growth in single parenthood was caused by availability of benefits to support lone mothers (Murray, 1988; Thatcher 1995: 561), Margaret Thatcher turned her attention to the system of child support. On the assumption that a man is more likely to provide for the family in which he is living rather than the family he has left, British social policy had allowed the first family to claim support from the state leaving the main breadwinner to sustain the second family. The Child Support Act 1991, initiated by Margaret Thatcher but implemented by John Major, reversed this assumption. It set up a Child Support Agency with responsibility for assessing and collecting maintenance according to a formula that presumed that the first family had priority entitlement to the income of an absent parent.

1990–1992: A CLASSLESS SOCIETY?

John Major's election as Prime Minister by the Conservative Party seemed to indicate a return to 'middle-way' conservatism associated with Harold Macmillan. Major stated that the welfare state was 'an integral part of the British instinct', and that he wanted to create 'a classless society'. Part of the value of Child Benefit, which had declined in the Thatcher era, was restored and a higher rate was paid to the first child. In a reversal of Thatcher's policy of resisting legal claims for compensation, £40 million was allocated to.help haemophiliacs who had been infected by contaminated blood products and a new Disability Working Allowance was introduced (Timmins, 1995: 480). The controversial internal market reforms required resources to lubricate their implementation and Education spending rose from 4.8 per cent of GDP in 1989/90 to 5.3 per cent in 1992/3 while health care and personal social service expenditure increased from 5.7 per cent to 6.8 per cent. Expenditure on social security also increased – from 10.7 per cent to 13.2 per cent of GDP – but this was 'demand driven' with expenditure on unemployment-related benefits doubling from £4.5 billion in 1989/90 to £9 billion in 1992/3 (Fleming and Oppenheimer, 1996) as the economy went into recession. The Community Charge was replaced by the lower and more progressive Council Tax based on each property being placed in one of eight bands according to its value. Discounts were made available to one-person and poorer households. However, the most important aspect of the new tax was not its form but its amount. In 1991, using revenue raised by increasing VAT to 17 per cent, central grants to local government were increased to keep the Council Tax at a modest level.

As the term 'quasi-market' suggests the internal markets introduced by Margaret Thatcher were, in some respects, at odds with the free market in welfare advocated by the radical right. The majority of health care remained publicly financed and the system of 'formula funding' for schools did not permit parents to add their own income to state funding to purchase a place at a better school. Nonetheless quasi-markets could be interpreted as a prelude to full markets – an interpretation that the Labour Party was keen to disseminate especially with regard to health care. The Citizen's Charter, launched in mid-1991, was the centrepiece of John Major's attempt to allay public anxiety about privatisation and marketisation and to inject an element of 'civic conservatism' into Margaret Thatcher's market philosophy. It portrayed wider competition, the management of public services to achieve performance targets set by the Government, information on standards and better redress of grievances as mechanisms for achieving higher standards of public service provision.

1992–1997: BACK TO BASICS?

The image of the Conservatives as the low tax party was the cornerstone of their 1992 election campaign and the 1992 Budget fortified this image by introducing a 20 per cent band of income tax on the first £2000 of taxable income. However, the budget deficit, forecast at £28 billion before the General Election, reached £50.2 billion in 1993/4 (Wilcox, 1997: 88). Immediate reductions in public expenditure to bring the budget closer to balance were difficult to achieve. The NHS reforms were expensive to implement and public suspicion that the service was 'not safe in Conservative hands' (Willetts, 1992: 137) needed soothing by cash. The changes in the educational system had removed local government from its dominant position as a distributor of resources leaving central government more exposed to the unpopularity associated with spending cuts. The 1988 Housing Act had set up an open ended commitment to use Housing Benefit to cushion the move to market rents with the result that expenditure on Housing Benefit soared from £4,059 million in 1988/9 to £10,440 million in 1993/4. The budget deficit was bridged by freezing income tax allowances, increasing NICs from 9 to 10 per cent, imposing VAT on fuel and reducing the value of the Married Couple's Allowance and tax relief on mortgage interest (Giles and Johnson, 1994: 3). These tax increases caused discontent in the Right of the party. In 1993 Michael Portillo, then Chief Secretary to the Treasury, announced a fundamental review of public expenditure to examine programmes 'where better targeting can be achieved, or from which the public sector can withdraw altogether' (Hansard, 8 February 1993: col. 683).

Three themes dominated social policy between 1992 and 1997: more responsive public services, the continued implementation and enhancement of quasi-markets and 'back to basics'. The 1992 Conservative Party manifesto continued the theme of the Citizen's Charter; public services had to become more consumer orientated. In the foreword to the manifesto John Major stated:

I do not believe the answer to every problem is simply for government to dig deeper in your pocket. I believe it often lies in changing the way government works; in making it respond to you. (Conservative Party, 1992)

Major's charterism attracted little attention in the election campaign and, although elements of the proposals such as published school league tables of attainment were of lasting importance, the Citizen's Charter gradually declined as the 'big idea' of government policy.

Education

Education remained high on the political agenda but initially choice and diversity lost ground to centralisation. Sixth-forms and further education colleges were stripped away from local councils and brought under the control of a new government quango, the Further Education Training Council. The 1993 Education Act promoted the establishment of more grant-maintained schools and created the Funding Agency for Schools with the task of monitoring and developing opted-out schools. As the General Election approached and the Labour leadership's commitment to comprehensive education waned the willingness of the Conservatives to endorse selection increased. The White Paper *Self-Government for Schools* declared that in 'too many places a comprehensive is the only choice, and some have not succeeded in meeting the full range of needs' (Department for Education and Employment, 1996: 36). Therefore 'to encourage diversity and choice' proposals were put forward to facilitate the creation of more grammar schools and to give greater freedom to schools to select pupils. The path for existing grant maintained secondary schools to become grammar schools would be made easier and the Funding Agency for Schools would be given the power to set up grammar schools. All schools would be encouraged to use powers to select up to 15 per cent of pupils on ability or aptitude in specific subjects and grant maintained schools would be able to introduce up to 50 per cent selection by 'ability or aptitude in one or more subjects or by general ability' (Department for Education and Employment 1996: 44). The Conservatives lost office before these proposals could be implemented.

Health care

John Major was highly sensitive to the vulnerability of the Conservatives on the healthcare issue and hence the implementation of the internal market proceeded with caution. The division between purchasers and providers was smoothly accomplished and the role of GPs as fundholders was enhanced. Nonetheless, the impact of the purchaser/provider split was modest. The notion of a quasi-market suggests that uncompetitive providers of health care should lose their contracts but such events were rare and purchasers and providers worked together to manage the market (Propper and Bartlett, 1997: 114). As Bartlett et al. (1998) have commented:

> Paradoxically, the ideological commitment to markets resulted in a transformation from a 'planned economy' of welfare towards a set of arrangements which had more in common with models of market socialism than with free market capitalism. (Bartlett et al., 1998: 1)

Political debate focused on the 'bureaucratic cost' of the new system as the number of general and senior managers increased by 133 per cent between 1990 and 1995 (Le Grand, 1998: 81). The Labour Party also argued that the ability of patients in fund-holding practices to receive treatment in hospital earlier than those in non-fundholding practices signalled the beginnings of a 'two tier' service.

Personal social services

Concern about its impact on the poll tax meant that implementation of the community care dimensions of the 1990 National Health Service and Community Care Act was phased over three years. The most significant phase was introduced in April 1993 when funds to meet the anticipated costs of new demands on residential and nursing home care were transferred from the central social security budget to local government. In order to ensure that local authorities moved from a provider to a purchasing/ 'enabling' role, 85 per cent of the transferred revenue had to be spent on services bought from the independent sector. Nonetheless, a clear division between purchasers and providers in the delivery of personal social services was not achieved. This was formally recognised in the White Paper *Social Services: Achievements and Challenge* (Department of Health, Welsh Office, 1997).

> Local authorities are also currently direct providers of care services. The Government does not however believe that this is a function for which they are well suited, and indeed the evidence suggests this may not be a cost effective use of their resources. (Department of Health, Welsh Office, 1997: 16)

The Government proposed to legislate in order to make it clear that the power of local government to provide residential care, home helps and home care should be used 'only where an authority can show the need to use it after a rigorous and objective review of independent sector alternatives' (Department of Health, Welsh Office, 1997: 17).

DISTRIBUTIVE PRINCIPLES IN 1997

A market in labour

In the late 1970s the state had intervened directly in the primary distribution of resources in numerous ways: prices and incomes policies, the ownership of industry, demand management, setting minimum wages in certain industries and policies for the regions. During the 1980s and 1990s this intervention was curtailed. One of Mrs Thatcher's first acts was to abandon direct state intervention in prices and incomes and replace it with the 'Medium Term Financial Strategy'. This set targets for the supply of money in the hope pay negotiators would adjust their behaviour in the knowledge that 'within a given money supply (provided that the government sticks to it), the more taken out in higher pay, the less available for investment, and the smaller the number of jobs' (Thatcher, 1993: 94). The role of Wage Councils in setting minimum wages in selected industries was gradually eroded prior to their abolition in 1993. Special assistance for the English regions was scaled down and the available resources more narrowly targeted.

Mrs Thatcher regarded excessive trade union power as 'poison' injected into British industry (Thatcher, 1993: 98). The following legislative measures were made between 1980 and 1990:

- the 'closed shop' became illegal;
- state benefits to those on strike were withdrawn;
- legal picketing was curtailed;
- compulsory ballots before a strike were introduced;
- unions became liable for damages arising out of certain forms of industrial action;
- secondary action affecting industries not party to a dispute was outlawed and trade unions were not allowed to discipline members for non-participation in industrial action.

These reforms, combined with privatisation and the impact of high unemployment, severely restrained the ability of organised labour to influence the operations of the labour market. Given the feebleness of the unions it is hardly surprising that membership declined by 3 per cent per year in the 1980s (Standing, 1999: 198).

What was the impact of the enhanced role of the market on the distribution of income? Having declined in the period 1968 to 1978, the relationship between the top decile of male earnings and the lowest decile increased from 2.4 to 3.3 between 1978 and 1996. The comparable gap in female earnings grew from 2.3 to 3 (Hills, 1998: 27). Overall, the proportion of the population with market incomes less than 50 per cent of the median increased from 18 per cent in 1979 to 27 per cent in 1991 (Mule, 2000: 111). The top decile of women earners increased their share relative to male median earnings whereas the share of the bottom decile of female earners remained static (Atkinson, 2000: 355) – a salutary reminder to those who ignore class in examining gender relationships. The number of two-earner couples increased rapidly between 1975 and 1993 and, as Johnson (1999: 23) has explained, 'married women's employment tends to be highest among the wives of relatively well-paid men, and wives' earnings tend to be positively correlated with those of their husbands'. The 1980s and 1990s were also marked by the decline in some high wage industries such as mining and their replacement by jobs in the lower wage service sector, an increase in the 'premiums' for skills and educational qualifications and a rise in self-employment, which contains a wide variety of earnings (Johnson, 1999: 17–23; Schmitt, 1994).

The abandonment of full employment as a policy goal meant that officially recorded unemployment increased from 4.1 per cent in 1979 to 11.1 per cent in 1986, declined to 5.8 per cent in 1990, then grew to 10.3 in 1993 before declining to 6.9 per cent in 1996. However, 'real' unemployment was camouflaged in the 1990s by the transfer of people from the unemployment registers to various forms of disability benefits. Lack of work was not evenly distributed between households; the proportion of households without someone in work increased from 9 per cent in 1979 to 18 per cent in 1997 (Hills, 1998: 31).

Changes in primary income distribution can also be explored through an examination of the Office of National Statistics' *Economic Trends* series although caution must be exercised in interpreting this data because of the numerous changes in the ways the statistics have been compiled. In 1978 the poorest decile of two-adult households with children received a work-derived income of 12.1 per cent of the income of the highest decile of similar households whereas the second lowest decile received 27.5 per cent. By 1995/6 the lowest decile received only 4.8 per cent of the income of the highest decile whereas the second lowest decile received 5.9 per cent – a very large increase in 'market-generated' inequality.

Universality and selectivity

The role of insurance benefits in social security was eroded in the 1980s and 1990s. The decision to increase the state pension only in line with prices meant its value, relative to average incomes, fell from 47 per cent in 1979 to 37 per cent in 1990 (Hills, 1998: 33). In real terms Unemployment Benefit remained static but declined from 36 per cent of average income in 1983 to 28 per cent in 1994 (Hills, 1998: 33). Eligibility rules excluded more people from benefits with the young unemployed, those with variable work histories and the self-employed hit particularly hard (Goodman et al., 1997: 223). Child Benefit declined in value in the 1980s but was briefly boosted by John Major's decision to increase it for the oldest child. The erosion of universal benefits in relative terms led to a greater reliance on means tested benefits. In 1979 48 per cent of out of work claimants were on income support compared to 68 per cent in 1993. The number of claimants of Housing Benefit increased from 1.5 million in 1979 to 4.5 million in 1995 and the recipients of Family Income Supplement/Family Credit increased from 85,000 to 608,000 in the same period. This growth in the reliance on means tested benefits for the non-elderly population was accompanied by a shift towards making the means tested benefits more selective. This was accomplished through lower eligibility thresholds – the exception being Family Credit – plus steeper cut-out rates, which produced quicker exits for those in the 'poverty trap' but sharper work disincentives for those still caught.

Area selectivity and 'challenge' funding

The Conservative's distrust of local government was reflected in inner city policy where planned expenditure by local government was substituted by private sector investment (Blackman, 1995: 43). The immediate cuts made to urban programmes when Margaret Thatcher first became Prime Minister suggests that she intended to withdraw the state from engagement in the 'inner city problem' but the riots in the summer of 1981 prompted a rethink. As Michael Heseltine, the Secretary of State for the Environment at the time, said, 'amid the personal tragedy and public disorder, something good emerged, because we were forced to rethink our strategy for the inner cities' (cited in Boyle, 1989: 31). The local authority urban programme was directed more firmly to economic projects and capital investment although grants to assist ethnic minority communities under Section 11 of the 1966 Local Government Act continued. Twenty-five Enterprise Zones were established in the early 1980s based on the premise of stimulating entrepreneurial activity by making capital expenditure tax deductible, abolishing planning controls and granting exemption from paying rates. Later, Urban Development Corporations became the centrepiece of the Conservative approach to inner-city regeneration. They were directly accountable to central government and commanded large resources, spent mainly on property-led urban redevelopment.

The return of Michael Heseltine to the Department of the Environment in 1990 gave the department the political clout to take control of the inner city agenda. Heseltine announced the launch of City Challenge whereby local authorities would submit bids for resources from a fund established by top-slicing the urban programme. This was followed in 1993 by the Single Regeneration Budget, which brought together 20 separate urban initiatives into a single programme. Like City Challenge, the available resources would be distributed according to the quality of the bids – as perceived by the Minister – and organisations other than local government would be able to take the lead in submitting schemes (Atkinson and Moon, 1994: 27). Other 'challenge' programmes emerged. 'Regional Challenge' related to European Union structural funds, 'Estates Renewal Challenge' to the transfer of local authority housing estates to the private sector and 'Capital Challenge' to mainstream capital spending by local government (Oatley, 1998: 13).

Need and desert

In the 1970s 'need' became the dominant distributive principle used in the social welfare system with 'desert' relegated to the sidelines. In the 1980s and 1990s, under the influence of neo-Conservative writers such as Charles Murray, 'desert' made a comeback. In his *In Pursuit of Happiness and Good Government* Murray asserted, 'The state's role in enabling the pursuit of happiness depends ultimately on nurturing not individuals, but the associations they form' (Murray, 1988: 260). Affiliations, he argued, are not contractual but develop through 'small step' interactions and are based on mutual respect for norms, on people fulfilling the obligations involved in being a good father, good mother, good neighbour and good friend. According to Murray, state welfare 'takes the trouble out of things' and thereby reduces the importance of duty in the maintenance of stable communities. Also, by mitigating the consequences of bad behaviour, state welfare undermines the self-respect derived from the correct performance of esteemed roles

So how are we to construct society so that anyone, no matter what his gifts, can reach the age of seventy, look back on his life, and be able to say it has been a happy life, filled with deep and justified satisfactions. The answer is clear, no matter what his gifts, he will, in a properly run society, be able to say things such as,
'I was a good parent to my children,'
'I was a good neighbor'
'I always pulled my own weight'
and that he lived among people who respected those achievements. (Murray, 1988: 282–3)

Murray claimed the 'perverse incentives' introduced by the state had created an 'underclass'. His solution was to abolish the 'assistance' elements of the welfare state so that 'little platoons' of like-minded, mutually obliged people could re-form.

In October 1993 John Major told the Conservative Party Conference 'it is time to return to core values, time to get back to basics … to accepting responsibility for yourself and your family and not shuffling it off on other people and the state'. Major's version of 'back to basics' was restrained; 'He sensed the dangers of investing [the idea] with a personal morality or a "moral majority" flavour' (Seldon, 1998: 403). Other cabinet members, taking their cue from Margaret Thatcher (Thatcher, 1995: 543–64), were more robust. They linked 'back to basics' to a national moral decline and associated this decline with the 'perverse incentives' of state welfare and the increase in single parenthood. Peter Lilley announced to the 1993 Conservative Party Conference that he had a 'little list, who never would be missed, of ladies who get pregnant just to jump the housing list'. John Redwood, having visited an estate in Wales with a high proportion of single parent families, declared that single parenthood was 'one of the biggest social problems of our day' (cited in Child Poverty Action Group, 1993).

An outbreak of sex scandals soon beached 'back to basics' and the Conservative Party was portrayed as having double standards – the rich taking the pleasure and the poor receiving the blame. Nonetheless, the theme remained a strong undercurrent in the social programmes of the Major administration and was at the core of attempts to curb public expenditure. A target of £320 million in annual savings was set for the Child Support Agency. The rapid growth in unemployment in the early 1980s had prompted the Conservatives to develop special employment and training schemes but, in deference to the market, these schemes 'became explicitly linked to the general strategy of reducing wage expectations and increasing work incentives' (Finn 2001: 74). Starting with the Restart programme, established in 1986, Conservative policy became more concerned with constructing an embryonic 'workfare' programme based on dovetailing unemployed people into the low paid jobs that the service sector had started to generate (Peck, 2001: 272). Jobseeker's Allowance, introduced in 1996, was the culmination of this approach. Jobseeker's Allowance was intended to be 'a means of support while an unemployed person looks for work, not an income for a lifestyle divorced from work' (Department of Employment/Department of Social Security, 1994: 10). Entitlement to Unemployment Benefit, without a test of means, was reduced to six months and the payment of Jobseeker's Allowance became conditional on compliance with the instructions of an employment service official. Such officials had the power to issue a 'Jobseeker's Directive' requiring the unemployed person, as a benefit condition, to seek work in a particular way and to participate in job search programmes.

The 1996 Housing Act represented the clearest attempt to apply 'underclass' theory to social policy. The 1977 Housing (Homeless Persons) Act had placed a duty on local authority housing departments to secure accommodation for homeless people. This was interpreted to mean that local authorities had to provide a *secure* tenancy (local authority or housing association accommodation) for those designated as homeless under the Act. Politicians and academics who had absorbed Murray's 'underclass' theory alleged that the 1977 Act provided a 'perverse incentive' for young women to become pregnant in order to qualify for social housing via the fasttrack homelessness route. According to Ridley 'a young lady with a child is in "priority housing need" – one without is not. It became a way of living for some to have one or more children by unknown men in order to qualify for a council house' (1991: 91). The Green Paper *Access to Local Authority and Housing Association Tenancies* (Department of the Environment, 1995) proposed to end this 'perverse incentive' by redefining homelessness to mean 'no accommodation whatsoever', providing only temporary accommodation for homeless people and ensuring that the homeless did not receive priority for rehousing. In the event the 1996 Housing Act did not change the statutory definition of homelessness but it did ensure that homeless people would not receive priority in securing a local authority or housing association tenancy.

THE DISTRIBUTION OF INCOME AND WEALTH

Income

The injection of market principles into the supply and demand for labour produced greatly increased inequality in the 1980s and 1990s. Did the operation of state welfare mitigate this increase in 'market' inequality? Assessed in terms of poverty indicators, it did not. If poverty is defined as less than 50 per cent of mean incomes then the proportion of working age people living in poverty (after housing costs) increased from 7 per cent in 1979 to 19 per cent in 1995/6 (Department of Social Security Analytical Services Division, 1999). Using the same definition, the proportion of *children* living in poverty increased from 10 per cent to 34 per cent in the some period (Department of Social Security Analytical Services Division, 1999). Absolute poverty also increased with the income of the poorest tenth of the population being 8 per cent lower in real terms in 1994/5 than in 1979 (Hills, 1998: 11, but see Green, 1988: 20 for a different interpretation).

Despite the 64 per cent real increase in average pensioner incomes between 1979 and 1997 (Department of Social Security, 2000: para. 1.2) the proportion of elderly people in relative poverty increased from 17 per cent to 28 per cent. The income of the bottom quintile of pensioners increased by 35 per cent in real terms between 1979 and 1997/8 but the income of the top quintile increased by 80 per cent (Department of Social

Table 7.1   *Income of Selected Deciles as a Percentage of 'Top' Decile: Households with Children, 1996/7*

	Lowest Decile	2nd Lowest	3rd Lowest	4th Lowest
Original income	4	7	12	19
Original income plus cash benefits	12	16	20	25
Disposable income	14	20	23	28
Income after indirect taxation	11	17	19	25
Final income (with value of 'in kind' services)	25	29	30	34
Equivalised disposable income	13	19	23	27

Source: Adapted from Studdard, N. (1998) 'The effects of taxes and benefits on household income: 1996/7' *Economic Trends*, No. 553, April, London: Stationery Office.

Table 7.2   *Income of Selected Deciles as a Percentage of 'Top' Decile: Two adults with children, 1978*

	Lowest Decile	2nd Lowest	3rd Lowest	4th Lowest
Original income (£)	12	28	34	39
Original income plus cash benefits	24	30	36	40
Disposable income	31	35	39	44
Income after indirect taxation	29	34	37	41
Final income (with value of 'in kind' services)	39	40	43	46

Source: Adapted from Central Statistical Office (1980) 'The effects of taxes and benefits on household income: 1978' *Economic Trends*, No. 315, January, London: HMSO.

Security, 2000: chart 1.3). This growing divide was mainly the result of increases in investment and occupational pension income: the inequalities of the economic system were reflected in pensioner incomes.

The above figures refer to cash incomes. What of the impact of state service provision on inequality? Table 7.1 gives the distribution of income at each stage of the redistributive process. It is worth repeating that comparisons of Central Statistical Office/Office for National Statistics figures on the redistribution of income over time are fraught with problems and there are particular difficulties in assessing the impact of the 'social wage' (Sefton, 1996). Nonetheless it can be seen that, although the activities of the state mitigated market inequality, the real standard of living of the poorest deciles in comparison with the highest decile was much lower in 1997 than in 1978 (see Table 7.2).

Wealth

The share of the top 5 per cent in total marketable wealth remained static between 1976 and 1996 at 52 per cent as did the share of the least wealthy 50 per cent who continued to obtain only 7 per cent of total wealth (Office for National Statistics, 2000: 97). This long-term stability in wealth owner-ship is surprising given that 1.5 million homes were transferred to council tenants, at substantial discounts, in the period. The stability can probably be explained by the gains made on the Stock Exchange (few of the least wealthy own shares) and movements in relative house prices counteracting the impact of the transfer of public assets (council housing) to the least wealthy.

8

New Labour, Social Exclusion and Social Justice

new, 'NEW', NEW LABOUR

> Labour had failed to understand that the old working class was becoming a new middle class: aspiring, consuming, choosing what was best for themselves and their families. They had outgrown crude collectivism and left it behind in the supermarket car-park. (Gould, 1998: 4)

In the mid-1980s the Labour Party was committed to demand management for full employment, a modest programme of public ownership, support for the 'producer' rights of trade unions and a universal welfare state financed from progressive taxation. After the 1987 election defeat, the 'modernisers' in the party denounced this programme as an electoral albatross and incompatible with economic success in a new global market. The quest began for new policies and a new image. Eventually a 'Third Way' in British politics was discovered (Blair, 1998, 2001).

Labour had been moving steadily to the right since the 1983 General Election when its radical, socialist manifesto – described as 'the longest suicide note in history' – helped to reduce Labour's share of the vote to 26.9 per cent. The 1987 General Election, with Labour obtaining 29.5 per cent of the vote compared to the Conservative's 46.1 per cent, accelerated the 'modernisation' process. A major policy review *Meet the Challenge, Make the Change* (Labour Party, 1989) endorsed the 'competitive economy'. It promised Labour would be 'the party of the consumer' and would endeavour to improve labour skills to enable Britain to capture world markets. Claiming the case against inequality rested as 'much on the need for economic efficiency as it does on social justice', the review identified the characteristics of Labour's new approach to social policy as promoting equal opportunities, creating 'pathways to independence', introducing a minimum wage and safeguarding the 'social wage'. Labour's 1992 manifesto *It's Time to Get Britain Working Again* claimed the release of capital receipts from local authority house sales and enhancing capital allowances to bring forward manufacturing investment would stimulate the economy at no cost to the taxpayer. The resources generated by an expanding economy would be invested in the National Health Service and the education and training necessary to enhance skills. The 'social wage' would be protected by higher pensions and extra child benefit, financed by additional NICs on earnings above £405 per week, plus a new top rate of income tax on incomes above £40,000 per year. Labour lost the 1992 election securing 35.2 per cent of the vote compared to the Conservative's 42.3 per cent.

The John Smith interlude

John Smith's Shadow Cabinet was divided into two camps; those who wanted to 'eliminate anything from the Labour programme which might give the electorate cause for concern' and those who 'thought it was better to be more positive about what we stand for' (Gould, 1995: 225). Smith belonged to the 'positive' camp – content with a dormant Clause Four, universal benefits and 'tax and spend' to promote social justice. After 'Black Wednesday' in September 1992, when Britain was forced to withdraw from Europe's exchange rate mechanism, Tory unpopularity meant change in Labour Party policy became less urgent. Nonetheless, despite Labour's 15 per cent poll lead, the 'modernisers' in the party, led by Blair and Brown, were deeply concerned about the party's election prospects. Labour had substantial majorities in the mid-term of previous Tory governments only to fail in the only poll that mattered. Labour's policies needed further amendment for electoral success. The party had to be seen as economically competent, tougher on crime and less willing to 'tax and spend' – a party 'where the upwardly mobile could feel at home, not unlike the one which David Owen tried to create a decade ago' (McSmith, 1996: 336). Blair, elected leader in 1994, moved quickly towards completing the 'modernisation' of his party. Within three years, through a sequence of inverted commas and lower and upper case letters, the Labour Party became New Labour.

The commission on social justice

Some of New Labour's distributive principles were derived from the report of the Commission on Social Justice, (CSJ) set up by John Smith, but strongly influenced by party 'modernisers' such as Patricia Hewitt, the Deputy Chair, and its Secretary, David Miliband.

Social Justice: Strategies for National Renewal (CSJ, 1994) emphasised the 'economic revolution' of the last 20 years. A 'global revolution of finance, competition, skill and technology' was occurring, which meant 'the notion of a job for life has disappeared and employment insecurity affects us all' (CSJ, 1994: 3). The Commission compared the 'old' economy of 'mass production', 'command and control', 'assets as things' and 'contracts' with the 'new' economy of 'mass customisation', 'empowerment/ decentralisation', 'assets are people' and 'trusts' (CSJ, 1994: 75). This 'new' economy had to be embraced by the creation of an 'Investors' Britain' as against the 'Deregulators' Britain' of free market Conservatives and the 'Levellers' Britain' of the 'Old Left'. The Levellers' strategy of the redistribution of wealth and income through the tax and benefits systems was dismissed and educational investment was embraced as the mechanism for 'increasing opportunities to compete in world markets' (CSJ, 1994: 96). Nonetheless, despite this rejection of redistribution via 'tax and spend', the Commission's specific ideas on how to construct 'an intelligent welfare state' involved large-scale public expenditure. The report advocated unemployment benefit for part-time workers; higher 'disregards' in assessing Income Support eligibility; an additional children's allowance added to unemployment benefit; higher universal 'bricks and mortar' subsidies to reduce rent levels; a comprehensive disability income; a minimum income guarantee for pensioners and an improved 'universal second pension'. The Commission was silent on the financing of these proposals but, if the poor were not to pay more for their welfare via indirect taxation, then a marked redistribution of income would be required. Blair and Brown, perhaps conscious of its implications for public expenditure, gave *Social Justice: Strategies For National Renewal* a tepid welcome. They were already working on a reformulation of Labour policies designed to eliminate Labour's reputation as a 'tax and spend' party and bolster confidence in Labour's ability to manage the economy.

NEW LABOUR'S DISTRIBUTIVE PRINCIPLES

Embracing the market

Kinnock's market endorsement was tainted by his earlier socialism (Hattersley, 1995: 306) whereas Blair's embrace of the market appeared genuine especially when seen in the context of the moat he constructed between 'Old' and 'New' Labour. Blair declared there was a 'limited but crucial role of government in a modern economy' to provide:

> A secure low-inflation environment and promote long-term investment; ensure that business has well-educated people to recruit into the workforce; ensure a properly functioning first-class infrastructure; work with business to promote regional development and small and growing firms; seek to open markets for our goods around the world; and create a strong and cohesive society which removes the drag on the economy of social costs. (Blair, 1996: 110)

As Shadow Chancellor, Gordon Brown flirted with 'EuroKeynesianism' by endorsing Jacques Delors' plan to use European Union spending power as a counter-cyclical force (Anderson and Mann, 1997: 95–7). However, as the British economy recovered, government spending as a route to economic recovery was downgraded and in 1995 Brown declared Labour's emphasis was on 'strengthening the supply-side foundations of the economy' (Brown, 1995).

In action, if not constitutionally, Labour abandoned nationalisation as the kernel of its programme in the 1960s (Dell, 2000) and adopted redistributive welfare as the means to eliminate unjustifiable inequalities. Nevertheless, Labour's 1996 repudiation of its constitutional commitment to public ownership was a powerful symbol of the remoulding of the party. In power, New Labour refined its endorsement of the global market. According to Brown, 'Policies for economic management must now recognise that in a global economy, there is no long-run trade off between growth and inflation' (Brown, 1997). A 'golden rule' on public finance was also announced: borrowing for investment was legitimate if it produced demonstrable returns over the economic cycle, but New Labour would not borrow to sustain revenue spending to promote full employment.

What works is what matters

New Labour elevated pragmatism into a political creed. Its guiding principle in assessing a course of action was potential for improvement, regardless of the ideological origins of the programme. This Benthamite philosophy (Wells, 2000: 40) sanctioned the adoption and expansion of many of the measures introduced by John Major. The Private Finance Initiative was enlarged with the private sector commissioned to build and service hospitals in return for an annual 'availability fee'. The transfer of local authority dwellings to registered social landlords – 20,000 in 1996/7 – increased to a projected 150,000 in 2000/2001 as New Labour geared up to its target of 200,000 transfers each year. Despite David Blunkett's pledge to the 1995 Labour Party Conference of 'watch my lips: no selection', existing grammar schools could only be abolished by a tortuous local procedure. Grant maintained schools (renamed Foundation Schools and brought back under local inspection and accountability) retained the right to select up to 15 per cent of their pupils by aptitude in a particular skill or curriculum area. Moreover, on the argument that performance was improved by diversity and competition, New Labour's 2001 manifesto promised to expand the number of 'specialist schools' – able to select up to 10 per cent of their pupils by 'aptitude in a particular skill or curriculum area' – to 'at least 1500 by 2006' (Labour Party, 2001: 15).

The 'what works' mantra also provided the cloak under which New Labour implemented its manifesto pledge to abolish the competitive tendering for local authority services. Competitive tendering was replaced by a requirement for local government to achieve 'best value' in the provision of services. 'Best value' was monitored by the Audit Commission, the DETR and a Housing Inspectorate. Education acquired a Standards and Effectiveness Unit and schools continued to be treated 'as producers of qualification output' (Smithers, 2001: 409). The National Health Service also received a strong dose of 'best value' albeit without the terminology. A Commission for Health Improvement was set up to supply advice to ministers and health authorities on the quality of local services and a National Institute for Clinical Excellence was established to measure the effectiveness of therapies and advise ministers about what should be available within the National Health Service. Performance targets permeated all dimensions of healthcare delivery.

Prudent for a purpose in public spending

As Shadow Chancellor, Brown abandoned Labour's 1992 spending proposals and portrayed New Labour's future expenditure commitments as likely to reduce costs in some areas to release resources for use elsewhere. The abolition of the assisted places scheme was presented as releasing finance to reduce class sizes in the state sector and the minimum wage was portrayed as passing some of the cost of social security onto the 'bad' employer.

Stop   Three months before the 1997 General Election, Brown announced that, for two years, New Labour would follow the spending plans set by the Conservatives, not just in total but in accordance with the departmental allocations set out in the 'Red Book'. The standard and higher rates of income tax, then 23 per cent and 40 per cent, would not be increased in the lifetime of the next parliament. A windfall tax on the 'undeserved' profits of the public utilities would pay for New Labour's welfare-to-work scheme and the 'phased' and 'prudent' release of the capital receipts from council house sales would supply capital finance for housing investment. In office, New Labour adhered to its pledge on implementing Conservative spending plans. This meant expenditure on state welfare services declined in real terms from £262 billion in 1996 to £257 billion in 1999 (Office for National Statistics 2001: 112). Total Government spending fell from 41.2 per cent of GDP in 1996/7 to 37.7 per cent in 1999/2000 (Toynbee and Walker, 2001: 102).

Go?   Information on the scale of public spending over the years 1999/2000 to 2003/4 was provided in New Labour's two comprehensive spending reviews (Chancellor of the Exchequer, 1998, 2000). According to Brown, prudence in public spending had allowed a reduction in the Public Sector Borrowing Requirement so now, with lower debt repayments, he could start to release the resources necessary to 'modernise' Britain. Spending on education, having received a modest 2 per cent increase in 1997/8 and 1998/9, was boosted and, over the four years of Blair's first administration, the annual growth rate was 3.6 per cent (Emmerson and Frayne, 2001: 5). These additional resources were spent on reducing class sizes in primary schools and on supporting schools to enable them to achieve performance targets set by the Government (Smithers, 2001). Further spending increases, averaging 5.6 per cent, were promised for 2001/2 to 2003/4. Resources for health care, after a modest annual growth of 2.2 per cent, increased by 5.5 per cent in 1999/2000, a projected 8 per cent in 2000/01 and were forecast to expand by 6.1 per cent each year until 2003/4 (Hansard, 2000a 14 March 2000; 2 April 2001). New Labour targeted these extra resources on bringing down waiting lists, reducing avoidable illness and improving co-operation between the NHS and other social services. The Conservative's quasi-market in health care was modified by the ending of GP fundholding and its replacement by 'commissioning' of 'secondary' health care by Primary Care Groups (PCGs) of GPs and other healthcare professionals in day-to-day contact with patients.

New Labour's manifesto pledge to release the capital receipts from the sale of local authority dwellings was implemented, but the spending was phased and accompanied by reductions in 'normal' borrowing approvals. This meant expenditure on housing declined in real terms in the late 1990s. As a consequence, the number of 'social housing' starts fell from 30,000 in 1996 to 18,000 in 2000 and the number of families in temporary accommodation increased from 45,000 to 75,000 (Department of Transport, Local Government and the Regions, 2001). The 2000 Comprehensive Spending Review boosted projected housing investment by an extra £2.5 billion each year up to 2004. A large share of the additional spending was targeted on the most run-down local authority estates by mechanisms such as the Major Repairs Grant, aimed at ensuring all council houses are above a 'decent' standard by 2010. Spending on urban regeneration declined significantly in the first years of New Labour governance (Urban Task Force, 1999: 286). However, the publication of the urban and rural white papers reflected an emerging consensus on the need for accelerated urban renewal to spare the countryside from development. Extra capital resources were promised for the period 2001–2004, supported by a package of fiscal measures such as a Community Investment Tax Credit and zero VAT for the sale of renovated houses empty for ten years or more. Social security spending was deemed 'annually managed expenditure', subject to change according to the demand generated by the system and yearly announcements about benefit levels. The 2000 Comprehensive

Spending Review projected only a modest increase of 1.5 per cent per annum up to 2003/4.

Equality of opportunity, not equality of outcome

New Labour repudiated equality of outcome as a policy objective. 'Whereas the left desired equality of outcome New Labour sets as its goal real equal opportunity for all and special privileges for none' (Mandelson and Liddle, 1996: 17). Blair agreed, stating 'I want to highlight opportunity as a key value ... the Left, at worst, has stifled opportunity in the name of abstract equality' (1998: 3). Brown, in declaring 'the essence of equality is equality of opportunity', claimed the search for equality of outcome had sent the Labour Party 'up the wrong roads' (1996, cited in Kellner, 1999: 161). Equality of outcome was not a feasible objective and its pursuit led to uniformity and the stifling of initiative. Far better for the Labour Party to pursue a 'maximalist equality of opportunity' policy involving 'recurrent, lifelong, and comprehensive political, social and economic opportunities for all' (Brown, 1999, cited in Callinicos, 2000: 38). The operation of a 'fully global economy' (Giddens, 1998: 30) was enlisted to support the claim that equality of outcome was a futile objective. The global economy would undo quickly any attempt by a national government to change its outcomes, and resistance to global forces would produce economic stagnation.

Including the excluded

In late 1997, a Social Exclusion Unit was set up in the Prime Minister's office. Blair described social exclusion 'as broadly covering those people who do not have the means, *material or otherwise*, to participate in social, economic, political and cultural life (Blair, 1998, cited in Scottish Office, 1998: 2, emphasis added). New Labour's approach to ending social exclusion contained five elements.

Work for those who can   Brown's secular economics combined with Blair's Christian morality to produce a stress on work as the route to well being (Rentoul, 2001: 373). Social inclusion would come mainly via participation in paid work. The windfall tax, promised in the 1997 manifesto, was introduced in New Labour's first budget when 30 companies, mainly the utilities privatised by the Conservatives, were selected to raise £5.2 billion to spend on reducing unemployment. New Labour's welfare to work strategy was grounded in the ideas of Lawrence Mead via their influence on the Conservative's benefits/work initiatives in the 1990s and contacts with the 'New Democrats' in the United States. Mead (1985, 1992) claimed a successful political strategy to end poverty must be built on getting the poor into jobs because, in the new politics of redistribution, those with jobs have virtue on their side. However, it was not sufficient to provide direct economic incentives because the poor had acquired a 'culture of poverty' and were immune from the normal economic baits. The state had to push the poor to display the behaviour required for self-reliance. Work must become a condition of state assistance and 'case managers' should be employed to be 'all over their clients like flypaper, every day' (Mead, 1997: 35) to ensure benefit recipients looked for work and kept their jobs. Although the New Labour welfare to work programme emphasised its 'help' dimensions – 'gateway to work' officials were called 'personal advisers' – the enforced obligations dimension of the strategy was revealed in Blair's declaration of 'Third Way' principles. An 'active supply-side labour policy was necessary to introduce targeted programmes for the long-term unemployed and other disadvantaged groups to give them the opportunity to reintegrate into the labour market on the principles of rights and responsibilities going together' (Blair and Schröder, 1999: 6).

Initially welfare to work – labelled the 'New Deal' – focused on young people aged 18 to 24 who had claimed Jobseeker's Allowance (JSA) for six months or more. The 'New Deal' begins with a period of up to four months – known as 'the Gateway' – aimed at improving job search activity and enhancing job readiness. Four options are then available to young people unable to find unsubsidised work: six months of work experience and training with a voluntary sector organisation paid at the benefit rate with a premium; six months with an Environmental Task Force also paid at the benefit rate plus a premium; up to a year of education or training with an allowance equal to benefit levels and subsidised employment with training paid at the rate for the job. Benefit sanctions are applied to those who do not participate fully in the New Deal; no 'fifth option of life on full benefit' is available because 'rights and responsibilities must go hand in hand' (Labour Party, 1997: 19). Later the New Deal was extended to other groups. People over 25, claiming JSA for more than 18 months, became eligible to be helped back to work by a government subsidy, paid to employers, of £75 a week and a single job grant of £100. A package involving personal advice, help with looking for a job and an employment credit was targeted on unemployed people over 50.

The dilemma of the public (work) and the private (care) roles of women with children bedevilled New Labour in its early years of office (Phillips, 1997). By 2000 the issue had been pushed firmly towards the conclusion 'all should work' – 'breadwinning' was to become universal. New Labour started the process of constructing obligations and associated rights for single parents to take paid work. The Treasury claimed single parents must become paid employees because work is the surest way out of poverty and 'couple women', with the same role in looking after children as lone mothers, were more often in work than single parents (HM Treasury, 1999: 15). The new childcare tax credit was designed to enable more women to work while at the same time supplying finance to prime the commodification of childcare. The availability of childcare places was also boosted by the National Childcare Strategy, launched in 1998, and aimed at creating 900 neighbourhood nurseries with 45,000 extra daycare places by 2004, targeted on deprived areas (HM Treasury, 2001: 4.20). In 2001, all single parents, as a condition of benefit entitlement, were required to attend gateway interviews to discuss work options with personal advisers. Failure to attend a 'gateway' interview resulted in a 20 per cent reduction in the adult rate of benefit. Following the election victory in June 2001 Blair announced the demise of the Department of Social Security and its replacement by a Department of Work and Pensions.

Measures aimed at boosting work income, when compared with the benefits available outside the workforce, accompanied New Labour's active promotion of work-seeking behaviour. The National Minimum Wage Act 1998 introduced a single National Minimum Wage (NMW) throughout the United Kingdom at a level based on advice from the Low Pay Commission. The Commission recommended a 'development rate' of £3.20 per hour for 18 to 20 year olds and a rate of £3.60 for those over 20. All those aged 16 and 17 and young people with apprenticeships would be exempt from the NMW (Low Pay Commission, 1998). In implementing the National Minimum Wage the Government reduced the 'development' rate to £3 – rising to £3.20 in April 2000 – and applied it to those under 22. According to estimates made by the Office for National Statistics 221,000 people aged 18 to 21 and 1,683,000 people aged over 22 would be likely to gain from the new statutory floor to wages (Lourie, 1999), which started in April 1999. In October 2001 the adult minimum wage was increased to £4.10 per hour and New Labour's 2001 manifesto promised a further increase, subject to economic circumstances, to £4.20 in October 2002 with young people entitled to £3.60.

Working Families Tax Credit (WFTC) replaced Family Credit in October 1999. WFTC applicants send their claims to a special unit located in the Inland Revenue rather than the Benefits Agency. The original idea had been to make all payments through the wages system, but fear of transferring income from the 'woman's purse to the man's pay-packet' led to a hybrid system whereby partners can choose who receives the payment. In fact, the majority of WFTC payments are made in the wage packet because most claimants are single parents. The noteworthy aspect of WFTC, in comparison to Family Credit, is its generosity. Eligibility is determined by 'credits' – a basic credit for each adult, additional credits depending on the number and age of the children and credits covering up to 70 per cent of childcare costs up to a specified ceiling. The point at which eligibility for WFTC ends was increased by £11 over the Family Credit threshold and the 'cut out' rate of benefit withdrawal was reduced from 70 per cent to 55 per cent. WFTC was complemented by additional support for families announced in the 1999 and 2000 budgets as Brown developed a strategy of combining universalism with selectivity. Child Benefit was increased above the rate of inflation and, by April 2001, had reached £15.50 per week for the first child and £10.35 for other children. A new children's tax credit was made available to families with one or more children under 16 living with them, tapered so that families with a member paying the 40 per cent rate of tax would not benefit. Revenue to help pay for the WFTC and the children's tax credit came from a reduction in tax relief on mortgage interest and the restriction of the tax relief available through the married couple's allowance. By October 2001 these measures would deliver, 'a minimum income guarantee' of £225 each week to a family working 35 hours with one child (HM Treasury, 2001: 4.58). The Treasury also put forward proposals for further integration of the tax and benefit systems. In 2003 an integrated child credit would be introduced, alongside an employment tax credit, aimed mainly at improving the take-home income of single people in work. Initially the policy of increasing the incomes of those in work was accompanied by reductions in the relative incomes of those not in work so 'the first two years of this Government's term in office were dire for poor children' (Bradshaw, 2000: 9). However, following the furore in the Labour Party over the October 1997 cuts in benefits for single parents, the Income Support scale rate for children under 11 was boosted to £31.45. This was a 80 per cent increase over the 1997 rate but this still left a couple with two young children 37.6 per cent below a poverty line set of 60 per cent of median income (Piachaud and Sutherland, 2001: 75).

Security for those who cannot work?   Tony Blair's foreword to *New Ambitions for our Country: A New Contract for Welfare*, promised 'Work for those who can; security for those who cannot' (Secretary of State for Social Security and the Minister for Welfare Reform, 1998: iii). New Labour claimed security for pensioners was provided by the Minimum Income Guarantee, a new name for means tested Income Support. In April 2001 it provided a minimum of £92.15 for a single pensioner and £140.55 for couples. The 'savings' disincentive, an inevitable outcome of reliance on means tested benefits, was modified by the promise of a 'pension tax credit' – a new name for higher levels of disregarded income when assessing entitlement to income support. The proposed State Second Pension, with its assurance of enhanced pension rights to contributors earning less than £9500 per year and/or with irregular contributions, was also targeted on low earners.

Attaching obligations to rights   In the countdown to the 1997 General Election 'rights require duties' became the central motif of New Labour's social policy. In 1995 Blair said 'We need a new settlement on welfare for a new age, where opportunity and responsibility go together' (Blair, 1995). He repeated the maxim in many subsequent speeches and articles (Blair, 1996).

David Marquand supplied a rationale for the revival of obligation as a distributive principle by claiming redistributive strategies require a moral order to sustain them. He attributed the neglect of obligation in the 1960s and 1970s to the influence of Richard Titmuss and Anthony Crosland. Titmuss was charged with so rarefying the notion of obligation that it disappeared into the ether. His call for universal altruism towards strangers had failed to establish *specific* obligations. 'Altruism did not capture the full flavour of words like "comradeship", "loyalty" and "duty" which lie at the heart of any notion of community. There is something a little watery about the concept, perhaps because it goes too wide and insufficiently deep' (Marquand, 1990: 9). In contrast, Crosland was accused of neglecting obligations. Under Crosland's 'passive, redistributive hedonism', the notion 'that rights should be balanced by duties ... that the point of collective provision was to foster self-reliance and civic activism came to be seen as patronising or elitist or (horror of horrors) judgmental' (Marquand, 1996: 23). Frank Field, then New Labour's foremost welfare expert, also affirmed the importance of duty. In the 1970s and 1980s Field was a 'passive hedonist' – a strong advocate of the unconditional redistribution of income. However, in 1996, he denounced Titmuss' view 'that welfare should be given as a right and free of any restrictions or stigma' (Field, cited in Willetts, 1996: 33). 'Taxpayers are likely to stump up a contribution for poorer stakeholders only if they approve of the behaviour of those for whom they are contributing' (Field, 1997: 25).

According to Phillip Gould, a key adviser to Tony Blair in the 1997 General Election campaign, 'the idea that individuals are defined by their relationship to the community, not in isolation from the community is Blair's grounding idea, his core political insight' (Gould, 1998: 233). Reading the work of John Macmurray had awakened this commitment to duty (Blair, 1996: 59–60). Macmurray was a student at Balliol College and there is a striking similarity between his philosophy and that of the 'New' Liberal, T.H. Green (Gould, 1998: 234). Both regarded a life of civic duty as a fundamental part of Christianity. Like Green, Macmurray thought the person, not the collective, was the primary element in society – a sentiment adopted by Blair in his claim that collective action should advance the interests of the *individual* not the collective (Blair, 2001: 10). Because action involves intentionality, then, according to Macmurray, self-realisation of the person could be achieved only in relationship to the 'Other' – the sum total of the network of personal relationships (Macmurray, 1995 [1961]: 157–8). He rejected the notion of 'natural rights'. Obligations and rights had to be linked otherwise mutuality was absent from human relationships and 'I make myself the giver and you the recipient' (Macmurray, 1995 [1961]: 189–90).

In power, the aphorism, 'rights require obligations', although focused on the obligation to work, influenced all dimensions of New Labour's social policy. Compulsory home–school agreements, setting out school and parental responsibilities were introduced. Entitlement to the payment of the Sure Start Maternity Grant became conditional on the obligations 'to keep appointments for child health advice and child health check-ups' and 'contacts with a healthcare professional to ensure expert advice on child development' (Chancellor of the Exchequer, 1999). New Labour's rough sleeping strategy allocated additional expenditure to assist rough sleepers to 'come out of the cold' into night shelters and hostels but concluded:

> Once we are satisfied that realistic alternatives are readily available we and the public at large are entitled to expect those working on the streets to seek to persuade people to take advantage of them. This includes the police. (Department of the Environment, Transport and the Regions, 2000a: 10)

Targeted local initiatives   Officially recorded unemployment, having reached 10 per cent in 1993, declined to 5.9 per cent in 1997 (Gregg and Wadsworth, 1999: 11). This fall in recorded unemployment, although mainly the result of an upturn in the economy, also reflected the transfer of workers from the unemployment registers to the ranks of the 'economically inactive' and hence potentially eligible for support from disability benefits. New Labour believed expanding the economy to a level necessary to bring the economically inactive back to work would result in 'overheating' and high inflation. Accordingly, despite its condemnation of Conservative 'initiative-itis', New Labour launched a series of initiatives targeted on selected local areas and aimed mainly at 'people change'.

The rationale of this 'small area' policy was provided in *The Goal of Full Employment: Employment Opportunity for all Throughout Britain* (HM Treasury, 2000a). According to the Treasury there had been a rapid decline in recorded unemployment, and job vacancies – estimated at 1 million in February 2000 – were at a record level. In addition, concentrated pockets of high unemployment were to be found in only 'a tail of around 15–20 local authority districts that have not enjoyed the fruits of recovery seen throughout the rest of Britain' (HM Treasury, 2000a: 1). This argument, supported by the claim that many of the high unemployment areas were next to places with a high number of job vacancies, justified a rigourously selective approach to area assistance plus a sharper focus on 'people change'. The list of special 'zones' and programmes directed to deprived areas soon became a long one. It included Community Legal Service Partnerships, the Crime Reduction Programme, Education Action Zones, Employment Zones, Health Action Zones, the New Deal for Communities, Newstart, Surestart, the Neighbourhood Renewal Fund, the Children's Fund and the Single Regeneration Budget, which was revamped to concentrate on the 65 most deprived local authorities. The flavour of New Labour's 'area' approach can be sampled by examining three programmes.

The Social Exclusion Unit's report *Bringing Britain Together: a National Strategy for Neighbourhood Renewal* (Social Exclusion Unit, 1998b) focused attention on the social pathology of deprived neighbourhoods. Compared to the rest of England, deprived neighbourhoods were characterised by such features as:

> nearly two thirds more unemployment ... almost one and a half times the proportion of lone parent households ... one and a half times the underage pregnancy rate ... 37 per cent of 16 year olds without a single GCSE at grades A–C, against 30 per cent for the rest of England. (Social Exclusion Unit, 1998b: para. 1.4)

The report concluded that the impact of earlier initiatives to combat neighbourhood deprivation had been limited because 'there had been too many different schemes each parachuted from outside that had lacked co-ordination and had concentrated too much on physical renewal and not enough on people' (Social Exclusion Unit, 1998b: 3). 'Joined up' thinking was the proposed solution. This was promoted, at central level, by the establishment of 18 action teams each with a 'champion' junior minister. The local 'initiative-itis' of the past would be overcome by a new initiative called *New Deal for Communities*. The Government set £800 million aside over three years for commissioned bids for local schemes. Each bid had to demonstrate 'connected' solutions to the problems identified in the deprived neighbourhoods and had to be compiled with the maximum feasible participation of the residents of the area.

Surestart was announced in 1998 as a scheme aimed at ensuring children, 'are ready to thrive when they get to school' (Chancellor of the Exchequer, 1998: 79). It was to 'be fully integrated into the New Deal for Communities' (Home Office, 1998: 15) and only local authorities with significant numbers of deprived neighbourhoods within their boundaries were invited to bid for funds. Bids had to be targeted at children under five and their parents through outreach services, home visiting, mentoring, befriending and advice about child health and development. Surestart made an unsure start. It took time to establish local schemes so that, by 2000, only a small part of the £453 million allocated to the initiative had been spent. The 2000 comprehensive spending review announced the extension of Surestart to cover one third of all poor children under four years old.

A National Strategy for Neighbourhood Renewal: a Framework for Consultation (Social Exclusion Unit, 2000), the outcome of the deliberations of the 18 policy action teams set up in 1998, attempted to bring some order to the hotchpotch of neighbourhood initiatives. It placed 'the onus firmly on the core public services – like schools, police and health services – as the Government's main weapons against deprivation' (Social

Exclusion Unit, 2000: 23). The special pots of money available to deprived neighbourhoods were to be targeted on innovation, joining up the core services, ensuring that pupils have at least three hours study support each week, supporting families and providing on-the-spot service delivery. The Government promoted new local strategic partnerships, to work up an agreed strategy between public services, the voluntary sector and private interests, and management of services at 'neighbourhood' level was endorsed. The 2000 Comprehensive Spending Review allocated £800 million over three years to a new *Neighbourhood Renewal Fund* for distribution to local authorities with concentrations of deprivation within their boundaries.

'Inclusive' mainstream services   Attempts to focus the attention of education and healthcare services on the needs of the socially excluded accompanied the attachment of special area-based initiatives to mainstream services. For example, the Government encouraged each primary school to concentrate on its least able pupils by announcing Level 4 in Mathematics and English was an attainment level to be expected from *all* pupils. Targets were established to act as markers on the route to achieving this goal. Performance measures set for the National Health Service incorporated similar attempts at 'inclusion' with the reduction in social class differences in healthcare outcomes a prominent target. Sometimes the Social Exclusion Unit took the initiative in encouraging mainstream services to become more inclusive. The increase in the number of pupils permanently excluded from school, from 3000 in 1991 to 12,688 in 1996/7 prompted the Prime Minister to ask the Social Exclusion Unit to investigate the problem. Its report included an action plan and £147 million per year was allocated to the provision of on-site learning support units where disruptive pupils could be placed quickly. By 2000 the number of pupils permanently excluded from school had been reduced to 8600.

SOCIAL JUSTICE AND SOCIAL EXCLUSION

According to New Labour the supply of enhanced opportunities to work, the bonding of obligations to rights, the injection of special resources into deprived neighbourhoods and 'targeted' spending in health and education amounts to promoting social justice, provided the programme is financed by 'fair' taxation. New Labour claims to be pursuing the Labour Party's traditional ends but by a 'Third Way', adapted to the new 'global' order (Blair, 1999a, 2001). New Labour's emphasis is on 'endowment social justice', aimed at creating work capabilities. Four propositions underpin the 'Third Way' when applied to the social welfare system.

- According to Blair:

  > The driving force behind the ideas associated with the Third Way is globalisation because no country is immune from the massive change that globalisation brings ... what globalisation is doing is bringing in its wake profound economic and social change. (Blair, 1999, cited in Savage and Atkinson, 2001: 8)

  This acceptance of the global market implies that individuals are entitled to the rewards they obtain. Any significant attempt at direct redistribution of global market rewards is probably unachievable and, if achieved, is likely to produce a stagnant national economy.
- The indifference of previous governments led to substantial growth in the number of individuals excluded from the rewards offered by participation in the global market.
- The promotion of social justice involves the creation of opportunities for socially excluded individuals. Such opportunities can be generated by a modest injection of income to those in work with family responsibilities, reconstructing state welfare as a form of 'social investment' (Giddens, 1998), preparing people for work and reattaching the 'excluded' to 'mainstream' values.
- The resources necessary for ending social exclusion can be obtained by reductions in certain forms of social security spending, economic growth and, when necessary, by raising additional taxation by 'fair' means. The impact of fiscal measures on the distribution of income, above the threshold deemed necessary to end social exclusion, is regarded as unimportant in the promotion of social justice (Hewitt, 2000). A 'decent floor, never mind the gap' is New Labour's guiding principle (Prowse, 2000).

As David Miller has said, this blending of social justice into the eradication of social exclusion reflects 'a striking fact about contemporary politics ... left or centre-left parties have, without exception, pared down their commitment to policies of social justice almost to vanishing point, even while continuing to use the term rhetorically' (Miller, 1999: x). Eliminating social exclusion is not the same as promoting social justice. Moreover, failure to advance social justice is likely to prejudice the goal of social inclusion.

Rawls, social inclusion and the third way

There are connections between the conception of social justice embodied in the Third Way and John Rawls' theory of justice. Rawls claimed inequalities should be attached to positions and offices accessible to all under the principle of fair equality of opportunity. New Labour's emphasis on more equal opportunities – with additional help for people living in deprived areas to help promote such equality of opportunity – can be interpreted as conforming to Rawls' theory (Buckler and Dolowitz, 2000: 102–9). Rawls' 'maximin' notion also appears to be one of New Labour's guiding principles and, in accordance with Rawls' recommendation that a distributive arm of government is necessary, New Labour has constructed new conduits to channel resource to the 'least advantaged'. According to the Treasury 1.2 million children will be lifted out of poverty by the minimum wage plus the measures announced in the 1998, 1999 and 2000 budgets (HM Treasury, 2000b). In addition New Labour's Minimum Income Guarantee and state second pension proposals will concentrate income on the poorest pensioners (Department of Social Security, 2000). Nevertheless, there are significant discrepancies between New Labour's formulation of social justice and that of Rawls. Rawls starts with a presumption of equality, arguing a departure from an equal distribution can be justified only by demonstrating how this retreat produces gains for the least advantaged above the share they could expect from an equal allotment. In contrast, New Labour starts from the distribution of income and wealth generated by the market transactions characteristic of the period 1979 to 1997, superimposed on a template of power and wealth forged in earlier times. New Labour has yet to supply reasons why the pattern of inequality it inherited from the Thatcher/Major governments is necessary for success in a global economy. Atkinson (1995) has reviewed nine empirical studies of the relationship between social security transfer spending and economic performance. Four studies found a negative relationship, three a positive relationship and two an insignificant relationship. Esping-Andersen's survey (1994), using total levels of spending as a proportion of GDP, found a similar mixture of relationships and Navarro (2000) has demonstrated how, in the past, redistributive social democratic states were the most closely integrated into the international economy. A recent review of the globalisation and welfare debate concluded:

> It has become increasingly common to argue that whatever the effects of globalization might be, these are intensely mediated by domestic arrangements and thus convergence in national Social Policy structures is not to be expected … All the authors in this volume share this view. (Pierson, 2001: 4)

If poverty is measured in relative terms then, almost by definition, the most egalitarian countries are likely to have the lowest poverty rates. But do low relative poverty rates undermine incentives to the extent that the 'poor' in egalitarian countries are less well off in *absolute* terms than the 'poor' in more unequal countries? Kangas (2000a, 2000b), using the Luxembourg Income Data Set, has related relative poverty rates in 20 countries to the absolute standard of living of the poor and found no strong relationship. Allowing for all the data problems, the relationship is likely to be a weak but negative one: the poor in unequal countries such as the USA and Britain are poorer in absolute terms than in, for example, the more egalitarian Nordic countries. Inequality produces no automatic 'trickle down' impact. Kangas also found social mobility to be lowest in the most unequal countries indicating little trade off between a higher risk of being poor and enhanced opportunity for social mobility.

New Labour's acceptance of inequality implies the existing holders of wealth and high income are entitled to their holdings because they acquired them in a context of global competition. Dominic Hobson has set out some of the evidence on this proposition in *The National Wealth: Who Gets What in Britain* (1999). He lists 90 aristocratic families with wealth ranging from the Duke of Westminster's £1700 million to the Earl of Aylesford's £15 million. He also quotes Rubenstein – 'Britain's premier historian of personal wealth' – as stating 'the most important qualification for achieving millionaire status in Britain has been to have a wealthy father' (Hobson, 1999: 531). Land ownership, the primary source of the 'undeserved' income identified by the 'new' Liberals at the turn of the century, remains an important source of unmerited income today (Banks et al., 2000). The value of residential land increased at a rate four times greater than the rate of inflation between 1970 and 1999 (Hallett, 1977: 103; Department of the Environment, Transport and the Regions, 2000b). Not only are many large fortunes undeserved but patterns of income owe more to state structured inequalities *within* nation-states than to global competition. Although it is commonplace to regard only the direct bene-ficiaries of state social protection as reliant on welfare, the state has also sheltered streams of income for state 'professionals' and, by regulating competition, it has protected large parts of the 'private' sector from global market forces (Schwartz, 2001). According to Burtless (1996, cited in Barr, 2000: 412) globalisation explains less than one-fifth of the increase in inequality in the USA since 1970. Moreover, all the erosion of gender dif-ference in incomes in Britain since 1979 has gone to women in social classes one and two (Atkinson, 2000) – an indicator of the entrenched influence of social class in income distribution.

Michael Walzer and the citizen as worker

New Labour's strong emphasis on the work/welfare association is in tune with Labour's demand for 'the right to work' made in the 1900s. It also reflects a long-standing Labour concern with the promotion of pro-duction and a reduction in 'involuntary' unemployment. The linking of the national minimum wage and the Working Families Tax Credit scheme offers the prospect of a 'living wage' for those in work – a core aspiration of the Labour movement since its foundation. So far, so good for social justice, but the erosion of the national insurance principle has meant choice of work, following a spell of unemployment, has been undermined and the New Deal programmes are aimed at lower level skills (Gray, 2001). This will maintain the flow of workers into low paid work at the national minimum wage with the associated risk that low paid workers will find it difficult to negotiate higher wages (Peck and Theodore, 2000). Moreover, having obtained low paid work, the extension of high marginal withdrawal rates, built into Working Families Tax Credit, 'may have long term implications for worker's human capital accumulation and earnings growth' (Brewer, 2001: 69).

New Labour has stretched its notion of 'work equals welfare' well beyond the 'economic' domain. The call for 'joined up' thinking across Whitehall has produced an early version of 'Housingfare', in the form of foyers combining accommodation for homeless people with training and the proposal to end Housing Benefit for unruly tenants (Department of the Environment, Transport and the Regions, 2000c: para. 5.46). 'Crimefare', embodied in the restrictions on benefits for people in breach of community service orders, is being developed and 'Healthfare', achievable through a reinvigorated occupational health service, has been promoted (Department of Health, 1998: 2). Such joined-up thinking has produced a twenty-first century version of the 'Industrial-Achievement Performance' model of welfare that

> ... incorporates a significant role for social welfare institutions as adjuncts to the economy. It holds that social needs should be met on the basis of merit, work performance and productivity ... It has been described as the 'Handmaiden Model'. (Titmuss, 1974: 31)

This model of the worker-citizen is at odds with Michael Walzer's idea of different spheres of life carrying different 'shared understandings'. According to Walzer, these varied understandings must be incorporated in heterogeneous social institutions if domination by a single distributive order is to be avoided. Under New Labour citizens appear to be valued in terms of a solitary 'sphere of justice', with loss of autonomy, financial exclusion and potential stigmatisation the consequences for those unable to achieve the elevated status of 'worker-citizen'. Indeed, as most workers have little more than their labour to sell on global markets, then New Labour's promotion of the worker-citizen has much in common with Hayek's elevation of the market.

Difference and the 'third' way

According to Iris Young (1990), mainstream political philosophy, with its emphasis on *individual* entitlements to material goods, has been incapable of accommodating the emergence of 'new' social movements, born of the experience of group oppression and a lack of respect for different cultures. Young has promoted the granting of *additional* 'representative rights' to excluded groups as the means to combat the existing cultural hegemony of white, heterosexual, middle-class males.

Whether such 'representational politics' is a valid dimension of social justice is contested. According to Miller (1999: 17), when disrespect for culture influences distributive outcomes, then it is a legitimate dimension of social justice whereas cultural disrespect alone, however undesirable, cannot be subsumed under 'social justice' without stretching the concept beyond any 'robust' meaning. Kelly (1998) adds the criticism that Young does not address adequately the issue of the selection of the identity-conferring groups to be allowed special representation. He argues, 'Not all identities are due public recognition as many of these are the basis of coercive relationships and oppression'. Young 'must employ a principle of inclusion which can discriminate among identity-groups but this raises the question of what principle of inclusion?' (Kelly, 1998: 193). In other words, Kelly thinks Young needs a prior theory of justice in distributive outcomes to justify her selection of the groups worthy of special treatment. In addition, there is the problem, identified by Rae (1981), that justice for one disadvantaged 'bloc' may produce injustice for other 'blocs'. For example, the promotion of equal representation rights for women may ignore the claims of working class women, older women and black women. Thus, as Taylor-Gooby explains, it may be the case that the promotion of equal opportunities for women will widen inequalities in *household* incomes because there is a tendency for 'women to partner with others in related social and economic positions' (2001: 81–2).

Nancy Fraser has also focused attention on the tensions between 'recognition' politics and the politics of distribution.

> Recognition claims often take the form of calling attention to, if not performatively creating, the putative specificity of some group, and then of affirming the value of that specificity. Thus, they tend to promote group differentiation. Redistributional claims, in contrast, often call for abolishing economic arrangements that underpin group specificity. (An example would be feminist demands to abolish the gender division of labour.) Thus the upshot is that the politics of recognition and the politics of redistribution appear to have mutually contradictory aims … The two kinds of claim thus stand in tension with each other; they can interfere with, or even work against, one another. (Fraser, 1998: 24)

She claims the politics of recognition has displaced claims for egalitarian redistribution because '"culturalist" theory asserts maldistribution is merely a secondary effect of misrecognition' (Fraser, 2000: 111). Phillips (1997), in endorsing Fraser's point on the strain between 'difference' and 'distribution' as criteria for social justice, has claimed 'the hegemonic status of difference in contemporary social and political thought can make it very difficult to talk about class' (Phillips, 1999: 42). Class, she says, refers to the positioning of people in a capitalist economy and 'we cannot plausibly present the working class as a cultural group fighting for recognition of its distinctive traditions' (Phillips, 1999: 42). Other authors have taken up the recent neglect of economic position in the analysis of social injustice. Milner (1999) attributes the decline of 'class' in social analysis to the rise of new social movements led by the 'intelligentsia' who remain reluctant to threaten class-based inequalities. Inasmuch as social change is sought, it is change that fine tunes the existing class-based order in ways conducive to the interests of the educated professionals who tend to dominate these movements (Milner, 1999: 166). In *Beyond Identity Politics: Emerging Social Justice Movements in Communities of Color*, John Anner argues:

> People-of-color organizations worry incessantly, as they should, about the number of representatives they have in Congress and in other political and administrative bodies. But that goal has been largely disconnected from the basic issues of providing adequate food, shelter, medical care, and education. The result has been a tremendous opening of opportunity for middle and upper-class women, people of color and other communities of interest while the working class and poor – finding that class trumps race after all – suffer increased deprivation. (Anner, 1996: 10).

In opposition New Labour made overtures to the 'politics of representation' by insisting on all-women shortlists for 50 per cent of vacant and winnable seats – an affirmative action that was not extended to ethnic minorities, gay people, elderly people, young people or to the working class. In power, although devolution and a new emphasis on pluralism in the delivery of welfare opened opportunities for representational politics, New Labour did not openly promote 'group' politics in public electoral systems, in the appointments made to public bodies and in the targets set in the Treasury in Public Service Agreements (Spencer, 2000). This may reflect concerns about the 'politics of difference' as expressed by Miller, Kelly, Rae, Fraser and Phillips. However, the declared death of 'class politics' (Blair, 1999b) suggests New Labour believes the promotion of *individual* work opportunities for the socially excluded is the main criterion on which progress towards 'social justice' is to be assessed.

SOCIAL INCLUSION WITHOUT SOCIAL JUSTICE?

The synthesis of social exclusion and social justice not only diminishes the idea of social justice it also hinders the attainment of a more inclusive society.

The underclass and social exclusion

As presented by New Labour the idea of social exclusion directs attention to the personal characteristics of the excluded rather than to the structures generating exclusion. The obscurity of the concept of social exclusion (Levitas, 1998) has enabled New Labour to emphasise different dimensions of the idea to different audiences. Nonetheless, a strong tone of the 'moral underclass' thesis initially underpinned New Labour's presentation of social exclusion. Geoff Mulgan, seconded to the Social Exclusion Unit from the think tank *Demos*, worked through the theoretical ideas underpinning the initial creation of the Social Exclusion Unit. According to John Lloyd of the *New Statesman*, Mulgan dismissed the view 'that sees society as composed of 30 per cent who are relatively wealthy, the 40 per cent getting by and 30 per cent poor' (Lloyd, 1997: 14). Instead he focused 'on the 8 to 10 per cent who stay poor: who leave school with no qualifications after a school life of inattention, truancy and disruption; who live in areas where nearly 50 per cent of all crimes are committed; who provide most of the single-parent families, the drug addicts, the chronic losers' (Lloyd, 1997: 14).

New Labour has stopped using the term 'underclass' but the moral delinquency it suggests remains an undercurrent flowing into its construction of social exclusion and the 'Third Way'. The Government's language represents social exclusion as a condition to be 'tackled' but, because New Labour has not identified any structural causal agents, the implication remains that the excluded have caused their own exclusion (Fairclough, 2000: 54–8). This 'choice' interpretation of exclusion is reflected in the way Giddens links the exclusion of the very rich with exclusion of the poor as if both have chosen their condition (Giddens, 1998: 103). Such 'blaming the victim' (Ryan, 1971) has implications for the potential stigmatisation of people who have been socially excluded. The incorporation of diverse groups within the remit of the social exclusion agenda enhances the potential for stigmatisation. In its 2001 report *Preventing Social Exclusion*, the Social Exclusion Unit subsumed rough sleepers, young runaways, prisoners, teenage mothers, low income families, drug addicts and deprived neighbourhoods in its account of social exclusion.

Positional goods

Some services are what Hirsch (1977) has called 'positional' – their value to the individual depends on the amount received *relative* to the amount obtained by others. Education has 'positional' attributes because certain occupations are rationed by qualifications and, as more people obtain qualifications, the 'entry level' for the occupation is raised. The retention of 'undeserved' income allows some people to buy privileged education for their children. In private schools the pupil–teacher ratio is half that of state schools. This inequality of input is reflected in access to university education with 88 per cent of children from private schools entering higher education compared to 27 per cent from state schools (Walden, 1996: 43). Within state schools, although the quality of an individual school can, against the odds, modify the link between deprivation and educational underachievement (Sparkes, 1999: 24) there is a potent association between deprivation and educational success. 3 per cent of 15-year-old pupils in the 200 schools with the highest levels of performance at GCSE were receiving free school meals compared to 42 per cent in the 200 lowest achieving schools (Hansard, 2000b, 21 March: col. 508). This relationship between deprivation and achievement persists into adult life even when allowance is made for other factors (Hopcraft, 1998). A recent review of the evidence on intergenerational social mobility concluded:

> Class boundaries seem to be neither more nor less permeable now than they have been in preceding decades. Rather, sectoral shifts towards non-manual work have created additional 'room at the top', but this has not been accompanied by greater equality in opportunities to get there from social origins embodying different degrees of class advantage. (Marshall et al., 1997: 59)

Statistics compiled by the Treasury confirm the entrenched relationship between disadvantage in childhood and future earnings.

> Children with advantaged parents are very likely to end up advantaged themselves ... around 80 per cent of boys whose fathers were in the top quarter of the earnings distribution end up in the top half of the earnings distribution. But the chances of ending up in the top half of the earnings distribution are much lower for boys whose fathers were in the poorest quarter. Just over a third of the boys with parents in the bottom quarter manage to move up to the top half of the earnings distribution. The pattern of mobility is not significantly different for girls. (HM Treasury, 1999: 31)

Housing is also a positional good in that its value is related closely to superior location. New Labour's 1997 manifesto promised to avoid 'boom and bust' in the housing market but, despite attempts to dampen demand by the withdrawal of mortgage income tax relief and an increase in Stamp Duty, prices increased by 32 per cent in real terms between May 1997 and November 2000. However, this house price inflation was not uniform and, in some areas, prices declined in real terms. Unable to afford a move to the suburbs, many homeowners remain trapped in the inner city.

Housing is also one of the domains in which the middle class 'hoard opportunities' by their ability to move into areas with the best state schools (Cabinet Performance and Innovation Unit, 2001: para. 41). This 'hoarding of opportunities' (Tilley, 1998) is becoming more important as an influence on life chances. Goldthorpe (2001) suggests that, in recent years, the educational attainment has declined as an influence on social mobility. The growth of credentials in the workforce has made qualifications less valuable as a passport to prestigious work and the 'softer' skills of personal style, team working and adaptability have become more significant in securing quality work. The elevation of these 'softer' skills allows the middle classes more opportunity to perpetuate themselves in high status jobs.

CONCLUSION: STATE WELFARE, SOCIAL INCLUSION AND SOCIAL JUSTICE

During the second part of the twentieth century, state redistribution of resources initially acquired through market transactions and inherited property rights became the main mechanism for the achievement of social justice. It remains so today not least because its major rivals – the common ownership of the means of production and class action to secure higher wages – have been so recently discredited (Castells, 1998; Mishra, 1999: 1–3). New Labour's principal argument against the welfare state of the 1970s is that its focus on equality of outcome undermined international competitiveness. State welfare must be reconstructed to promote human and social capital and, as a spin off, this 'smart' welfare state will persuade those who pay taxation to assist those who receive welfare.

New Labour's inertia in promoting social inclusion in its first years of office is demonstrated in the figures on the incidence of poverty and the statistics on the impact of taxation and welfare benefits on income redistribution. Although absolute poverty declined, if poverty is measured on the benchmark of 50 per cent of equivalised mean income before housing costs, then pensioner poverty increased under New Labour governance from 22 per cent in 1995/6 to 23 per cent in 1999/00 (Department of Social Security Analytical Services, 2001: 157). Child poverty increased from 19 per cent of the child population in 1995/6 to 22 per cent in 1999/00 (Department of Social Security Analytical Services, 2001: 154). Table 8.1 and 8.2 show how the poorest decile households with children lost ground between 1997 and 2000 in comparison to the richest decile and those with average incomes. The Gini coefficient, calculated on equivalised disposable income, provides a measure of overall inequality. It increased from 33 to 35 between 1997 and 2000, almost reaching its 1990 high point of 36 (Lakin, 2001: 43). Why did inequality increase and the poorest fall behind despite New Labour's minimum wage legislation, the introduction

Table 8.1 *Income of Selected Deciles as a Percentage of 'Top' Decile: Non-retired Households with Children: 1996/7 and 1999/2000*

	Lowest Decile		2nd Lowest		3rd Lowest		4th Lowest	
	1996/97	1999/00	1996/7	1999/00	1996/97	1999/00	1996/97	1999/00
Original income	3.8	3.4	6.8	5.7	11.6	10.1	18.8	17.4
Original income plus cash benefits	12.1	10.0	16.3	13.0	19.6	16.0	25.2	22.0
Disposable income	14.2	11.7	19.5	15.1	22.8	17.9	28.3	23.7
Income after indirect taxation	10.7	9.3	16.6	12.8	19	15	24.6	20.0
Final income (with value of 'in kind' services)	24.5	20.1	28.6	22.1	30	24	34.4	28.8
Equivalised disposable income	13.0	11.5	18.6	16.5	23	20	27	23.8

Sources: Adapted from Studdard, N. (1998) 'The effects of taxes and benefits on household income: 1996/7' *Economic Trends*, No. 553, April, London: Stationery Office and Lakin, C. (2001) 'The effects of taxes and benefits on household income: 1999/2000, *Economic Trends*, No. 569, 2001', London: Stationery Office.

Table 8.2   *Income of Lowest Decile as a Per Cent of Mean Income of Families with Children*

	1978	1996/7	1999/00
Original income	24.9	10.7	10.4
Original income plus cash benefits	46.5	30.4	27.8
Disposable income	56.8	33.7	31.8
Income after indirect taxation	56	27.1	25.4
Final income (with value of 'in kind' services)	68.2	51.8	49.3
Equivalised disposable income	na	32.4	30.9

Sources: Adapted from Central Statistical Office (1980) 'The effects of taxes and benefits on household income: 1978' *Economic Trends*, No. 533, April, London: Stationery Office.
Studdard, N. (1998) 'The effects of taxes and benefits on household income: 1996/7', *Economic Trends*, No. 533, April, London: Stationery Office.
Lakin, C. (2001) 'The effects of taxes and benefits on household income: 1999/2000', *Economic Trends* No. 569, London: Stationery Office.

of Working Families Tax Credit plus other pro-poor policy measures? First, the richest decile continued to pull away from the poorest deciles in terms of 'market' income, especially income from investment and self-employment. Second, the Government's 'direct' redistributive measures were compromised by increases in indirect taxation (up by £378 per year for the poorest households with children). Third, the contributory principle as the basis of entitlement to benefit was eroded. In the past the contract between government and citizen – benefit is due in return for a specified contributory record – supplied part of the rationale for universal entitlements to cash benefits. However, successive government breaches of the 'legitimate expectations' of the National Insurance contract, such as restrictions on pension levels and reductions in entitlements to Unemployment Benefit (Department of Employment, 1994), were compounded by New Labour. National Insurance benefits for widows were cut to save £500 million per year (Vidler, 1998: 15), Incapacity Benefit was means tested and, between 1997 and 2000, basic insurance benefits for adults declined to their lowest ever level in relationship to average earnings (Department of Social Security, 2001). The Select Committee on Social Security concluded that 'The National Insurance Scheme has been undermined, both directly as a result of successive governments' policies and indirectly as a result of economic and social change' (Select Committee on Social Security, 2000: para. 42), a judgement Frank Field endorsed when reflecting on New Labour's policies after he was ousted from his post as Minister for Welfare Reform (Field, 1998). Fourth, the income from Working Families Tax Credit was counted in determining entitlement to

Housing Benefit, Council Tax Benefit and a move from Income Support to work involved loss of free school meals and help with mortgage costs. Thus a claim for Working Families Tax Credit could result in a reduction in income (National Association of Citizen's Advice Bureau 2001: 4.9; Gray, 2001). Finally, the limited growth in spending on universal services restricted the redistributive potential of 'targeted' universalism.

In New Labour's second policy phase, started in April 2000, the resources available for health, education, housing, personal social services and regeneration were increased and the Government directed more cash to poor working families in its 2000 and 2001 budgets. Labour's 2001 manifesto also promised to add a 'fourth pillar' to the welfare state – the pillar of asset creation – in the forms of measures to give council tenants an equity stake in the value of local authority housing and the setting up of an interest-bearing Child Trust Fund, in name of each newly born child, 'with an initial endowment from the government, with more for poorer children' (Labour Party, 2001: 27).

The impact of Blair's emphasis on opportunity creation – his 'endowment' notion of fairness – will take many years to show through in changes in the distribution of adult incomes, but the impact of the new direct redistributive measures is starting to be identified. Simulations of the impact of all the 'cash' measures announced by the Government since 1997 indicate an impressive net gain of 13 per cent for the poorest decile and 0.5 per cent for the richest decile (Clark et al., 2001: 7). However, 'the percentage gains shown ... would only occur if all the changes were introduced at once. In practice, reforms are spread over a number of years' (Goodman, 2001: 97) so the figures take no account of any future increases in taxation. Movements in and out of the labour force and the take-up rates of means tested benefits are also discounted as is the real value of universal services. Even if New Labour's second policy phase is completed as intended, the share of the GDP devoted to public spending will be 40.6 per cent as against 41.2 per cent in John Major's last year in office.

New Labour's focus on improving the bank of individual opportunities available to the socially excluded echoes the political and social thinking of early twentieth century 'new' Liberalism. However, New Labour's approach has more in common with Green's 'hindering of hinderences' than with the radical 'social' liberalism of Hobhouse and Hobson. Indeed, the missing element of New Labour's interpretation of fairness is a developed notion of social justice in taxation. Additional resources, well above those already promised for 2001–2004, are necessary to regenerate the inner cities and to develop the high quality public services required to bind 'Middle England' to universal provision. Within these universal services resources can then be targeted on the people who have not received their fair share of the 'social surplus' (Skocpol, 1991). Without this extra investment, the disaffection – manifested in the extremely low voter turnout in deprived districts in the 2001 General Election and the revival of far-Right parties – will grow. Raising these resources requires the rejuvenation of the 'new' Liberal and socialist principle of the taxation of 'undeserved' income. As Hobhouse said:

> The man who, without further aid than the universally available shares in the social inheritance which is to fall to him as a citizen, pays his way through life, is to be justly regarded as self-supporting. (Hobhouse, 1974 [1911]: 24)

Bibliography

Abel-Smith, B. (1953) *The Reform of Social Security*. London: Fabian Society.

Abel-Smith, B. (1964) *The Hospitals: 1800–1948*. London: Heinemann.

Abel-Smith, B. and Townsend, P. (1965) *The Poor and the Poorest*. London: Bell and Son.

Alberti, S. (1996) *Eleanor Rathbone*. London: Sage.

Aldcroft, D.T. (1970) *The Inter-War Economy*: Britain 1919–1939, London: B.T. Batsford.

Aldridge, N. (1996) 'Only demi-paradise?: Women in garden cities and new towns', *Planning Perspectives*, 11, 23–49.

Alexander, A. (1985) *Borough Government and Politics: Reading 1835–1985*. London: George Allen & Unwin.

Ambrose, P. (1994) *Urban Process and Power*. London: Routledge.

Anderson, T., and Sim, D. (2000) (eds) *Housing and Social Exclusion Context and Challenges*. Coventry: Chartered Institute of Housing and Housing Studies.

Anner, J. (1996) *Beyond Identity Politics: Emerging Social Justice Movements: Communities of Color*. New York: South End Press.

Ashley, W. (1925) *The Economic Organisation of England: An Outline History*. London: Longmans, Green and Co.

Atkinson, A.B. (1969) *Poverty in Britain and the Reform of Social Security*. Cambridge: Cambridge University Press.

Atkinson, A.B. (1972) *Unequal Shares*. Harmondsworth: Penguin.

Atkinson, A.B. (1983) *The Economics of Inequality*. Oxford: Clarendon Press.

Atkinson, A.B. (1991) *Social Insurance*. London: Suntory-Toyota International Centre for Economics and Related Disciplines.

Atkinson, A.B. (1995) *Incomes and the Welfare State*. Cambridge: Cambridge University Press.

Atkinson, A.B. (2000) 'Distribution of income and wealth in Britain over the twentieth century' in A.H. Halsey and J. Webb (eds), *British Social Trends*. Basingstoke: Macmillan.

Atkinson, R. and Moon, G. (1994) *Urban Policy in Britain: The City, the State and the Market*. Basingstoke: Macmillan.

Audit Commission (1985) *Managing Social Services for the Elderly More Effectively*. London: HMSO.

Audit Commission (1986) *Making A Reality of Community Care*. London: HMSO.

Bacon, R. and Eltis, W. (1976) *Britain's Economic Problem: Too Few Producers*, Basingstoke: Macmillan.

Baker, K. (1993) *The Turbulent Years: My Life in Politics*. London: Faber.

Banks, J., Blundell, R. and Smith, J.P. (2000) *Wealth Inequality in the United States and Great Britain*. London: Institute for Fiscal Studies.

Barber, M. (1994) *The Making of the 1944 Education Act*. London: Cassell.

Barlow, J., Cocks, R. and Parker, M. (1994) *Planning For Affordable Housing*. London: Department of the Environment.

Barlow Report (1940) *Report of the Royal Commission on the Geographical Distribution of the Industrial Population*, Cmd 6153. London: HMSO.

Barna, T. (1945) *The Redistribution of Incomes Through Public Finance in 1937*. Oxford: Clarendon Press.

Barnes, J. and Lucas, H. (1975) *Educational Priority*. London: HMSO.

Barnett, C. (1986) *The Audit of War: The Illusion and Reality of Britain as a Great Nation*. Basingstoke: Macmillan.

Barnett, C. (1995) *The Lost Victory: British Dreams, British Realities 1945–1950*. Basingstoke: Macmillan.

Barr, N.A. (1980) 'Taxation, benefits and pay; action on the social division of welfare' in M. Brown, and S. Baldwin (eds), *The Yearbook of Social Policy in Britain 1977*. London: Routledge and Kegan Paul.

Barr, N.A. (1998) *The Economics of the Welfare State*. Oxford: Oxford University Press.

Barr, N.A. (2000) *The Economics of the Welfare State*. Oxford: Oxford University Press.

Barrett, M. and McIntosh, M. (1982) *The Anti-Social Family*. London: Verso.

Barry, N. (1990) *Welfare*, Buckingham: Open University Press.

Bartlett, W. and Le Grand, J.A. (1993) *Quasi-Markets and Social Policy*. Basingstoke: Macmillan.

Bartlett, W., Roberts, J.A. and Le Grand, J.A. (1998) *Revolution in Social Policy: Quasi-Market Reforms in the 1990s*. Bristol: Policy Press.

Bebbington, D.W. (1982) *The Nonconformist Conscience: Chapel and Politics 1870–1914*. London: George Allen and Unwin.

Bedarida, F. (1990) *A Social History of England 1851–1990*. London: Routledge.

Beddoe, D. (1989) *Back to Home and Duty: Women Between the Wars 1918–1939*. London: Pandora.

Beenstock, M. and Brasse, V. (1986) *Insurance for Unemployment*. London: Allen & Unwin.

Bellamy, C. (1988) *Administering Central-Local Relations 1871–1919*. Manchester: Manchester University Press.

Benn, C. and Chitty, C. (1996) *Thirty Years On: Is Comprehensive Education Alive and Well or Struggling to Survive?* Harmondsworth: Penguin.

Bentham, J. (1948) [1776] *A Fragment of Government*. Oxford: Blackwell.

Bentham, J. (1970a) [1781] *An Introduction to the Principles of Morals and Legislation*. London: Athlone Press.

Bentham, J. (1970b) [1798] *Pauper Management Improved*. London: Baldwin and Ridgeway.

Bernstein, G.L. (1986) *Liberalism and Liberal Politics in Edwardian England*. London: Allen and Unwin.

Bevan, A. (1946) Speech to House of Commons.

Bevan, A. (1952) *In Place of Fear*. London: Heinemann.

Beveridge, W.H. (1906) 'The problem of the unemployed', *Sociological Papers*, Vol. 3.

Beveridge, W.H. (1909) *Unemployment: a Problem of Industry*. London: Longmans, Green and Co.

Beveridge, W.H. (1942) *Social Insurance and Allied Services*. Cmd 6404. London: HMSO.

Beveridge, W.H. (1943) *The Pillars of Security and Other War-Time Essays*. London: George Allen & Unwin.

Birch, R.C. (1974) *The Shaping of the Welfare State*. London: Longman.

Blackley, W.L. (1905) *Thrift and National Insurance as a Security against Pauperism*. London: Kegan Paul and Co.

Blackman, T. (1995) *Urban Policy in Practice*. London: Routledge.

Blackstone, T. (1971) *A Fair Start: the Provision of Pre-school Education*. London: Allen Lane.

Blair, T. (1995) 'The Rights We Enjoy, the Duties We Owe', The Spectator Lecture, London.

Blair, T. (1996) *New Britain: My Vision of a Young Country*. London: Fourth Estate.

Blair, T. (1998) *The Third Way*. London: Fabian Society.

Blair, T. (1999a) 'Beveridge revisited: a welfare state for the 21st century', in R. Walker (ed.), *Ending Child Poverty: Popular Welfare for the 21st Century*. Bristol: Policy Press.

Blair, T. (1999b) Speech to Labour Party Conference, September.

Blair, T. (2001) 'Third way, phase two', *Prospect*, March, 10–13.

Blair, T. and Schröder, G. (1999) *Europe: The Third Way/Die Neue Mitte. www.labour.org.uk*.

Blaug, M. (1990) *John Maynard Keynes: Life, Ideas, Legacy*. Basingstoke: Macmillan/Institute of Economic Affairs.

Bliss, A.D.P. (1909) (ed.) *The New Encyclopaedia of Social Reform*. London: Punk and Wagnalls.

Board of Education (1938) *Report of the Consultative Committee on Secondary Education with Special Reference to Grammar Schools and Technical High Schools* (The Spens Report). London: HMSO.

Boddy, M. and Gray, F. (1979) 'Filtering theory: housing policy and the legitimation of inequality', *Policy and Politics*, 7, 39–54.

Bolderson, S. (1991) *Social Security, Disability and Rehabilitation: Conflicts in the Development of Social Policy 1914–1946*. London: Jessica Kingsley Publishers.

Booth, C. (1969) [1892] *Labour and Life of the People in London*. First series: Poverty 11, New York: Augustus M. Kelly.

Booth, C. (1902) *Labour and Life of the People of London* (2nd Edition). London: Macmillan.

Bosanquet, B.P. (1893) *The Civilisation of Christendom and Other Studies*. London: Swan Sonnenschein.

Bosanquet, B.P. (1917) *A Handy Book for Visitors of the Poor in London*. London: Longmans.

Bosanquet, H. (1902) *The Strength of the People: A Study in Social Economics*. London: Macmillan.

Bosanquet, H. (1906) *The Family*. London: Macmillan.

Bosanquet, H. (1909) *The Poor Law Report of 1909*. London: Macmillan.

Boss, P. (1971) *Exploration into Child Care*. London: Routledge and Kegan Paul.

Bottomore, T. and Rubel, M. (1990) *Karl Marx: Selected Writings in Sociology and Social Philosophy*. Harmondsworth: Penguin.

Bourke, J. (1994) *Working-Class Cultures in Britain 1890–1960: Gender, Class, Ethnicity*. London: Routledge.

Bovenkerk, F. (1984) 'The rehabilitation of the rabble: how and why Marx and Engels wrongly depicted the lumpen-proletariat as a reactionary force', *The Netherlands Journal of Sociology*, 20 (1), 13–42.

Bowlby, M. (1945) *Housing and the State 1919–1944*. London: George Allen and Unwin.

Bowley, A.L. (1919) *The Change in the Distribution of the National Income 1880–1913*. Oxford: Oxford University Press.

Bowmaker, E. (1895) *The Housing of the Working Classes*. London: Methuen.

Bowpitt, G. (2000) 'Poverty and its early critics: the search for a value-free definition of the problem' in J. Bradshaw and R. Sainsbury (eds), *Getting the Measure of Poverty: The Early Legacy of Seebohm Rowntree*. Aldershot: Ashgate.

Boyle, D. (1989) *Building Futures: Layman's Guide to the Inner City Debate*. London: W.H. Allen.

Bradshaw, J. (2000) 'Child poverty under Labour' in G. Fimister (ed.), *End in Sight? Tackling Child Poverty in the UK*. London: Child Poverty Action Group.

Braithwaite, W.J. (1957) *Lloyd George's Ambulance Wagon*. London: Cedric Chivers Ltd.

Branson, N. and Heinemann, M. (1973) *Britain in the Nineteen Thirties*. Herts: Panther.

Brewer, M. (2001) 'Comparing in-work benefits and the reward to work for families with children in the US and the UK', *Fiscal Studies*, 22 (1), 41–78.

Bridgen, P. and Lowe, R. (1998) *Welfare Policy under the Conservatives*. London: Public Records Office.

Briggs, A. (1969) 'The welfare state in historical perspective' in C. Schottland (ed.), *The Welfare State*. New York: Harper and Row.

British Medical Association (1969) *Health Services Financing*. London: British Medical Association.

Brown, G. (1995) Speech to the Labour Finance and Industry Group, 17 May 1995.

Brown, G. (1997) 'Responsibility in public finance', speech at the Queen Elizabeth Conference Centre, 20 January.

Brown, J.C. (1990) *Victims or Villains? Social Security Benefits in Unemployment*, York: Joseph Rowntree Memorial Trust.

Brown, J.C. (1992) *Social Security for Retirement*. York: Joseph Rowntree Foundation.

Brown, K.D (1971) *Labour and Unemployment 1900–1914*, Newton Abbott, David and Charles.

Bruce, M. (1973) *The Rise of the Welfare State: English Social Policy 1601–1971*. London: Weidenfeld and Nicolson.

Buckler, S. and Dolowitz, D. (2000) 'New Labour's ideology: a reply to Michael Freeden', *Political Quarterly*, February 2000, 102–9.

Bunbury, H. (1957) 'Introduction to Lloyd George's Ambulance Wagon' in W.J. Braithwaite, *Lloyd George's Ambulance Wagon*. London: Cedric Chivers Ltd.

Burden, T., Cooper, C. and Petrie, S. (2000) *Modernising Social Policy: Unravelling New Labour's Welfare Reforms*. Aldershot: Ashgate.

Burgess, S. and Propper, C. (1999) 'Poverty in Britain' in P. Gregg, and J. Wadsworth (eds), *The State of Working Britain*. Manchester: Manchester University Press.

Burgess, T. and Travers, T. (1980) *Ten Billion Pounds: Whitehall's Takeover of Town Halls*. London: Grant MacIntyre.

Burke, E. (1790) 'Reflections on the revolution in France' in *The Works of the Right Honourable Edmund Burke*, Vol. 2, London: Henry G. Bohn.

Burnett, J. (1994) *Idle Hands: The Experience of Unemployment*. 1790–1990. London: Routledge.

Butler, A.R. (1971) *The Art of the Possible*. London: Hamish Hamilton.

Cabinet Office Performance and Innovation Unit (2001) *Social Mobility: A Discussion Paper*. London: Cabinet Office.

Callaghan, J. (1987) *Time and Chance*. London: Collins.

Callinicos, A. (2000) *Equality*. Cambridge: Polity.

Campbell, J. (1987) *Nye Bevan and the Mirage of British Socialism*. London: Weidenfeld and Nicolson.

Campbell, T. (1983) *The Left and Rights: A Conceptual Analysis of the Idea of Socialist Rights*. London: Routledge and Kegan Paul.

Campbell, J. (2000) *Margaret Thatcher, Volume One: The Grocer's Daughter*. London: Jonathan Cape.

Carey, J. (1992) *The Intellectuals and the Masses*. London: Faber and Faber.

Carling, E.R. and McIntosh, T.S. (1945) *The Hospital Services of the North-Western Area*. London: HMSO.

Castells, M. (1998) *End of Millennium*. Oxford: Blackwell.

Castle, B. (1994) *Fighting All The Way*. London: Pan Books.

Central Advisory Council for Education (1963) *Half Our Future* [Newsom Report]. London: HMSO.

Central Advisory Council for Education (1966) *Children and their Primary Schools* [Plowden Report]. London: HMSO.

Central Housing Advisory Committee (1955) *Unsatisfactory Tenants*. London: HMSO.

Central Housing Advisory Committee (1969) *Council Housing: Purposes, Procedures and Priorities*. London: HMSO.

Central Statistical Office (1980) 'The effects of taxes and benefits on household income: 1978' *Economic Trends*, 533, 99–115, London: Stationery Office.

Chadwick, E. (1842) *Report of the Sanitary Conditions of the Labouring Population of Great Britain*. M. Flynn (ed.), 1965, Edinburgh: Edinburgh University Press.

Chancellor of the Exchequer (1976) *Public Expenditure to 1979–80*, Cmnd 6393. London: HMSO.

Chancellor of the Exchequer (1998) *Modern Public Services for Britain: Investing in Reform*, Cm 4011. London: Stationery Office.

Chancellor of the Exchequer (1999) *Economic and Fiscal Report Statement and Budget Report*, House of Commons Paper No. HC 298, London: Stationery Office.

Chancellor of the Exchequer (2000) *Prudent for a Purpose: Building Opportunity and Security for All*, Cm 4807. London: Stationery Office.

Chamberlain, J. (1885) The Radical Programme, in D.A. Hamer (ed.) (1971) *The Radical Programme*. London: Harvester Press.

Charity Organisation Society (1881) *Dwellings of the Poor*. London: Charity Organisation Society.

Charnley, J. (1996) *A History of Conservative Politics 1900–1996*. Basingstoke: Macmillan.

Checkland, S.G. (1983) *British Public Policy 1776–1939*. Cambridge: Cambridge University Press.

Checkland, S.G. and Checkland, E.O. (eds) (1974) *The Poor Law Report of 1834*. Harmondsworth: Penguin.

Cherry, G.E. (1988) *Cities and Plans: The Shaping of Urban Britain in the Nineteenth and Twentieth Centuries*. London: Edward Arnold.

Cherry, S. (1996) *Medical Services and the Hospitals in Britain 1860–1939*. Cambridge: Cambridge University Press.

Child Poverty Action Group (1993) 'Main events', *Poverty*, 86, Winter 5.

Chitty, C. (1992) *The Education System Transformed*. Manchester: Baseline Books.

Clark, T., Myck, M. and Smith, J. (2001) *Fiscal Reforms Affecting Households, 1996–2001*. London: Institute for Fiscal Studies.

Clarke, A. (1998) *The Tories: Conservatives and the Nation State 1922–1997*. London: Weidenfeld and Nicholson.

Clarke, J. and Langan, M. (1993) 'The British welfare state: foundation and modernization', in A. Cochrane and J. Clarke (eds), *Comparing Welfare States: Britain in International Context*. London: Sage.

Clarke, J., Cochrane, A. and Smart, A. (1987) *Ideologies of Welfare: From Dreams to Disillusion*. London: Hutchinson.

Clarke, J.J. (1937) *The Local Government of the United Kingdom and the Irish Free State*. London: Isaac Pitman and Sons.

Clarke, P. (1978) *Liberals and Social Democrats*, Cambridge: Cambridge University Press.

Clough, R. (1992) *Labour: A Party Fit For Imperialism*. London: Larkin.

Cockett, R. (1995) *Thinking The Unthinkable*. London: HarperCollins.

Coleman, D. (1988) 'Population', in A.H. Halsey (ed.), *British Social Trends Since 1900*. Basingstoke: Macmillan.

Colledge, D. (1989) *Labour Camps: The British Experience*. Sheffield: Sheffield Popular Publishing.

Collini, S. (1979) *Liberalism and Sociology*. Cambridge: Cambridge University Press.

Commission on Social Justice (1993) *The Justice Gap*. London: Institute for Public Policy Research.

Commission on Social Justice (1994) *Social Justice: Strategies For National Renewal*. London: Vintage.

Conservative Party (1951) *Manifesto*. London: Conservative Party.

Conservative Party (1970) *A Better Tomorrow*. London: Conservative Party.

Conservative Party (1979) *The Best Future for Britain*. London: Conservative Party.

Conservative Party (1987) *The Next Moves Forward: The Conservative Party Manifesto 1987*. London: Conservative Party.

Conservative Party (1992) *The Best Future for Britain*. London: Conservative Party.

Constantine, S. (1983) *Social Conditions in Britain 1918–1939*. London: Methuen.

Copley, S. and Sutherland, K. (1995) *Adam Smith's Wealth of Nations*. Manchester: Manchester University Press.

Cox, C.B. and Boyson, R. (1975) *Black Paper 1975: The Fight For Education*. London: Dent and Sons.

Cox, C.B. and Dyson, R. (1977) *Fight for Education*. London: Critical Quarterly Society.

Craig, F.W.S. (1975) British General Election Manifestos. Basingstoke: Macmillan.

Cronin, J.E. (1991) *The Politics of State Expansion: War, State and Society in Twentieth Century Britain*. London: Routledge.

Crosland, C.A.R. (1962) *The Conservative Enemy: a Programme for Radical Reform in the 1960s*. London: Jonathan Cape.

Crossman, R.H.S. (1969) *Paying for the Social Services*, Fabian Tract 399. London: Fabian Society.

Crowther, M.A. (1978) 'The later years of the workhouse 1890–1929' in P. Thane (ed.), *The Origins of British Social Policy*. London: Croom Helm.

Crowther Report (1959) *Fifteen To Eighteen*. London: HMSO.

Culyer, A.J. (1976) *Need and the National Health Service: Economics and Social Change*. London: Martin Robertson.

Cummins, P. (ed.) (1993) *Combating Exclusion in Ireland 1990–1994: A Midway Report*. Brussels: European Commission, Brussels.

Curtis, L. (1956) *Octavia Hill: Pioneer of the National Trust and Housing Reformer.* London: Hutchinson.

Darley, G. (1990) *Octavia Hill: A Life.* London: Constable.

Daunton, M.J. (1995) *Progress and Poverty: An Economic and Social History of Britain 1700–1850.* Oxford: Oxford University Press.

Davidof, L. (1990) 'The family in Britain' in F.M.L. Thomson (ed.), *The Cambridge Social History of Britain 1750–1950 Vol. 2.* Cambridge: Cambridge University Press.

Davies, B. (1968) *Social Needs and Resources in Local Services.* London: Michael Joseph.

Davies, B. and Reddin, M. (1978) *Universality, Selectivity and Effectiveness in Social Policy.* London: Heinemann.

Davin, A. (1996) *Growing Up Poor: Home, School and Street in London, 1870–1914.* London: Rivers Oram Press.

Davis, E. (1998) *Public Spending.* Harmondsworth: Penguin.

Deacon, A. (1982) 'An end to the means test? Social security and the Atlee government', *Journal of Social Policy*, 11 (3), 289–306.

Deacon, A. and Bradshaw, J. (1983) *Reserved For The Poor.* Oxford: Martin Robinson.

Deakin, N. (1969) *Colour, Citizenship and British Society.* London: Panther.

Dean, M. (1991) *The Constitution of Poverty: Towards a Genealogy of Liberal Governance.* London: Routledge.

Dell, E. (2000) *A Strange Eventful History: Democratic Socialism in Britain.* London: HarperCollins.

Denham, A. and Garnett, M. (2001) *Keith Joseph.* Bucks: Acumen.

Dennis, N. and Halsey, A.H. (1988) *English Ethical Socialism.* Oxford: Clarendon Press.

Department for Education and Employment (1996) *Self-Government for Schools,* Cm 3315. London: HMSO.

Department of Employment/Department of Social Security (1994) *Jobseeker's Allowance,* Cm 2687. London: HMSO.

Department of the Environment (1973) *Better Homes, The Next Priorities.* London: HMSO.

Department of the Environment (1987) *Housing: The Governments Proposals,* Cm 214. London: HMSO.

Department of the Environment (1995) *Access to Local Authority and Housing Association Tenancies: A Consultation Paper.* London: Department of the Environment.

Department of the Environment, Transport and the Regions (2000a) *Come In Out of the Cold.* London: Department of the Environment, Transport and the Regions.

Department of the Environment, Transport and the Regions (2000b) *Quality and Choice: A Decent Home for All: The Housing Green Paper.* London: Stationery Office.

Department of the Environment, Transport and the Regions (2000c) *Housing and Construction Statistics: Great Britain.* June Quarter 1999 Part 2. London: Stationery Office.

Department of Health (1989) *Working For Patients.* London: HMSO.

Department of Health (1998) *Towards Occupational Health Solutions.* London: Stationery Office.

Department of Health, Welsh Office (1997) *Social Services: Achievements and Challenge.* London: Stationery Office.

Department of Health and Social Security (1974) *Report of the Committee on One-Parent Families* Cmnd 5629, [The Finer Report] Vol. 1. London: HMSO.

Department of Health and Social Security (1975) *Better Services For The Mentally Ill.* Cmnd 6233. London: HMSO.

Department of Health and Social Security (1976) *Priorities for Health and Personal Social Services.* London: HMSO.

Department of Health and Social Security (1981a) *Care In Action.* London: HMSO.

Department of Health and Social Security (1981b) *Growing Older.* London: HMSO.

Department of Health and Social Security (1985a) *Reform of Social Security: Programme for Change,* Cmnd 9517. London: HMSO.

Department of Health and Social Security (1985b) *Reform of Social Security: Programme for Change.* Vol. 2, Cmnd 9518. London: HMSO.

Department of Health and Social Security (1985c) *Reform of Social Security: Programme for Action.* London: HMSO.

Department of Social Security (2000) *The Changing Welfare State: Pensioner Incomes.* London: Department of Social Security.

Department of Social Security (2001) *The Abstract of Statistics for Social Security Benefits and Contributions and Indices of Prices and Earnings, 2000 Edition.* London: Department of Social Security.

Department of Social Security Analytical Services Division (1999) *Opportunity For All: Indicators of Success: Definitions, Data and Baseline Information.* London: Stationery Office.

Department of Social Security Analytical Services Division (2001) *Households Below Average Income 1994/5 to 1999/2000.* London: Stationery Office.

Department of Transport, Local Government and the Regions (2001) *Statutory Homelessness: England – First Quarter 2001.* London: Department of Transport, Local Government and the Regions.

Dicey, A.V. (1981) [1914] *Lectures on Law and Public Opinion in England During the Nineteenth Century.* New York: Transaction Books.

Digby, A. (1989) *British Welfare Policy: Workhouse to Workfare.* London: Faber & Faber.

Digby, A. (1996) 'Poverty, health and the politics of gender in Britain, 1870–1948' in A. Digby, and Stewart, J. (eds), *Gender, Health and Welfare.* London: Routledge.

Digby, A. and Stewart, J. (eds) (1996) 'Welfare in context' in A. Digby, and Stewart, J. (eds), *Gender, Health and Welfare.* London: Routledge.

Dilnot, A., Kay, J. and Morris, C. (1984) *The Reform of Social Security.* Oxford: Oxford University Press.

Dilnot, A., Disney, R., Johnson, P. and Whitehouse, E. (1994) *Pensions Policy in the UK: An Economic Analysis.* London: The Institute of Fiscal Studies.

Donnison, D. (1962) *Health, Welfare and Democracy in Greater London.* Greater London Papers. London: London School of Economics.

Donnison, D. (1965) *Social Policy and Administration.* London: George Allen & Unwin.

Douglas, I. and Lord, S. (1986) *Local Government Finance: A Practical Guide.* London: Local Government Information Unit.

Douglas, J.W.B. (1964) *The Home and the School.* London: Macmillan.

Driver, F. (1993) *Power and Pauperism: The Workhouse System 1834–1884.* Cambridge: Cambridge University Press.

Dupree, M. (2000) 'The provision of social services' in M. Daunton (ed.), *The Cambridge Urban History of Britain: Volume III 1840–1950.* Cambridge: Cambridge University Press.

Dugdale, R.L. (1877) *The Jukes: A Study in Crime, Pauperism, Disease and Heredity*. New York: G.P. Putnam and Sons.

Dunleavy, P. (1981) *The Politics of Mass Housing in Britain, 1945–1975*. Oxford: Clarendon Press.

Dutton, D. (1991) *British Politics Since 1945: The Rise and Fall of Consensus*. Oxford: Basil Blackwell.

Dwork, D. (1987) *War is Good for Babies and Other Young Children: A History of the Infant and Child Welfare Movement in England 1898–1918*. London: Tavistock Publications.

Eckstein, H. (1958) *The English Health Service*. Harvard: Harvard University Press.

Edgar, A. and Sedgwick, P. (1999) *Key Concepts in Cultural Theory*. London: Routledge.

Edsell, N.C. (1971) *The Anti-Poor Law Movement 1834–54*. Manchester: Manchester University Press.

Edwards, J. (1995) *When Race Counts: The Morality of Racial Preference in Britain and America*, London: Routledge.

Eisenstein, Z. (1980) 'The state, the patriarchal family and working mothers', *Kapitaliststate*, Vol. 8 (1), pp. 43–66.

Ellison, N. (1994) *Egalitarian Thought and Labour Politics: Retreating Visions*. London: Routledge.

Emmerson, C. and Frayne, C. (2001) *Election 2001: Overall Tax and Spending*. London: Institute for Fiscal Studies.

Englander, D. (1998) *Poverty and Poor Law Reform in Britain: From Chadwick to Booth*. Harlow: Longman.

Enthoven, A.C. (1988) *Theory and Practice of Managed Competition in Health Care Finance*. Amsterdam: North-Holland.

Esping-Andersen, G. (1994) 'Welfare states and the economy' in N.J. Smelser and R. Swedberg (eds), *Handbook of Economic Sociology*. Princeton, NJ: Princeton University Press.

Etzioni, A. (1995) *The Spirit of Community*. London: Fontana.

Evans, E.J. (1978) *Social Policy 1830–1914: Individualism, Collectivism and the Origins of the Welfare State*. London: Routledge and Kegan Paul.

Evans, M. and Glennerster, H. (1993) *Squaring the Circle? The Inconsistencies and Constraints of the Beveridge Plan*. London: Suntory-Toyota International Centre for Economics and Related Disciplines.

Evy, H.V. (1971) 'The land campaign: Lloyd George as social reformer 1909–14' in A.J.P. Taylor (ed.), *Lloyd George: Twelve Essays*. London: Hamish Hamilton.

Fabian Society (2000) *Paying for Progress: A New Politics for Public Spending*. London: Fabian Society.

Fairclough, N. (2000) *New Labour, New Language*. London: Routledge.

Faulks, K. (1998) *Citizenship in Modern Britain*. Edinburgh: Edinburgh University Press.

Fforde, M. (1990) *Conservatism and Collectivism 1886–1914*. Edinburgh: Edinburgh University Press.

Fido, L. (1977) 'The charity organization society and social casework in London 1869–1900' in A.P. Donajgrodzki (ed.), *Social Control in Nineteenth Century Britain*. London: Croom Helm.

Field, F. (1971) *Poor People and the Conservative Government*. London: Child Poverty Action Group.

Field, F. (1981) *Inequality in Britain: Freedom, Welfare and the State*. London: Fontana.

Field, F. (1997) *Reforming Welfare*. London: Social Market Foundation.

Field, F. (1998) *Reflections on Welfare Reform*. London: Social Market Foundation.

Field, F., Meacher, M. and Pond, C. (1977) *To Him Who Hath*. Harmondsworth: Penguin.

Fielding, S. (1998) 'The good war 1939–45' in N. Tiratsoo (ed.), *From Blitz to Blair*. London: Phoenix.

Fimister, G. (1995) *Social Security and Community Care in the 1990s*. Sunderland: Business Education Publishers.

Finlayson, G.B.A.M. (1994) *Citizenship and Social Welfare in Britain 1830–1990*. Edinburgh: Edinburgh University Press.

Finn, D. (2001) 'Welfare to work? New Labour and the unemployed' in S.P. Savage and R. Atkinson (eds), *Public Policy Under Blair*. Basingstoke: Palgrave.

Finn, M. (1993) *After Chartism: Class and Nation in English Radical Politics, 1848–1874*. Cambridge: Cambridge University Press.

Fisk, M. (1996) *Housing in the Rhondda 1800–1940*. Cardiff: Merton Priory Press.

Fleming, J. and Oppenheimer, P. (1996) 'Are government spending and taxes too high (or too low)? National Institute Economic Review, July 1996.

Floud, R. (1997) *The People and the British Economy 1830–1914*. Oxford: Oxford University Press.

Forster, W.E. (1870) Speech to the House of Commons, 17 February.

Forsyth, G. (1966) *Doctors and State Medicine*. London: Pitman Medical.

Foster, P. and Wilding, P. (2000) 'Whither welfare professionalism?' *Social Policy and Administration*, Vol. 24, No. 2, June 143–149.

Francis, M. (1997) *Ideas and Policies under Labour 1945–1951: Building a New Britain*. Manchester: Manchester University Press.

Francis, M. and Morrow, J. (1994) *A History of English Political Thought in the Nineteenth Century*. London: Duckworth.

Fraser, N. (1998) 'From redistribution to recognition? Dilemmas of justice in a "post-socialist" age' in C. Willett (ed.), *Theorising Multiculturalism: A Guide to the Current Debate*. Oxford: Blackwell.

Fraser, N. (2000) 'Rethinking recognition', *New Left Review*, 3, May/June, 2000, 107–121.

Fraser, N. and Gordon, L. (1994) 'Civil citizenship against social citizenship' in B. van Steenbergen (ed.), *The Condition of Citizenship*. London: Sage.

Frazer, W.M. (1950) *A History of English Public Health*. Bailliere: Tindall and Cox.

Freeden, M. (1978) *The New Liberalism: An Ideology of Social Reform*. Oxford: Clarendon Press.

George, H. (1979) [1879] *Progress and Poverty*. London: Hogarth Press.

George, V. (1968) *Social Security: Beveridge and After*, London: Routledge and Kegan Paul.

George, V. and Wilding, P. (1994) *Welfare and Ideology*. Hemel Hempstead: Harvester.

Giddens, A. (1998) *The Third Way*. Cambridge: Polity Press.

Giddens, A. (2000) *The Third Way and its Critics*. Cambridge: Polity Press.

Gilbert, B.B. (1966) *The Evolution of National Insurance in Great Britain: The Origins of the Welfare State*. London: Michael Joseph.

Gilbert, B.B. (1970) *British Social Policy 1914–39*. London: B.T. Batsford Ltd.

Gilbert, B.B. (1987) *David Lloyd George: The Architect of Change 1863–1912*. Ohio: Ohio State University.

Giles, J. (1995) *Women, Identity and Politics, 1900–1950*: Basingstoke: Macmillan.

Giles, C. and Johnson, P. (1994) *Taxes Down, Taxes Up, The Effects of a Decade of Tax Changes*, London: The Institute for Fiscal Studies.

Gillie, A. (2000) 'Rowntree, poverty lines and school boards' in J. Bradshaw and R. Sainsbury (eds), *Getting the Measure of Poverty: The Early Legacy of Seebohm Rowntree*. Aldershot: Ashgate.

Ginsburg, N. (1992) 'Racism and housing: concepts and reality' in P. Braham, A. Rattans and R. Skellington (eds), *Racism and Antiracism*. London: Sage.

Gladstone, D. (1999) *The Twentieth Century Welfare State*. Basingstoke: Macmillan.

Gladstone, F.J. (1979) *Voluntary Action in a Changing World*. London: Bedford Square Press.

Glennerster, H. (1995) *British Social Policy Since 1945*. Oxford: Blackwell.

Glennerster, H., Hills, J., Travers, T. with Hendry, J. (2000) *Paying for Health, Education, and Housing: How Does the Centre Pull the Purse Strings?* Oxford: Oxford University Press.

Glynn, S. and Oxborrow, J. (1976) *Interwar Britain: A Social and Economic History*. London: Allen and Unwin.

Goddard, H.H. (1912) *The Kallikak Family: A Study in the Heredity of Feeblemindedness*. New York: Macmillan.

Goldthorpe, J. (2001) *Mobility, Education and Meritocracy*. Maxwell Cummings Lecture, Montreal: McGill University.

Goodin, R.E. (1988) *Reasons For Welfare*. Princeton: Princeton University Press.

Goodin, R.E. and Le Grand, J. (1987) *Not Only The Poor: The Middle Classes and the Welfare State*. London: Unwin Hymen Ltd.

Goodman, A., Johnson, P. and Webb, S. (1997) *Inequality in the UK*. Oxford: Oxford University Press.

Goodman, A. (2001) 'Income inequality: what has happened under New Labour?', *New Economy*, Vol. 8, No. 2, June, 92–97.

Gough, I. (1979) *The Political Economy of the Welfare State*. Basingstoke: Macmillan.

Gould, B. (1995) *Goodbye To All That*. Basingstoke: Macmillan.

Gould, P. (1998) *The Unfinished Revolution*. London: Little, Brown and Co.

Gorsky, M. (1999) *Patterns of Philanthropy, Charity and Society in Nineteenth-Century Bristol*. London: Royal Historical Society.

Gosden, P.H.J.H. (1961) *The Friendly Societies in England 1815–1875*. Manchester: Manchester University Press.

Gray, A. (2001) '"Making work pay" – devising the best strategy for lone parents in Britain', *Journal of Social Policy*, 10 (2), 189–207.

Gray, J. (1995) *Enlightenment's Wake: Politics and Culture at the Close of the Modern Age*. London: Routledge.

Green, D.G. (1985) *Working – Class Patients and the Medical Establishment*. London: Gower/Maurice Temple Smith.

Green, D.G. (1999) *An End to Welfare Rights: The Rediscovery of Independence*. London: Civitas.

Green, J. and Thorogood, N. (1998) *Analysing Health Policy: A Sociological Approach*. London: Addison Wesley Longman.

Green, T.H. (1881) *Liberal Legislation and Freedom of Contract*. London: Simpkin Marshall.

Green, T.H. (1883) *Prolegomena to Ethics*. Oxford: Oxford University Press.

Green, T.H. (1988) [1895] *Lectures on the Principle of Political Obligation* in P. Harris, and J. Morrow (eds), Cambridge: Cambridge University Press.

Greenleaf, W.H. (1983) *The British Political Tradition Volume Two: The Ideological Heritage*. London: Methuen.

Greenwood, A. (1930) *Labour's Plan To Abolish The Slums*. Labour Party.

Gregg, P. (1967) *The Welfare State: An Economic and Social History of Great Britain from 1945 to the Present Day*. London: George G. Harrap and Co.

Gregg, P. and Wadsworth, J. (eds) (1999) *The State of Working Britain*. Manchester: Manchester University Press.

Greve, J. (1971) *Homelessness in London*. Edinburgh: Scottish Academic Press. Edinburgh.

Griffiths, J.A.G. (1966) *Central Departments and Local Authorities*. London: George Allen and Unwin.

Griffiths, J. (1947) Speech to the House of Commons, 24 November. Hansard, Fifth Series Vol. 44 London.

Griffiths, R. (1988) *Community Care: Agenda for Action*. London: HMSO.

Grimes, S.S. (1991) *The British National Health Service*. New York: Garland Publishing.

Habermas, J. (1994) 'Citizenship and national identity' in B. van Steengergen (ed.), *The Condition of Citizenship*. London: Sage.

Hall, R.H. (1979) *The Professionals*. Buckinghamshire: Open University Press.

Hall, P., Land, H., Parker, R. and Webb, A. (1975) *Change, Choice and Conflict in Social Policy*. London: Heinemann.

Hall, P., Thomas, R., Gracey, H., Drewett, R. (1973) *The Containment of Urban England*, Vol. 1. London: George Allen and Unwin.

Hall, P. and Ward, C. (1998) *Sociable Cities: The Legacy of Ebenezer Howard*. Chichester: John Wiley and Sons.

Hallett, G. (1977) *Housing and Land Policies in West Germany and Britain: A Record of Success and Failure*. Basingstoke: Macmillan.

Halsey, A.H. (ed.) (1972) *Educational Priority, Vol. 1: E.P.A. Problems and Policies*. London: HMSO.

Hampshire, S. (1999) *Justice is Conflict*. London: Duckworth.

Hannington, W. (1937) *The Problem of the Distressed Areas*. London: Victor Gollanz.

Hansard (1993) Col. 638, 8 February.

Hansard (2000a) Col. 100, 14 March.

Hansard (2000b) Col. 308, 21 March.

Hansard (2001) Col. 43, 2 April.

Hanson C.G. (1972) 'Welfare before the welfare state' in R.M. Hartwell (ed.), *The Long Debate on Poverty*. London: Institute of Economic Affairs.

Hardwick, P., Khan, B. and Langmead, S. (1994) *An Introduction To Modern Economics*. 4th edition. Harlow: Longman.

Hardy, A. (2001) *Health and Medicine in Britain Since 1860*. Basingstoke: Palgrave.

Harris, J. (1972) *Unemployment and Politics: A Study in English Social Policy 1886–1914*. Oxford: Oxford University Press.

Harris, J. (1993) *Private Lives, Public Spirit: A Social History of Britain 1870–1914*. Oxford: Oxford University Press.

Harris, J. (1999) 'Beveridge and the Beveridge Report – life, ideas, influence' in R. Walker (ed.), *Ending Child Poverty: Popular Welfare for the 21st Century*. Bristol: Policy Press.

Harris, T. (2000) 'The effects of taxes and benefits on household income, 1998–99', *Economic Trends*, No. 557, April 45–75.

Hattersley, R. (1995) *Who Goes Home?: Scenes From Political Life*. London: Warner Books.

Hay, J.R. (1975) *The Origins of the Liberal Reforms*. Basingstoke: Macmillan.

Hay, J.R. (1978) *British Welfare State 1880–1975*. London: Edward Arnold.

Hayek, F.A. (1944) *The Road to Serfdom*. London: Routledge and Kegan Paul.

Hayek, F.A. (1976a) *Law, Legislation and Liberty, Vol. 1, Rules and Social Order*. London: Routledge.

Hayek, F.A. (1976b) *Law, Legislation and Liberty, Vol. 2, The Mirage of Social Justice*. London: Routledge.

Hayek, F.A. (1976c) *Law, Legislation and Liberty, Vol. 3, The Political Order of a Free People*. London: Routledge.

Hayek, F. (1988) *The Fatal Conceit: The Errors of Socialism*, Chicago: University of Chicago Press.

Haynes, R. (1985) *The Geography of Health Services in Britain*. London: Croom Helm.

Heald, D. (1983) *Public Expenditure*. London: Martin Robertson.

Heasman, K. (1962) *Evangelicals in Action: An Appraisal of Their Social Work in the Victorian Era*. London: Geoffrey Bles.

Heath, E. (1998) *The Course of My Life: The Autobiography of Edward Heath*. London: Hodder and Stoughton.

Heb, J. (1981) 'The social policy of the Atlee government', in W.J. Mommsen (ed.), *The Emergence of the Welfare State in Britain and Germany*. London: Croom Helm.

Heilbroner, R.L. (1955) *The Worldly Philosophers*. London: Allen Lane.

Heller, A. (1974) *The Theory of Need in Marx*. London: Allison and Busby.

Henderson, H.D. (1942) 'The principles of the Beveridge Plan: memoranda written while at the Treasury during the war', in H. Clay (ed.), *The Inter-War Years and Other Papers: A Selection from the Writings of Hubert Douglas Henderson*. Oxford: Clarendon Press.

Henderson, P. (ed.) (1950) *Letters of William Morris*. London: Longman.

Hendrick, H. (1994) *Child Welfare: England 1872–1989*. London: Routledge.

Hennessy, P. (1992) *Never Again*. London: Jonathan Cape.

Hennock, E.P. (1987) *British Social Reform and German Precedents: the Case of Social Insurance 1880–1914*. Oxford: Clarendon Press.

Herbert, S.M. (1939) *Britain's Health*. Harmondsworth: Penguin.

Her Majesty's Treasury (1999) *The Modernisation of Britain's Tax and Benefit System, Number Four: Tackling Poverty and Extending Opportunity*. London: HM Treasury.

Her Majesty's Treasury (2000a) *The Goal of Full Employment: Employment Opportunity For All Throughout Britain*. London: HM Treasury.

Her Majesty's Treasury (2000b) *Prudent for a Purpose: Working for a Stronger and Fairer Britain: Financial Statement and Budget Report*. London: Stationery Office.

Her Majesty's Treasury (2001) *Investing for the Long Term: Building Opportunity and Prosperity for All*. London: HM Treasury.

Heseltine, M. (1987) *Where There's A Will*. London: Arrow.

Hewitt, P. (2000) 'How an egalitarian can also be an elitist', *New Statesman*, 21 February, 25–27.

Hickman, M.J. (1998) 'Education for "minorities": Irish Catholics in Britain' in G. Lewis (ed.), *Forming Nation, Framing Welfare*. London: Routledge.

Hicks, U.K. (1954) *British Public Finances: Their Structure and Development 1880–1952*. Oxford: Oxford University Press.

Hill, O. (1889) 'A few words to fresh workers', *The Nineteenth Century*, Vol. XXVI, No. 151, September.

Hills, J. (ed.) (1991) *The State of Welfare: The Welfare State in Britain Since 1974*, Oxford: Clarendon Press.

Hills, J. (1998) *Income and Wealth: The Latest Evidence*. York: Joseph Rowntree Foundation.

Himmelfarb, G. (1984) *The Idea of Poverty: England in the Early Industrial Age*. New York: Alfred A. Knoph.

Himmelfarb, G. (1991) *Poverty and Compassion: The Moral Imagination of the Late Victorians, England in the Early Industrial Age*. London: Faber and Faber.

Himmelfarb, G. (1995) *The De-Moralisation of Society: From Victorian Virtues to Modern Values*. London: Institute of Economic Affairs.

Hirsch, F. (1977) *The Social Limits to Growth*. London: Routledge and Kegan Paul.

Hobhouse, L.T. (1893) *The Labour Movement*. London: Williams and Norgate.

Hobhouse, L.T. (1974) [1911] *Liberalism*. New York: Galaxy Books.

Hobhouse (1911) *Social Evolution and Political Theory*. New York: Columbia College.

Hobson, D. (1999) *The National Wealth: Who Gets What in Britain*. London: HarperCollins.

Hobson, J.A. (1891) *The Problem of Poverty: An Inquiry into the Industrial Condition of the Poor*. London: Methuen.

Hobson, J.A. (1901) *The Social Problem*. London: Nisbet.

Hobson, J.A. (1910) *The Industrial System: An Inquiry into Earned and Unearned Income*. London: Longmans, Green and Co.

Hobson, J.A. (1926) [1894] *The Evolution of Modern Capitalism*. London: Walter Scott.

Hole, J. (1866) *The Homes of the Working Class With Suggestions For Their Improvement*. London: Garland.

Holland, R. (1904) *Heller's Annotated Edition of the New Code for Public Elementary Schools*. London: Bemrose and Son.

Holtermann, S. (1978) 'The Welfare economics of priority area policies', *Journal of Social Policy*, 7 (1), 23–40.

Holman, R., Lafitte, F., Spencer, K. and Wilson, E. (1970) *Socially Deprived Families in Britain*. London: Bedford Square Press.

Holmans, A.E. (1987) *Housing Policy in Britain: A History*. London: Croom Helm.

Home Office (1998) *Supporting Families: a consultation paper*. London: Stationery Office.

Hopcraft, J. (1998) *Intergenerational and Life-Course Transmission of Social Exclusion*. London: Centre for the Analysis of Social Exclusion.

Hopkins, E. (1994) *Childhood Transformed: Working-Class Children in Nineteenth-Century England*. Manchester: Manchester University Press.

Hopkins, E. (1995) *Working-Class Self Help in the Nineteenth Century*. London: UCL Press.

Hoppen, K.T. (1998) *The Mid-Victorian Generation, 1846–1886*. Oxford: Clarendon Press.

Howard, C. (1997) *The Hidden Welfare State: Tax Expenditures and Social Security Policy in the United States*. Princeton, New Jersey: Princeton University Press.

Hughes, G. and Lewis, G. (eds) (1998) *Unsettling Welfare: the Reconstruction of Social Policy*. London: Routledge.

Humphreys, R. (1995) *Sin, Organized Charity and the Poor Law in Victorian England*. London: St. Martins Press.

Humphreys, R. (1999) *No Fixed Abode: A History of Responses to the Roofless and the Rootless in Britain*. Basingstoke: Macmillan.

Humphries, S. and Gordon, P. (1994) *Forbidden Britain*. London: BBC Books.

Hunt, E.H. (1981) *British Labour History 1815–1914*. London: Weidenfeld and Nicolson.

Hunter, J. (1997) *Who Owns Scotland?* Edinburgh: Canongate.

Hurry, J.B. (1910) *Poverty and Its Vicious Circles*. London: J. and A. Churchill.

Hurt, J. (1971) *Education in Evolution: Church, State, Society and Popular Education 1800–1870*. London: Rupert Hart-Davis.

Hutt, A. (1972) *The Post-War History of the British Working Class*. London: EP Publishing Ltd.

Hyndman, H.M. (1887) 'English workers as they are', *Contemporary Review*, 52 (3), 122–36.

Inland Revenue (1997) *Inland Revenue Statistics 1997*. London: HMSO.

Jackson, D., Turner, H.A. and Wilkinson, F. (1972) *Do Trade Unions Cause Inflation?* Cambridge: Cambridge University Press.

Jacobs, L.R. (1993) *The Health of Nations*. New York: Cornell University Press.

Jacobs, S. (1976) *Science and British Liberalism: Locke, Bentham, Mill and Popper*. Aldershot: Avebury.

Jacobs, S. (1985) 'Race, empire and the welfare state: council housing and racism', *Critical Social Policy*, 5 (1), 6–29.

James, S. and Nobbs, C. (1998) *The Economics of Taxation*. Hemel Hempstead: Prentice Hall Europe.

Jarvis, M. (1998) 'The 1958 Treasury Dispute', *Contemporary British History*, 12 (2), 22–50.

Jay, D. (1946) *The Socialist Case*. London: Faber and Faber.

Jeffreys, K. (1987) 'British politics and social policy during the Second World War', *Historical Journal*, 30/1, 123–44.

Jenkins, R. (1966) *Speech to the Committee for Commonwealth Immigrants*, 20 May.

Jenkins, R. (1998) *The Chancellors*. London: Macmillan.

Johnson, P. (1999) 'Inequality, redistribution and living standards in Britain since 1945' in H. Fawcett and R. Lowe (eds), *Welfare Policy in Britain: The Road From 1945*. Basingstoke: Macmillan Press.

Johnston, D. (2000) *Equality*. Indianapolis: Hackett Publishing Company.

Jones, G.S. (1984) *Outcast London: A Study of the Relationship between Classes in Victorian Society*. Harmondsworth: Allen Lane.

Jones, G.S. (1985) 'The Language of Chartism', in J. Epstein and D. Thompson (eds), *The Chartist Experience: Studies in Working-Class Radicalism and Culture, 1830–1860*. London: Macmillan.

Jones, M.E. (1952) *Hannah Moore*. Cambridge: Cambridge University Press.

Jones, K. (1960) *Mental Health and Social Policy 1845–1959*. London: Routledge and Kegan Paul.

Jones, K., Bradshaw, J. and Brown, J. (1983) *Issues in Social Policy*. London: Routledge and Kegan Paul.

Jones, R. (1914) *The Nature and First Principle of Taxation*. London: P.S. King and Son.

Joseph, K. and Sumption, J. (1979) *Equality*. London: John Murray.

Kangas, O. (2000a) 'Distributive justice and social policy: some reflections on Rawls and income distribution', *Social Policy and Administration*, 34 (5), 510–28.

Kangas, O. (2000b) *Distributive Justice and Social Policy*, Maxwell School of Citizenship and Public Affairs, Working Paper 221. New York: Syracuse University.

Kaufman, M. (1975) [1907] *The Housing of the Working Classes and the Poor*. Wakefield: EP Publishing Ltd.

Kay, J.P. (1970) [1832] *The Moral and Physical Condition of the Working Classes Employed in the Cotton Manufacture in Manchester*. London: Cass.

Kay, J.A. and King, M.A. (1986) *The British Tax System*: Oxford: Oxford University Press.

Kellner, P. (1999) 'Equality of access' in D. Leonard (ed.), *Crosland and New Labour*. London: Fabian Society.

Kelly, P. (1998) 'Contractarian social justice: An overview of some contemporary debates', in D. Boucher and P. Kelly (eds), *Social Justice from Hume to Walzer*. London: Routledge.

Kent, S.K. (1999) *Gender and Power in Britain 1640–1990*. London: Routledge.

Kevles, D.J. (1986) *In The Name of Eugenics: Genetics and the Uses of Human Heredity*. Harmondsworth: Pelican.

Keynes, J.M. (1936) *The General Theory of Employment, Interest and Money*. London: Macmillan.

Kincaid, J. (1975), *Poverty and Equality in Britain*. Harmondsworth: Penguin.

King, A. (1975) 'Overload: problems of governing in the 1970s', *Political Studies*, 23 (2), 162–174.

King, D. (1995) *Actively Seeking Work?: The Politics of Unemployment and Welfare Policy in the United States and Great Britain*. Chicago: University of Chicago Press.

King, D. (1999) *In the Name of Liberalism: Illiberal Social Policy in the United States and Britain*. Oxford: Oxford University Press.

King, S. (2000) *Poverty and Welfare in England 1700–1850: A Regional Perspective*. Manchester: Manchester University Press.

Kirkman-Gray, B. (1908) *Philanthropy and the State or Social Politics*. London: P.S. King and Son.

Kley, R. (1994) *Hayek's Social and Political Thought*. Oxford: Clarendon Press.

Krieger, L. (1974) 'The idea of the welfare state' in P. Anderson (ed.), *Lineages of the Absolute State*. London: New Left Books.

Kymlicka, W. (1990) *Contemporary Political Philosophy*. Oxford: Clarendon Press.

Labour Party (1945) *Let Us Face The Future*. London: Labour Party.

Labour Party (1964) *Let's Go with Labour for the New Britain*. London: Labour Party.

Labour Party (1974a) *Let Us Work Together – Labour's Way Out of the Crisis*. London: Labour Party.

Labour Party (1974b) *Britain Will Win With Labour*. London: Labour Party.

Labour Party (1989) *Meet the Challenge, Make the Change*. London: Labour Party.

Labour Party (1992) *It's Time to Get Britain Working Again*. London: Labour Party.

Labour Party (1997) *New Labour Because Britain Deserves Better*. London: Labour Party.

Labour Party (2001) *Ambitions for Britain: Labour's Manifesto 2001*. London: Labour Party.

Lafitte, F. (1945) *Britain's Way to Social Security*. London: Pilot Press.

Lakin, C. (2001) 'The effects of taxes and benefits on household income: 1999–2000'. *Economic Trends* No. 569, 35–72, London: Stationery Office.

Land, A., Lowe, R. and Whiteside, N. (1992) *The Development of the Welfare State 1939–1951*. London: HMSO.

Land, H. (1995) 'Families and the law' in J. Muncie, M. Wetherall, R. Dallos, and A. Cochrane (eds), *Understanding The Family*. London: Sage.

Lavalette, M. and Mooney, G. (2000) *Class Struggle and Social Welfare*. London: Routledge.

Law, B. (1999) *Oldham, Brave Oldham*. Oldham: Oldham Arts and Heritage.

Lawson, N. (1992) *The View From No. 11*. London: Transworld Publishers.

Laybourn, K. (1990) *Britain On The Breadline: A Social and Political History Of Britain Between The Wars*. Gloucester: Allen Sutton.

Laybourn, K. (1995) *The Evolution of British Social Policy and the Welfare State*. Keele: Keele University Press.

Lees, L.H. (1998) *The Solidarities of Strangers: The English Poor Laws and the People 1700–1948*, Cambridge: Cambridge University Press.

Le Grand, J. (1998) *Learning from the NHS Internal Market; A Review of the Evidence*. London: King's Fund.

Letwin, S.R. (1992) *The Anatomy of Thatcherism*. London: Fontana.

Levin, P. (1997) *Making Social Policy*. Buckingham: Open University Press.

Levitas, R. (1998) *The Inclusive Society: Social Exclusion and New Labour*. Basingstoke: Macmillan.

Levy, H. (1944) *National Health Insurance: A Critical Study*. Cambridge: Cambridge University Press.

Lewis, G. (ed.) (1998) *Forming Nation, Framing Welfare*. London: Routledge.

Lewis, J. (1991) *Women and Social Action in Victorian and Edwardian England*. Aldershot: Edward Elgar.

Lewis, J. (1995) *The Voluntary Sector, the State and Social Work in Britain: The Charity Organisation Society/Family Welfare Association since 1869*. Aldershot: Edward Elgar.

Lewis, J. (1999) 'The voluntary sector and the state in twentieth century Britain' in H. Fawcett and R. Lowe (eds), *Welfare Policy in Britain: The Road from 1945*. Basingstoke: Macmillan.

Lidbetter, E.J. (1933a) *Handbooks for Public Assistance Officers, Part 1*. London: Law and Local Government Publications.

Lidbetter, E.J. (1933b) *Heredity and the Social Problem Group*. London: Edward Arnold.

Lister, R. (1997) *Citizenship: Feminist Perspectives*. Basingstoke: Macmillan Press.

Lloyd George, D. (1909) *The New Liberalism: Speeches by the Right Hon. David Lloyd George*. London: Daily News.

Lloyd, J. (1997) 'A plan to abolish the underclass', *New Statesman*, 29 August 13–15.

Local Government Act (1929) London: HMSO.

Loch, C.S. (1895) 'Manufacturing a new pauperism', *The Nineteenth Century*, Vol. XVI, No. 1, April.

Longmate, N. (1974) *The Workhouse*. London: Temple Smith.

Loughlin, M. (1986) *Local Government and the Modern State*. London: Sweet and Maxwell.

Lourie, J. (1999) *National Minimum Wage*, House of Commons Research Paper 99/18, London: House of Commons.

Lowe, R. (1867) Speech to the House of Commons, 1 July, Hansard, Third Series. London: Cornelius Buck.

Lowe, R. (1999) 'Introduction: The Road from 1945' in H. Fawcett and R. Lowe (eds) *Welfare Policy in Britain: The Road from 1945*, Basingstoke: Macmillan Press.

Low Pay Commission (1998) *First Report of the Low Pay Commission*, Cm 3976. London: Stationery Office.

Lydall, H.F. (1959) 'The long-term trend in the size and distribution of income' *Journal of the Royal Statistical Society*, Series A 147, 1–22.

Lynes, T. (1963) *Pension Rights and Wrongs*. London: Fabian Society.

Lynes, T. (1974) 'Policy on social security', in M. Young (ed.), *Poverty Report 1974*. London: Temple Smith.

Mabbott, J.D. (1948) *The State and the Citizen*. London: Hutchinson.

Macfarlane, L.J. (1998) *Socialism, Social Ownership and Social Justice*. Basingstoke: Macmillan.

Mackay, T. (1889) *The English Poor*. London: John Murray.

MacKenzie, D. (1999) 'Eugenics and the rise of mathematical statistics in Britain' in D. Dorling, and S. Simpson (eds), *Statistics in Society: The Arithmetic of Politics*. London: Arnold.

Maclean, M. (1998) 'The origins of child support in Britain and the case for a strong child support system' in R. Ford, and J. Millar (eds), *Private Lives and Public Responses*. London: Policy Studies Institute.

Macleod, I. and Powell, E. (1952) *The Social Services: Needs and Means*. London: Conservative Political Centre.

Maclure, J.S. (1973) *Educational Documents: England and Wales 1816 to the Present Day*. London: Methuen and Co Ltd.

Macmurray, J. (1995) [1961] *The Form of the Personal, Vol. 11: Persons in Relation*. London: Faber and Faber.

Macnicol, J. (1978) 'Family allowances and less eligibility' in P. Thane (ed.), *The Origins of British Social Policy*. London: Croom Helm.

Macnicol, J. (1998) *The Politics of Retirement in Britain 1878–1948*. Cambridge: Cambridge University Press.

Macnicol, J. (1999) 'Problem families to underclass' in H. Fawcett and R. Lowe (eds), *Welfare Policy in Britain: The Road from 1945*. Basingstoke: Macmillan Press.

MacRaild, D.M. (1999) *Irish Migrants in Modern Britain 1750–1922*. Basingstoke: Macmillan.

Mallet, B. (1913) *British Budgets 1887 to 1912–13*. Basingstoke: Macmillan.

Mallock, W.H. (1896) *Classes and Masses, Wealth, Wages and Welfare in the United Kingdom. A Handbook of Social Facts for Political Thinkers and Speakers*. London: A & C Black.

Malpass, P. (1990) *Reshaping Housing Policy: Subsidies, Rents and Residualisation*. London: Routledge.

Malthus, T.R. (1803) *An Essay on the Principle of Population or, A View of its Past and Present Effects on Human Happiness*. 2nd edition. Cambridge: Cambridge University Press.

Mandelson, P. and Liddle, R. (1996) *The Blair Revolution: Can New Labour Deliver?* London: Faber and Faber.

Mann, K. (1992) *The Making of an English 'Underclass'? The Social Divisions of Welfare and Labour*. Buckingham: Open University Press.

Marlow, J. (1997) 'Metaphor, intertextuality, and the political consensus', *Politics*, 17 (2), 127–34.

Marquand, D. (1990) 'A language of community' in B. Pimlott, A. Wright, and T. Flower (eds), *The Alternative: Politics for a Change*. London: W.H. Allen.

Marquand, D. (1996) 'Moralists and hedonists', in D. Marquand, and A. Seldon (eds), *The Ideas That Shaped Post-War Britain*. London: Fontana.

Marquand, D. (1997) *The New Reckoning: Capitalism, States and Citizens*. Oxford: Polity Press.

Marshall, G., Swift, A. and Roberts, S. (1997) *Against the Odds? Social Class and Social Justice in Industrial Societies*. Oxford: Clarendon Press.

Marshall, T.H. (1963) [1950] 'Citizenship and social class' in Marshall, T.H., *Sociology at the Crossroads and Other Essays*. London: Heinemann.

Marshall, T.H. (1981) *The Right to Welfare and Other Essays*. London: Heinemann Educational Books.

Marx, K. (1968) [1875] *Critique of the Gotha Programme*. London: Lawrence and Wishart.

Marx, K. and Engels, F. (1969) *Basic Writings on Politics and Philosophy*. L. Feuer (ed.). London: Collins.

Mason, T. (1998) '"Hunger is a very good thing": Britain in the 1930s' in N. Tiratsoo (ed.), *From Blitz to Blair*. London: Phoenix.

Masterman, C.F.G. (1909) *The Condition of England*. London: Methuen.

Mazumdar, P.M.H. (1992) *Eugenics, Human Genetics and Human Failings: The Eugenics Society, its Sources and its Critics in Britain*. London: Routledge.

McBriar, A.M. (1987) *An Edwardian Mixed Doubles: The Bosanquets versus The Webbs*. Oxford: Clarendon Press.

McCoy, L. (1998) 'Education for Labour: social problems of nationhood' in G. Lewis (ed.), *Forming Nation, Framing State*. London: Routledge.

McCrudden, C. (1990) 'Law and positive discrimination: a British perspective' in S.K. Mitra (ed.), *Politics of Positive Discrimination: A Cross National Perspective*. Aldershot: Dartmouth Press.

McKibbin, R. (1998) *Classes and Cultures: England, 1918–1951*. Oxford: Oxford University Press.

McSmith, A. (1996) *Faces of Labour – the Inside Story*. London: Verso.

McWilliam, R. (1998) *Popular Politics in Nineteenth Century England*. London: Routledge.

Mead, L.M. (1985) *Beyond Entitlement*. New York: Basic Books.

Mead, L.M. (1992) *The New Politics of Poverty*. New York: Basic Books.

Mead, L.M. (1997) *From Welfare to Work: Lessons from America*. London: Institute of Economic Affairs.

Mearns, A. (1983) [1883] *The Bitter Cry of Outcast London*, Leicester: Leicester University Press.

Means, R. and Smith, R. (1998) *Community Care Policy and Practice*. Basingstoke: Macmillan.

Mellor, J.M. (1977) *Urban Sociology in an Urbanized Society*. London: Routledge and Kegan Paul.

Mencher, S. (1967) *Poor Law to Poverty Program*. Pittsburg: University of Pittsburg Press.

Merrett, S. (1979) *State Housing In Britain*. London: Routledge and Kegan Paul.

Merrison, A. (Sir) (1979) *Royal Commission on the National Health Service*, Cmnd 7615, London: HMSO.

Micklewright, J. (1989) 'The strange case of British earnings-related unemployment benefit', *Journal of Social Policy*, 19 (2), 527–48.

Middleton, N. (1971) *When Family Failed*. London: Victor Gollancz.

Middleton, R. (1996) 'The size and scope of the public sector' in S.J.D. Green and R.C. Whiting (eds), *The Boundaries of the State in Modern Britain*. Cambridge: Cambridge University Press.

Midwinter, E.C. (1967) 'State intervention at the local level: the new poor law in Lancashire', *Historical Journal*, 10 (1), 106–12.

Mill, J.S. (1996) [1861] *Considerations On Representative Government*. London: J.M. Dent.

Miller, D. (1999) *Principles of Justice*. Cambridge, MA: Harvard University Press.

Millett J.D. (1940) *The Unemployment Assistance Board*. London: George Allen and Unwin.

Millward, M. and Sheard, S. (1995) 'The urban fiscal problem, 1870–1914: government expenditure and finance in England and Wales', *Economic History Review*, 48 (3), 501–35.

Milner, A. (1999) *Class*. London: Sage.

Ministry of Health (1920) [The Dawson Report] *Interim Report of the Consultative Council on Medical and Allied Services*. London: HMSO.

Ministry of Health (1921) [The Cave Report] *Final Report of the Voluntary Hospitals Committee*. London: HMSO.

Ministry of Health (1927) *Annual Report*. London: HMSO.

Ministry of Health (1947) *Not Yet Five*. London: HMSO.

Ministry of Housing and Local Government (1965) *The Housing Programme: 1965 to 1970*, Cmnd 2838. London: HMSO.

Ministry of Pensions and National Insurance (1958) *Provision for Old Age: The Future Development of the National Insurance Scheme*, Cmnd 538. London: HMSO.

Ministry of Pensions and National Insurance (1959) *Improvements in National Assistance*, Cmnd 782. London: HMSO.

Ministry of Reconstruction (1944a) *Employment Policy*, Cmd 6527. London: HMSO.

Ministry of Reconstruction (1944b) *Social Insurance*, Cmd 6500. London: HMSO.

Ministry of Social Security (1966a) *Circumstances of Families*. London: HMSO.

Ministry of Social Security (1966b) *Financial and Other Circumstances of Retirement Pensioners*. London: HMSO.

Ministry of Social Security (1967) *Supplementary Benefits Commission Annual Report*. London: Ministry of Social Security.

Minor, I. (1979) 'Working-class women and matrimonial law reform' in D.E. Martin and D. Rubinstein (eds), *Ideology and the Labour Movement*. London: Croom Helm.

Mishra, R. (1981) *Society and Social Policy: Theories and Practice of Welfare*. Basingstoke: Macmillan.

Mishra, R. (1984) *The Welfare State in Crisis*. Brighton: Harvester Wheatsheaf.

Mishra, R. (1999) *Globalization and the Welfare State*. Cheltenham: Edward Elgar.

Mohan, J. (1998) 'Uneven development, territorial politics and the British health care reforms', *Political Studies*, 46 (2), 309–27.

Monck, E. and Lomas, G. (1980) *Housing Action Areas: Success and Failure*. London: Centre For Environmental Studies.

Money, C.L.G. (1910) *Riches and Poverty*. London: Methuen.

Moroney, R.M. (1976) *The Family and the State*. London: Longman.

Morton, J. (1991) *'Cheaper Than Peabody': local authority housing from 1890 to 1919*. York: Joseph Rowntree Foundation.

Mule, R. (2000) *Political Parties, Games and Redistribution*. Cambridge: Cambridge University Press.

Murie, A. (1997) 'The social rented sector, housing and the welfare state in the UK', *Housing Studies*, 12 (4), 437–61.

Murray, C. (1988) *In Pursuit of Happiness and Good Government*. New York: Simon and Schuster.

Murray, C. (1999) *The Underclass Revisited*. London: American Enterprise Institute.

Murray, P. (1999) *Poverty and Welfare 1830–1914*. London: Hodder and Stoughton.

Musgrove, F. (1964) *Youth and the Social Order*. London: Routledge and Kegan Paul.

National Assistance Act (1948) London: Stationery Office.

National Association of Citizen's Advice Bureaux (2001) *Work in Progress: Client Experience of Working Families Tax Credit*. London: National Association of Citizen's Advice Bureaux.

National Health Service Act (1946) London: Stationery Office.

National Insurance Act (1911) in Cooke, O.H. (1911) *The National Insurance Act, 1911*, London: Toplen and Peacock.

Navarro, V. (2000) 'Are pro-welfare and full-employment policies possible in the era of globalization?', *International Journal of Health Services*, 30 (2), 231–51.

Nazroo, J.Y. (1997) *The Health of Britain's Ethnic Minorities: Findings from a National Survey*. London: Policy Studies Institute.

Nevile, C. (1838) *The New Poor Law Justified: With Suggestions for the Establishment of Insurance Offices for the Poor*. London: Ridgeway.

Newman, T.S. (1945) *The Story of Friendly Societies and Social Security*. London: Hearts of Oak Benefit Society.

Newton, K. (1980) 'Central government grants, territorial justice and local democracy in post war Britain' in D.E. Ashford (ed.), *Financing Urban Government in the Welfare State*. London: St. Martin's Press.

Newton, K. and Karran, T.J. (1985) *The Politics of Local Expenditure*. Basingstoke: Macmillan.

Nicholson, J.L. (1964) *Redistribution of Income in the United Kingdom in 1949, 1957 and 1953*. London: Bowes and Bowes.

Nicholson, P. (1990) *The Political Philosophy of the British Idealists*. Cambridge: Cambridge University Press.

Niner, P. (1975) *Local Authority Housing Policy and Practice – A Case Study Approach*. Centre for Urban and Regional Studies. Birmingham: University of Birmingham.

Niskanen, W.A. (1973) *Bureaucracy: Servant or Master?* London: Institute of Economic Affairs.

Noddings, N. (1986) *Caring, a Feminine Approach to Ethics and Moral Education*. California: University of California Press.

Nozick, R. (1974) *Anarchy, State and Utopia*. Oxford: Blackwell.

Oakley, A. (1996) *Man and Wife Richard and Kay Titmuss: My Parents' Early Years*. London: HarperCollins.

Oatley, N. (1998) (ed.) *Cities, Economic Competition and Urban Policy*. London: PCP.

O'Brien, M. and Penna, S. (1998) *Theorising Welfare: Enlightenment and Modern Society*. London: Sage.

Offe, C. (1984) *Contradictions of the Welfare State*. London: Hutchinson.

Office for National Statistics (2000) *Social Trends 30*. London: Stationery Office.

Office for National Statistics (2001) *Social Trends 31*. London: Stationery Office.

Old Age Pensions Act (1908) c. 40, London: HMSO.

Oldham Borough Council (1949) *Annual Report*. Oldham: Oldham Borough Council.

Olecnowicz, A. (1997) *Working-Class Housing in England between the Wars: The Becontree Estate*. Oxford: Clarendon Press.

Oliver, M. and Barnes, C. (1998) *Disabled People and Social Policy*. Harlow: Longman.

Ormerod, P. (1991) 'Incomes policy' in M. Artis, and D. Cobham (eds) *Labour's Economic Policies 1974–79*. Manchester: Manchester University Press.

Owen, D. (1965) *English Philanthropy: 1660–1960*, Oxford: Oxford University Press.

Page, R.M. (1996) *Altruism and the British Welfare State*. Aldershot: Avebury.

Parekh, B. (1991) 'British citizenship and cultural difference' in G. Andrews (ed.), *Citizenship*. London: Lawrence and Wishart.

Parekh, B. (2000) *The Future of Multi-Ethnic Britain: Report of the Commission on the Future of Multi-Ethnic Britain*. London: Profile Books.

Parker, H. (1998) *Low Cost but Acceptable: A Minimum Income Standard for the UK*. Bristol: Policy Press.

Parker, R. (1970) 'The future of the personal social services' in W.A. Robson, and B. Crick (eds), *The Future of the Social Services*. Harmondsworth: Penguin.

Parrott, A.L. (1984) *The Iron Road to Social Security*. Sussex: The Book Guild Ltd.

Parry, J. (1993) *The Rise and Fall of Liberal Government in Victorian Britain*. New Haven, CT: Yale University Press.

Parsons, L.G., Clayton Fryers, S. and Godber, G.E. (1945) *Hospital Survey: The Hospital Services of the Sheffield and East Midlands Area*. London: HMSO.

Pateman, C. (1995) 'The fraternal social contract' in R.E. Goodin and P. Pettit (eds), *Companion to Contemporary Political Philosophy*. Oxford: Blackwell.

Peacock A.T. and Wiseman, J. (1961) *The Growth of Public Expenditure*. Princeton, NJ: Princeton University Press.

Pearson, N. (1911) 'The idle poor', *Nineteenth Century and After*, No. 70, 903–27.

Peck, J. (2001) *Workfare States*. New York: Guilford Press.

Peck, J. and Theodore, N. (2000) ' "Work first": workfare and the regulation of contingent labour markets'. *Cambridge Journal of Economics*, 24, 119–138.

Peden, G.C. (2000) *The Treasury and British Public Policy, 1906–1959*. Oxford: Oxford University Press.

Pederson, S. (1993) *Family, Dependents and the Origins of the Welfare State: Britain and France, 1914–1945*. Cambridge: Cambridge University Press.

Phillips, A. (1999) *Which Equalities Matter?* Cambridge: Polity Press.

Phillips Committee (1953) *Report of the Committee on the Economic and Financial Problems of the Provision for Old Age*, Cmd 9333. London: HMSO.

Phillips, M. (1997) 'Workfare for lone mothers: a solution to the wrong problem' in A. Deacon (ed.), *From Welfare to Work*. London: Institute of Economic Affairs.

Piachaud, D. and Sutherland, H. (2001) 'Child poverty: aims, achievements and prospects for the future', *New Economy*, 8 (2), 71–77.

Pierson, P. (1994) *Dismantling the Welfare State: Reagan, Thatcher and the Politics of Retrenchment*. Cambridge: Cambridge University Press.

Pierson, P. (ed.) (2001) *The New Politics of the Welfare State*. Oxford: Oxford University Press.

Pierson, S. (1979) *British Socialists: The Journey from Fantasy to Politics*. Cambridge, MA: Harvard University Press.

Pimlott, B. (1989) 'Is post war consensus a myth'?, *Contemporary Record*, 2 (6), 12–14.

Plant, R. (1991) *Modern Political Thought*. Oxford: Blackwell.

Plant, R., Lesser, H. and Taylor Gooby, P. (1980) *Political Philosophy and Social Welfare*. London: Routledge.

Pope, R., Pratt, A. and Hoyle, B. (1986) *Social Welfare in Britain 1885–1985*. London: Croom Helm.

Powell, J.E. (1972) *Joseph Chamberlain*. London: Thames and Hudson.

Powell, J.E. (1975) *Medicine and Politics: 1975 and After*. Kent: Pitman Medical. (First published in 1966 as *A New Look At Medicine and Politics*.)

Powell, M. (1997a) 'An expanding service: municipal acute medicine in the 1930s', *Twentieth Century History*, 8 (3), 334–57.

Powell, M. (1997b) *Evaluating the National Health Service*. Buckingham: Open University Press.

Propper, C. and Bartlett, W.J. (1997) *Providers, Purchasers and Contracts: Economic Effects of Institutional Reform in the NHS*. London: Economic and Social Research Council.

Prowse, M. (2000) 'Mind the gap', Prospect, January. *www.prospect-magazine.co.uk/highlights/mind_gap/index.html*.

Pugh, M. (1992) *Women and the Women's Movement in Britain 1914–1959*. Basingstoke: Macmillan.

Quandagno, J. (1982) *Ageing in Early Industrial Society: Work, Family, and Social Policy in Nineteenth-Century England*. London: Academic Press.

Race Relations Act (1976) Chapter 74, London: Stationery Office Books.

Radice, L. (1984) *Beatrice and Sidney Webb: Fabian Socialists*. Basingstoke: Macmillan.

Rae, D. (1981) *Equalities*. Cambridge, MA: Harvard University Press.

Ramsay, M. (1997) *What's Wrong With Liberalism: A Radical Critique of Liberal Political Philosophy*. Leicester: Leicester University Press.

Ranade, W. (1997) *A Future for the NHS?: Health Care for the Millennium*. Harlow: Longman.

Ranelagh, J. (1991) *Thatcher's People*. London: Fontana.

Rathbone, E. (1986) [1924] *The Disinherited Family*. Bristol: Falling Wall Press.

Rawls, J. (1971) *A Theory of Justice*. Oxford: Oxford University Press.

Rawls, J. (1987) Preface to the French edition of *A Theory of Justice* in S. Freeman (ed.), *John Rawls: Collected Papers*. Cambridge, MA: Harvard University Press.

Reisman, D. (1977) *Richard Titmuss: Welfare and Society*. London: Heinemann.

Rentoul, J. (2001) *Tony Blair: Prime Minister*. London: Little, Brown and Company.

Resource Allocation Working Party (1976) *Sharing Resources for Health in England*, London: HMSO.

Rhodes, T. and Bailey, S.J. (1979) 'Equality, statistics and the distribution of the rate support grant', *Policy and Politics*, 7 (1), 83–97.

Ricardo, D. (1971) [1817] *Principles of Political Economy and Taxation*. Harmondsworth: Penguin.

Richter, M. (1996) *The Politics of Conscience: T.H. Green and His Age*, Bristol: Thoemmes Press.

Ridley, N. (1991) *'My Style of Government': The Thatcher Years*. London: Hutchinson.

Roberts, A. (1999) *Salisbury: Victorian Titan*. London: Weidenfeld and Nicolson.

Robson, W. (1976) *Welfare State and Welfare Society*. London: Allen and Unwin.

Rodger, J.J. (2000) *From a Welfare State to a Welfare Society: The Changing Context of Social Policy in a Postmodern Era*. Basingstoke: Macmillan.

Rose, M.E. (1971) *The English Poor Law 1780–1930*. Newton Abbott: David and Charles.

Rose, M.E. (1988) 'The disappearing pauper: victorian attitudes to the relief of the poor in E.M. Sigsworth (ed.), *In Search of Victorian Values*. Manchester: Manchester University Press.

Rossiter, C. and Wicks, M. (1982) *Crisis or Challenge? Family Care, Elderly People and Social Policy*. London: Study Commission on the Family.

Rowntree, B.S. (1901) *Poverty: A Study of Town Life*. London: Macmillan and Co.

Rowntree, B.S. (1937) *Human Needs of Labour*. London: Longmans, Green and Co.

Rowntree, B.S. and Lavers, G. (1951) *Poverty and the Welfare State*. London: Longman Green.

Royal Commission on Health Insurance (1926) *Minority Report*, Cmd 1596. London: HMSO.

Rubinstein, D. (1984) 'Comprehensive education' in *Education: A Second Level Course*. Buckingham: Open University Press.

Ryan, W. (1971) *Blaming the Victim*. New York: Vintage.

Sanderson-Furniss, A.D. and Phillips, M. (1920) *The Working Woman's House*. London: Swarthmore Press.

Savage, M. and Miles, A. (1994) *The Remaking of the British Working Class, 1840–1940*. London: Routledge.

Savage, P. and Atkinson, R. (2001) *Public Policy Under Blair*. Basingstoke: Palgrave.

Saville, J. (1957) 'The welfare state: an historical approach', *The New Reasoner*, 1 (3), 5–15.

Schifferes, S. (1976) 'Council tenants and housing policy in the 1930s' *in Housing and Class in Britain*. London: Political Economy of Housing Workshop.

Schmidtz, D. and Goodin, R.E. (1998) *Social Welfare and Individual Responsibility*. Cambridge: Cambridge University Press.

Schmitt, J. (1994) 'The changing structure of male earnings in Britain, 1974–88' in R. Freeman, and L. Katz (eds), *Changes and Differences in Wage Structures*. Chicago: University of Chicago Press.

Schwartz, H. (2001) 'Round up of the usual suspects! Globalization, domestic politics, and welfare state change in P. Pierson (ed.), *The New Politics of the Welfare State*. Oxford: Oxford University Press.

Scott Committee (1942) *Report of the Committee on Land Utilisation in Rural Areas*, Cmd 6378. London: HMSO.

Scott, J. (1994) *Poverty and Wealth: Citizenship, Deprivation and Privilege*. Harlow: Longman.

Scottish Office (1998) *Social Exclusion in Scotland*. Edinburgh: Stationery Office.

Searle, G.R. (1976) *Eugenics and Politics in Britain, 1900–1914*. Leyden, Netherlands: Noordhoff International.

Searle, G.R. (1977) *The Quest for National Efficiency: The Study in British Politics and Political Thought, 1899–1914*. Oxford: Basil Blackwell.

Searle, G.R. (1998) *Morality and the Market in Victorian Britain*. Oxford: Clarendon Press.

Secretary of State for the Environment (1971) *Fair Deal For Housing*, Cmnd 4728. London: HMSO.

Secretary of State for the Environment (1977) *Housing Policy: A Consultative Document*, Cmnd 4851. London: HMSO.

Secretary of State for Social Security and the Minister for Welfare Reform (1998) *New Ambitions for Our Country: A New Contract For Welfare*, Cm 3805. London: Stationery Office.

Secretary of State for Social Services (1985) *Reform of Social Security: Programme for Change*. Vol. 2, Cmnd 9518. London: HMSO.

Secretary of State of the Department of Health and Social Security (1971) *Strategy for Pensions*, Cmnd 4755. London: HMSO.

Seebohm Committee (1968) *Report of the Committee on Local Authority and Allied Personal Social Services*, Cmnd 3703. London: HMSO.

Seers, D. (1951) *The Levelling of Incomes Since 1938*. Oxford: Blackwells.

Sefton, T. (1996) *The Changing Distribution of the Social Wage*. London: STICERD.

Seldon, A. (1986) *The Riddle of the Voucher*. London: Institute of Economic Affairs.

Seldon, A. (1998) *Major: A Political Life*. London: Phoenix.

Select Committee on Social Security (2000) *Fifth Report: The Contributory Principle*. London: House of Commons.

Shannon, R. (1996) *The Age of Salisbury 1881–1902: Unionism and Empire*. Harlow: Longman.

Shaw, J.B. (1908) *The Commonsense of Municipal Trading*. London: Fabian Society.

Shehab, F. (1953) *Progressive Taxation*. Oxford: Clarendon Press.

Shklar, J. (1990) *The Faces of Injustice*. New Haven, CT: Yale University Press.

Sidgwick, H. (1883) *The Principles of Political Economy*. London: Macmillan.

Simon, B. (1965) *Education and the Labour Movement 1870–1920*. London: Lawrence and Wishart.

Simon, S.D. (1938) *A Century of City Government: Manchester 1838–1938*. London: George Allen and Unwin.

Skidelsky, R. (1967) *Politicians and the Slump: The Labour Government of 1929–1931*. London: Macmillan.

Skocpol, T. (1991) 'Targeting within universalism: politically viable policies to combat poverty in the United States' in C. Jencks, and P.E. Peterson (eds), *The Urban Underclass*. Washington, DC: Brookings Institute.

Slater, G. (1930) *The Poor and the State*. London: Constable.

Smellie, K.B. (1937) *A Hundred Years of English Government*. London: Duckworth.

Smith, A. (1970) [1776] *Inquiry into the Nature and Causes of the Wealth of Nations*. Harmondsworth: Penguin.

Smithers, A. (2001) 'Education policy' in A. Seldon (ed.), *The Blair Effect: The Blair Government 1997–2000*. London: Little, Brown and Co.

Social Exclusion Unit (1998a) *Rough Sleeping – Report by the Social Exclusion Unit*, Cm 4008. London: Stationery Office.

Social Exclusion Unit (1998b) *Bringing Britain Together: A National Strategy for Neighbourhood Renewal*, Cm 4045. London: Stationery Office.

Social Exclusion Unit (2000) *A National Strategy for Neighbourhood Renewal: a Framework for Consultation*. London: Stationery Office.

Social Exclusion Unit (2001) *Preventing Social Exclusion*. London: Stationery Office.

Southall, H. (1999) 'Working with historical statistics on poverty and economic distress' in D. Dorling and S. Simpson (eds), *Statistics in Society: The Arithmetic of Politics*. London: Arnold.

Sparkes, J. (1999) *Schools, Education and Social Exclusion*. London: Centre for the Analysis of Social Exclusion.

Spence, J., Walton, W.S., Miller, F.J.W. and Court, S.D.M. (1954) *A Thousand Families in Newcastle upon Tyne*, Oxford: Oxford University Press.

Spencer, H. (1884a) 'The sins of the legislators', *Contemporary Review*, 45, 761–74.

Spencer, H. (1884b) *Man 'Versus' the State*. London: Williams and Norgate.

Spencer, S. (2000) 'Making race equality count: measuring progress towards race equality', *New Economy*, 7 (1), 35–41.

Standing, G. (1999) *Global Labour Flexibility: Seeking Distributive Justice*. Basingstoke: Macmillan.

Stanton, R. (1996) *Capital Allocations: Method of Determination by Central Government*. London: London Research Centre.

Starkey, P. (2000) 'The feckless mother: women, poverty and social workers in wartime and post-war England', *Women's History Review*, 9 (3), 539–57.

Statute of Artificers (1563) reprinted in Pickering, D. (1769) *The Statutes at Large, from Magna Carta to 1761*. London: Butterworth.

Stevenson, J. (1976) *Social Conditions in Britain Between The Wars*. Harmondsworth: Penguin.

Stevenson, J. (1984) *British Society 1914–45*. London: Pelican.

Stevenson, J. and Cook, C. (1977) *The Slump: Society and Politics During the Depression*. London: Cape.

Stewart, M. (1972) 'The distribution of income' in W. Beckerman (ed.), *The Labour Government's Economic Record 1964–1970*. London: Duckworth.

Studdard, N. (1998) 'The effects of taxes and benefits on household income: 1996/7' *Economic Trends*, 533, 33–67, London: Stationery Office.

Sullivan, M. (1998) 'Democratic socialism and social policy' in R.M. Page and R. Silburn (eds), *British Social Welfare in the Twentieth Century*. Basingstoke: Macmillan.

Supplementary Benefits Commission (1974) *Supplementary Benefits Handbook*. London: HMSO.

Tawney, R.H. (1975) [1931] *Equality*. London: Allen and Unwin.

Tawney, R.H. (1938) *Equality* (Workers Educational Association Edition). London: Allen and Unwin.

Taylor, R. (1975) *Lord Salisbury*. Harmondsworth: Allen Lane.

Taylor-Gooby, P. and Dale, J. (1981) *Social Theory and Social Welfare*. London: Edward Arnold.

Taylor-Gooby, P. (2001) 'Complex equalities – redistribution, class and gender' in R. Edwards and J. Glover (eds), *Risk and Citizenship: Key Issues in Welfare*. London: Routledge.

Tennyson, A. (1856) *The Northern Farmer: New Style*. London: Strahan Press.

Thane, P. (1998) 'Gender, welfare and old age in Britain, 1870s–1940s in A. Digby, and J. Stewart (eds), *Gender, Health and Welfare*. London: Routledge.

Thane, P. (2000) *Old Age in English History: Past Experiences, Present Issues*. Oxford: Oxford University Press.

Thatcher, M. (1987) *Speech to Conservative Party Conference*, Brighton 9 October.

Thatcher, M. (1993) *The Downing Street Years*. London: HarperCollins.

Thatcher, M. (1995) *The Path To Power*. London: HarperCollins.

Thompson, L. (1988) *An Act of Compromise*, London: Shelter.

Thomson, D. (1984) 'The decline of social welfare: falling state support for the elderly since early Victorian times', *Ageing and Society*, 4, 451–482.

Thomson, M. (1998) *The Problem of Mental Deficiency, Eugenics, Democracy, and Social Policy in Britain 1870–1959*. Oxford: Clarendon Press.

Tilly, C. (1998) *Durable Inequality*. California: University of California.

Timmins, N. (1995) *The Five Giants: A Biography of the Welfare State*. London: Fontana.

Tinker, A. (1981) *The Elderly in Modern Society*. Harlow: Longman.

Titmuss, R.M.T. (1950) *The Problems of Social Policy*. London: HMSO.

Titmuss, R.M.T. (1968) *Commitment to Welfare*. London: George Allen & Unwin.

Titmuss, R.M.T. (1970) *The Gift Relationship*. London: Allen & Unwin.

Titmuss, R.M.T. (1974) *Social Policy: An Introduction*. London: George Allen & Unwin.

Tomlinson, J. (1997) *Democratic Socialism and Economic Policy: The Attlee Years, 1945–1951*. Cambridge: Cambridge University Press.

Tomlinson, J. (1998) 'Why so austere?: The British welfare state of the 1940s', *Journal of Social Policy*, 27 (1), 63–77.

Townsend, P. (1968) *Social Services for All?* London: Fabian Society.

Townsend, P. (1973) 'Poverty as relative deprivation' in D. Wedderburn (ed.), *Poverty, Inequality and Class Structure*. Cambridge: Cambridge University Press.

Townsend, P. (1979) *Poverty in the United Kingdom*. Harmondsworth: Penguin.

Townsend, P. and Wedderburn, D. (1965) *The Aged in the Welfare State*. London: Bell and Sons.

Townsend, P. and Bosanquet, N. (1972) *Labour and Inequality*. London: Fabian Society.

Townshend, J. (1990) *J.A. Hobson*. Manchester: Manchester University Press.

Townshend, Mrs. (1910) *The Case Against the Charity Organisation Society*, Fabian Tract 158. London: Fabian Society.

Toynbee, P. and Walker, D. (2001) *Did Things Get Better? An Audit of Labour's Successes and Failures*. Harmondsworth: Penguin.

Tucker, R.V. (1972) *The Marx-Engels Reader*. New York: Norton.

Twigger, R. (1998) *The Barnett Formula*, House of Commons Research Paper 98/8. London: House of Commons.

Twigger, R. (2000) *The Burden of Taxation*, House of Commons Research Paper 00/65. London: House of Commons.

Unwin, R. (1902) *Cottage Plans and Common Sense*, Fabian Tract No. 109. London: Fabian Society.

Urban Task Force (1999) *Towards an Urban Renaissance*. London: E & F.N. Spon.

Uthwatt Committee (1942) *Final Report of the Expert Committee on Compensation and Betterment*, Cmd 6386. London: HMSO.

Veit-Wilson, J. (1995) 'Paradigms of poverty: a rehabilitation of B.S. Rowntree' in D. Englander and R. O'Day (eds), *Retrieved Riches: Social Investigation in Britain 1840–1914*. Aldershot: Scholar Press.

Veit-Wilson, J. (1999) 'The National Assistance Board and the "rediscovery" of poverty' in H. Fawcett, and R. Lowe (eds), *Welfare Policy in Britain: The Road from 1945*. Basingstoke: Macmillan.

Vidler, G. (1998) *Widow's Benefits*, House of Commons Research Papers, 98/100. London: House of Commons.

Vincent, A. and Plant, R. (1984) *Philosophy, Politics and Citizenship: The Life and Thought of the British Idealists*. Oxford: Basil Blackwell.

Waddington, K. (1996) '"Grasping gratitude"; charity and hospital finance in late-Victorian London' in M. Daunton (ed.), *Charity, Self-Interest and Welfare in the English Past*. London: UCL Press.

Waites, B. (1987) *A Class Society at War*. Lemington Spa: Berg.

Walden, G. (1996) *We Should Know Better: Solving the Educational Crisis*. London: Fourth Estate.

Walker, C. (1983) *Managing Poverty: the Limits of Social Assistance*. London: Routledge.

Walsh, A.J. (1972) 'Tax allowances and fiscal policy' in P. Townsend and N. Bosanquet (eds), *Labour and Inequality*. London: Fabian Society.

Wasson, E. (2000) *Born to Rule: British Political Elites*. Stroud: Sutton Publishing.

Walters, W. (2000) *Unemployment and Government*. Cambridge: Cambridge University Press.

Walzer, M. (1983) *Spheres of Justice*. Oxford: Martin Robertson.

Watts, D. (1992) *Joseph Chamberlain and the Challenge of Radicalism*. London: Hodder and Stoughton.

Webb, B. (1979) *My Apprenticeship*. Cambridge: Cambridge University Press.

Webb, B. and Webb, S. (1909) *The Break-up of the Poor Law*. London: Longmans and Co.

Webb, B. and Webb, S. (1929) *English Local Government, Part 11: The Last Hundred Years*. London: Longmans, Green and Co.

Webb, S. (1907a) *The Decline in the Birth Rate*. Fabian Tract 131, London: Fabian Society.

Webb, S. (1907b) *Paupers and Old Age Pensions*. Fabian Tract No. 135, London: Fabian Society.

Webb, S. (1962) [1913] 'The basis of socialism: historic' in G.B. Shaw (ed.), *Fabian Essays in Socialism*. London: George Allen & Unwin.

Webb, S. and Webb, B. (1913) 'What is Socialism?' *New Statesman*, May 10.

Webster, C. (1988) *The Health Services Since the War, Vol. 1: Problems of Health Care: The National Health Service before 1957*. London: HMSO.

Webster, C. (1996) *The Health Services since the War, Vol. 11: Government and Health Care: The British National Health Service 1958–1979*. London: HMSO.

Webster, C. (1998) *The National Health Service: A Political History*. Oxford: Oxford University Press.

Wells, D. (2000) *Tony Blair: Making Labour Liberal*. Beckenham: Rains Press.

West, E.G. (1965) *Education and the State*. London: Institute of Economic Affairs.

Wheen, F. (1999) *Karl Marx*. London: Fourth Estate.

Whiteside, N. (1991) *Bad Times: Unemployment in British Social and Political History*. London: Faber and Faber.

Whiteside, N. (1999) 'Private provision and public welfare: health insurance between the wars' in D. Gladstone (ed.), *Before Beveridge: Welfare Before The Welfare State*. London: Institute of Economic Affairs.

Whiting, R.C. (2000) *The Labour Party and Taxation: Party Identity and Political Purpose in Twentieth Century Britain*. Cambridge: Cambridge University Press.

Wilcox, S. (1997) *Housing Finance Review 1997/8*. York: Joseph Rowntree Foundation.

Wilkinson, H. (1939) *The Town That Was Murdered*. London: Victor Gollancz.

Willcocks, A.J. (1967) *The Creation of the National Health Service*. London: Routledge and Kegan Paul.

Willetts, D. (1992) *Modern Conservatism*. Harmondsworth: Penguin.

Willetts, D. (1996) *Blair's Gurus*. London: Institute of Economic Affairs.

Williams, T. (1943) 'The finance of the social services' in W.A. Robson (ed.), *Social Security*. New York: Garland Publishing.

Williamson, J.G. (1985) *Did British Capitalism Breed Inequality?* London: Allen and Unwin.

Wilson, E. (1977) *Women and the Welfare State*. London: Tavistock.

Wistow, G., Knapp, M., Hardy, B. and Allen, C. (1994) *Social Care in a Mixed Economy*. Buckingham: Open University Press.

Wohl, A.S. (1983) *Endangered Lives: Public Health in Victorian Britain*. London: Methuen.

Wolfe, A. (1977) *The Limits of Legitimacy*. New York: Free Press.

Wolfe, A. and Klausen, J. (1997) 'Identity politics and the Welfare State', *Social Philosophy and Policy*, 14 (2), 231–57.

Woodroofe, K. (1962) *From Charity to Social Work in England and the United States*. London: Routledge and Kegan Paul.

Wrigley, C. (1976) *David Lloyd George and the Labour Movement*. Brighton: Harvester Wheatsheaf.

Yelling, J.A. (1986) *Slums and Slum Clearance in Victorian London*. London: Allen & Unwin.

Yelling, J.A. (1992) *Slums and Redevelopment: Policy and Practice in England with Particular Reference to London*. London: UCL Press.

Young, H. (1991) *One of Us*, Basingstoke Macmillian.

Young, I. (1990) *Justice and the Politics of Difference*. Princeton NJ: Princeton University.

Young, J.D. (1989) *Socialism and the English Working Class*. Hemel Hempstead: Harvester Wheatsheaf.

Young, K. and Laffin, M. (1990) *Professionalism in Local Government*. Harlow: Longman.

Young, K. and Rao, N. (1997) *Local Government Since 1945*. Oxford: Blackwell.

Index